The gathering storm / *Paul N Siegel*

Shakespeare's English and Roman history plays : a *Marxist* analysis / Redwords

REDWORDS

The gathering storm
Shakepeare's English and Roman history plays : a Marxist analysis / Paul N Siegel
November 1992 / Redwords
31 Cottenham Road
Walthamstow, London E17 6RP

ISBN 1 872208 045
Design and production: Roger Huddle and Sofie Mason.
Cover picture: Oscar Zarate
Set in Monotype Gill Sans Light and Galliard
Imagesetting by East End Offset Bureau
Printed by Great Britain by St Austell Printing Company

Shakespeare's history plays / *Paul N Siegel* / a Marxist analysis

The gathering storm

Contents

Redwords would like to thank
Catherine Allison
Paul Cooper
Cyrus Gilbert-Rolfe
Mike Gonzalez
Peter Marsden
Phil Mellows
John Rees
Megan Trudell
Dot Pearce
Thomas Yoseloff at *Associated University Presses*
and Oscar Zarate
for helping us publish this book.

Shakespeare in these times / *Mike Gonzalez*

Whose Shakespeare?

We can be certain that William Shakespeare, playwright and actor, lived and died between 1564 and 1616. Beyond that, everything about Shakespeare is open to debate and conjecture; he has spawned an apparently endless stream of speculation.

In our times he has come to epitomise all that is most conservative in British and American cultural life. Why then does a Marxist like Paul Siegel devote 25 years of his life to the study and exploration of his work? The ill-conceived National Curriculum for British schools, born of a conservative reaction to liberal child-centred learning, appears to regard Shakespeare as second only to corporal punishment as a disciplinary device. It will be compulsory now for all British 14 year olds to read and answer questions on a Shakespeare play. This year the chosen work will deal with the dramatic conflict between the powerful sexual desire of youth and the social constraints that make it impossible and unbearable to explore that physical awakening (*Romeo and Juliet*). In other years, students may be expected to know by heart the speeches that reveal the intense corruption of power, and the contempt of the leaders of society for those who entrust them with their rule (*Coriolanus*) or expose how our masters murder one another in its pursuit (*Julius Caesar*). Those who worship the market and ignore its obvious contempt for human need insist on the greatness of *The Merchant of Venice* that showed how money destroys honour; and the slow disintegration of a megalomaniac king at the hands of daughters he has allowed to flatter and cajole him into rejecting the one child capable of genuine and unacquisitive love (*King Lear*) should give some pause to the champions of family values.

Yet the ministers of Her Majesty's British Government perceive no irony there. On the contrary, for them – in some way as yet unspecified – Shakespeare represents 'Englishness', an unchanging and deeply conservative national tradition yearning for empire. For the speech writers Shakespeare offers an inexhaustible fund of sound-bites invested with the authority of an undeniable general truth. The bourgeoisie reaches back beyond its own historical advent and claims comtinuity from a heritage lost in the past, but representing the proud fusion of bourgeoisie and aristocracy, parliament and monarchy, which is 'English culture' with the Bard of Avon at its heart. Shakespeare thus is rendered 'timeless', 'perfect', 'pure', exemplary not of *a* culture but of culture itself, not of a language set in time and place but of Language in its highest form.

In the late 20th century Shakespeare occupies an unchallenged central place – so exemplary is he that every other writer for the stage is eclipsed before the fact. It seems to work retrospectively too. In his own time, Shakespeare was one among many writers for an expanding stage – a jobbing playwright who as often as not wrote parts or scenes or shared the authorship of hurriedly written pieces. In his time Ben Jonson was a mightier figure and in subsequent years Shakespeare was less significant than Webster or Fletcher or Middleton. During the Restoration, when his work returned to some favour, many of his plays were only acceptable in bowdlerised form or frequently interrupted by musical interludes and comic episodes. And the English literature establishment was by no means always in agreement about Shakespeare's greatness and superiority. Yet he has since come to be regarded with awe, and others cower in his shadow. The vagaries of his reputation seem to be closely intertwined with the fortunes of the British ruling class, echoing its changing relationship with a wider world. With customary imperial arrogance the presumed dominion of Shakespeare implies too a dismissal of all the other aspiring universal cultures where Shakespeare receives polite acknowledgment but no more; in the Orient, in the Hispanic world, in Russia, in northern Europe, very few would see any reason to shift Chekhov or Calderon or Ibsen from their well-earned pedestals.

A case of them and us ?

There is an apparent logic, therefore, in a simple case of negation; if Shakespeare belongs to the ruling class then we will have none of him. To the refuse dump of history with this scribbler, where he can be left to rot with the chauvinist poets and the forgotten poetasters, the Southeys and their ilk! Such a view would have found sympathy among one group of critics claiming their ascendancy from the Marxist tradition; the popular culturalists, as they might be called, would regard all the products of the past as irredeemably corrupt, tainted with the bourgeois stain, and offering nothing to a movement whose object is the transformation of the world and the creation of a new proletarian culture. Only the elements of popular culture under capitalism might be worth salvaging. But just as Lenin, Trotsky and Lunacharsky were critical of their forbears in the Proletkult movement that exploded out of the October Revolution in Russia, so our response to Shakespeare should draw on the rejoinders of the Bolshevik leaders. The culture of the past did not belong to the bourgeoisie; it was appropriated by that burgeoning class and was assimilated to its visions. The bourgeoisie paid for artists, rendered art a commodity to be bought and sold like any other whose content was measured in exchange and not use values; and its universe of ideas set the imprisoning frame for the artists and writers working in its service. Yet all art is a field of conflict between those values and others, implied or expressed, whose fullest development requires a different framework and different horizons. Just as the future socialist society will recover all the fruits and products of the general development of humanity, so it will celebrate that content of rebellion and resistance, of questioning and discomfort, which marks all creative activity in a society where the activity of the majority of human beings is rendered uncreative. Art celebrates the potentiality for men and women to consciously shape the world to the fulfilment of human purposes – even where it can do no more than bewail the impediments to the fulfilment of that most human vocation.

For socialists, the significance of literature and art is not proscriptive – there is no schedule of acceptable works or forms, whether judged by their contents or the behaviour of their authors. The value of art for Marxists is not the same as its worth, the price set by a group of market analysts called critics whose job it is too often to preserve the hierarchy of market quantities. Such criticism is an adjunct of the business of selling culture, its judgments equivalent to advertising copy where, as often as not, possession of the book or painting is sufficient evidence of cultural superiority. It is a parody of Marxism, however, to simply reverse the procedure and erect a negative index.

There is such a plethora of Shakespeare scholarship that it is impossible even to categorize, let alone to read. But the body of work that has an impact for Marxists will address two things. First, what moment produced this work – for the material of drama above all is the language of shared experience, realized in an act of recognition (which is not the same as approval or empathy – indeed for Brecht is precisely the opposite). The meaning of the work arises from that dialogue with the world of values and expectations to which it is addressed. Secondly, what new meanings emerge when each successive period reappropriates the work, and presumably makes sense of it again in relation to a new prevailing culture?

These questions assume that the value of Shakespeare is given in history. If it is not then we are left with an idea of art and culture that is eternal and universal, a single body of truths to which 'great art' adds new components which simply repeat or reproduce those universal truths. There is a particular irony in ascribing such a status to Shakespeare, for the power of his drama flows more than anything else from a recognition that human beings change constantly and that each moment of transformation is pregnant with unknown and unforeseeable outcomes.

We are to the gods like flies to wanton boys,
they use us for their sport.

If we are to believe the National Heritage lobbies, *Shakespeare's Complete Works* become a kind of Universal Dictionary of Great Truths and Conservative Precepts, learned by rote by tens of generations of schoolchildren for whom Shakespeare was simultaneously closed off and made the touchstone of basic cultural completeness. Small wonder that those clamouring for access to the inner sanctum, but unable to make it past the solemn refusal of endless generations of critics to touch the Holy Writ and make it understandable, have 'translated' Shakespeare into modern worlds – Julius Capone of Chicago, the Capulets and Montague of the Lower East Side, Coriolanus as Hitler. Or there is Jan Kott's existential Lear or David Morgan's hippy reject Hamlet or the Macbeth set in an outworld space satellite that I saw recently at the Citizen's Theatre in Glasgow.

Paul N Siegel's achievement is to have been seduced by none of these approaches, but instead to situate and address Shakespeare amid the dilemmas and tensions of his time. And here – and we shall return to this issue – is the answer to the mystery of Shakespeare's survival outside the commercial enterprise of the Stratford industry or the Heritage Shakespeare so beloved of the British ruling class. For Shakespeare has a poetic power and a dramatic impact that derives from the living of a history riven with pain, destruction and human anguish – and punctuated by nobility and grace. Sadly, it remains our history, not yet by far a chapter in our social archaeology, we still inhabit a society wrenched apart by the struggle of class interests.

In his historical moment Shakespeare can be understood and acknowledged without falling into the traps set for us. Because his time was part of our own history, the dilemmas and contradictions of his protagonists are recognisable in the present. Not in a direct sense of course; there are few remaining believers in the monarchy as representative of the divine will, fewer still share a belief in a destiny to which each human being is subject. If some of Shakespeare's predecessors have been lost to us, it is not because of a conspiracy of exclusion but because they did not write against the pressing current of historical change – Shakespeare did. There is no need to squabble about whether he or some other dramatist was the greatest – the comparison between Shakespeare, Shaw, Osborne, Brecht, Shaffer, is a meaningless game among those whose sole concern is to erect a canon, a scale of simple measurement. What does matter is the capacity of each to reveal aspects of the complexity of human experience. In this, Shakespeare's plays have something important to offer.

Shakespeare's language and dramatic structure were as varied as any other – with fine and moving moments, and others trite and awkward. But Shakespeare's most modern and powerful plays are those in which individual protagonists encounter the encroachments of a burgeoning new world – a world of money, of power, of human beings setting out to shape not only their own destiny but the lives and futures of others. It is the drama of human beings breaking out of the circle of destiny and divine planning and finding their humanity in forging the world. There is nothing inevitable, however, about the outcome of the confrontation, nothing certain about the liberating result of the decision to act. On the contrary, for Richard III, for Hamlet, for Macbeth, the decision to act against the gods has terrible and fatal consequences –

no less moving because they were deserved. The world to come is yet to be formed, the world of the past is in decline and moving to destruction; nothing is certain, all is in doubt. The wry commentaries of the few working people in the plays are sharp and telling, but there is no sense that they are actors in the history we see. They are as yet in the wings of the drama – a drama acted out by those who may shape the world, the 'noble minds' of Shakespeare's still medieval universe. The artisans and labourers who stood in the yard of the Elizabethan theatres understood and were moved by the great dramas on the stage, and laughed at the rebellious wit and satire the comedies provided. But they were in every sense still spectators at the drama of a history whose evolution would later place them at the centre of the stage.

At the heart of his explanation of Shakespeare, Siegel places the dynamics of the 'Elizabethan compromise' – the moment of Shakespeare. 1588 was the turning point, as the wreckage of the Spanish Armada marked the end of the fragile balance of different and opposing forces. Elizabeth I oversaw within her court a faithful representation of a wider reality; the inner factions vying for her attention and patronage spoke for a range of classes each of which sought in her protection the guarantee of different social orders. Elizabeth had created a strong state – an absolutist structure which, for a time at least, located itself above the warring factions and tried to maintain a fragile balance of forces. On one side were the old landowning aristocracy with Sussex as their advocate at court. This once autonomous group no longer enjoyed their own provincial rule or the right to raise private armies at will; Elizabeth inherited the results of her father Henry VIII's successful confrontation with that class. He it was who laid the foundation of the absolutist state. Weakened by the growing power of the monarchy, by its economic failures and by the sale and transfer of its lands, the feudal landowners could no longer defy the court or the burgeoning state. They could lobby for their interests and try by every means to undermine the burgeoning classes which would profit by their disappearance. But they had no independent power – only the ability to convince the queen that her interests would be served by protecting theirs.

At the other end of the spectrum stood a new emerging merchant class, the foundation of the new capitalism. Their source lay in the towns and cities, and particularly in London, where the bankers and financiers of a new world of trade and commerce were exhibiting a growing confidence. In the post-1492 world American gold circulated around northern Europe, purchasing manufactures and stimulating trade; the plantations of the New World demanded labour transported from Africa to South America in ships financed and organised from English ports. And in exchange for the human cargo they delivered, they brought back the goods and the spices that were the motor of trade. The growth of the towns hastened in its turn the movement of land, and the enclosure of the commons. The old feudal aristocracy became increasingly dependent on this new class but was itself fading from history and could do little to halt the growing power of its antagonists.

The Elizabethan state, however, did for a time succeed in diverting that emergent class from its historical course. The so-called 'eleven wonderful years' (1577-88) in some ways held the balance in a long pause; but it could not last. For those years the Elizabethan state held power by balancing the hostile classes and by creating a new class of its own dependent on the queen's will and working in the institutions of the state that she was forging. This was the new aristocracy – Dudley and above all Raleigh – whose fate was linked with the emerging bourgeoisie, on which they depended for their commercial and economic power, but which tried at the same time to carve an independent space for itself at court. As Siegel himself says 'they represented the topmost reaches of the enterprising gentry'. The period of the Elizabethan compromise was a time of equilibrium but underneath it tensions and conflicts were mounting that were inexorably approaching explosion point. On the one hand, the tension was the product of success and prosperity itself; after 1575 the growth of manufacturing industry and the expansion of trade gathered pace. At first, the absolutist state provided a framework for that growth, a constraint on the reactionary resistance of the feudal landowners and an organised national political state to underpin the expansion of trade. Yet it rapidly became a restraint upon expansion, as 1588 showed. For it was only under pressure from the merchant classes that Elizabeth attacked the Great Armada and took on at home and abroad the might of Spanish expansionism.

In submitting to the pressure, Elizabeth marked the end of that fragile equilibrium; prosperity itself tipped the balance towards the future. Rising prices for agricultural and manufactured goods benefited the merchants and the bankers rather than the landowners; the dispossessed peasantry were now absorbed into an expanding and changing agriculture. In the aftermath of 1588, Elizabeth defended the Crown's monopoly of trade by turning again to an alliance with the institutions of the old order – the Church and the aristocracy – spurning the new aristocrats who were her own creation, yet also the stalking horses of a very different order. But the Tudor state could not hold back the dynamics of history; an increasingly confident bourgeoisie grew restive with the Crown, and began to withdraw from the compromise on which that state was built. In Siegel's words, 'the war with Spain was in reality the first phase of the English Civil War'. The first casualty of that lurch towards the future was the new aristocracy, crushed between the rising bourgeoisie and the absolutist state.

The balance of thought

This correlation of forces had its expression and its foundation in ideas. The feudal order produced little in the way of public culture; the English aristocrat had little time for learning and existed in a world where the shape of things was given in a divinely-established order of things. There was continuity within that order, but there was no sense of change and progress, no concept of history. The new aristocracy were functionaries, products of the absolutist state, who evolved a different and more complex perception of the relations between human beings and the organisation of society, a complexity, furthermore, that was echoed in what can be called the ideology of the Elizabethan compromise.

This body of thinking, which Siegel describes as Christian humanism, drew a paradox into the centre of its system. The order of things was given, the hierarchies on which society was built were reflections of the divine will. Thus the authority of the state derived from sources greater than the balance of interest between monarchy and aristocracy. Yet at the same time the human protagonist of that order possessed a power of will and a responsibility to fulfil the universal order. Individuals, in other words, could act in evil ways and distort and corrupt the shape of things – and others could assume the duty of reestablishing the balance of society, the compromise between the warring forces within society and within the individual.

Like the compromise on which it rested, such thinking corresponded to a time of transition and change, and could not long outlast the encounter between incompatible social forces, though it could perhaps survive the immediate clash. It is, therefore, a vision imbued with tragedy, with the inevitability of its own passing, and thus too filled with a sense of loss and longing for another better past time, perhaps the Illyrian paradise in which some of the comedies are set or the unnamed gardens where wit enacted a shallow and always ultimately resolved conflict of wills.

William Shakespeare stood astride these times and dramatised the powerful sense of change that gave them their identity. It was an irony that the most profound expression of the moment of transformation from the point of view of the new aristocratic class should come just as that class was entering a decline – as the new bourgeoisie prepared the challenges that would later explode in the English Revolution beginning in 1640.

It is that sense of a world in flux and change that provides the dramatic power in Shakespeare, and that makes his preoccupations meaningful several centuries later.

Yet there are contradictions within his position as an artist as well. Shakespeare stands not only at a moment of philosophical transition, but also at the threshold of fundamental changes in the role and nature of theatre. For while his glance was in many ways nostalgic, his patrons were no longer the aristocracy who paid for and commissioned the masques and private satires of earlier times, but the market place, the crowds who paid the wages of the new permanent companies of actors.

A populated stage

Shakespeare helped to usher in a commercial theatre financed by the bourgeoisie and attended often by a radical class of the 'middle sort' the craftsmen and journeymen, the farmers and clerks of a new age. How then did they respond to the tragedy of men in confrontation with the divine plan? It is futile to try to guess at that response here but it is clear that for many of them, at least, the power of the play must have lain in the defeat of the mighty, who abused their power, reviled justice and pursued their own interests. For most of them the revenge which came to Macbeth, Richard III, and Claudius, must have seemed like a just sanction – though not one as yet that they could execute themselves. Yet in little more than a generation the children of that noisy public were offered the possibility of transforming the world themselves, of turning it all upside down. The Shakespearean moment, however, was a bridge between these epochs, and one where the visions appropriate to the old order and the new met. The shift in Shakespeare's time, however, is marked through the plays – from a time of imagined utopia and romance, of wit and stability, to a world shaped by living forces and real actions whose corresponding form was realism. The historical backgrounds of the Henry plays, for example, are known but the characters that move within them are the recognisable figures of a contemporary world.

Henry V is the exemplary symbol of the modern state, the forger of a united nationhood, subjecting both the internal and the external enemy to that purpose.

Falstaff, on the other hand, belongs to the underworld of a decomposing feudal order cast out now to live and die on his wits in a world where his masters are no longer powerful. Once the object of young Prince Hal's bewildered admiration, he must leave behind his memory and his companions (Pistol, Bardolph etc.) to forge the future state. Falstaff, the bloated wit with his entourage of chancers and ne'er-do-wells, has little space in this new world of money and commodities. In the other world he could offer sycophancy, flattery and amusement to entertain some feudal lord who would keep him in return – he had no need of the encumbrance of money. But in the new order he is a disappearing breed, and he and his ilk are consumed by the new rules; it is only those who can manipulate the money economy like Mistress Quickly who survive into the new age. Falstaff has rightly been compared to the Knight of the Baleful Countenance, Don Quixote, for both are survivors of one age whose consciousness is too narrow to function in this wider and more ruthless world of markets and money.

The transition is already visible in the encounter between Shylock, the functionary of a money economy, and Bassanio who tries (and fails) to function in it with his honour only. And Hamlet expresses in his agonised dilemmas an issue constantly confronted in this shifting universe. On the one hand, the divine order is given – but on the other it is ever threatened and undermined by those who put themselves outside it for gain or power lust or even, as in Hamlet's case, in order to wreak a just revenge. Yet the just cause does not eliminate the evil that flows from it – the disengagement of men from the will of God, and the disruption of His order. And yet in a time of change that freeing of human beings from the constraints of providence is inescapable. Time and again the great tragedies of Shakespeare's drama stem from this exercise of a free will, an arbitrary will, that brings disaster in its wake; the Venice of *Othello* is a place under siege, yet its collapse comes not from external forces but from within as Iago sows the jealousy and bitterness that makes Othello assume the right to kill.

It is perhaps in *King Lear* that the moral corruption at the heart of the tragedies achieves its most profound expression. Lear throws aside wisdom and judgment (his Fool tells him 'Thou shoulds't not have been old nuncle till thou hadst been wise') – qualities of which in the cosmic system of Shakespeare's class he should have been the guarantor – out of pique and jealousy. The consequences are devastating for good and evil characters alike. The saintly Cordelia dies as do her scheming sisters and the blind Lear reels about on the symbolic 'blasted heath' which could be seen to represent the barren moral landscape of the age.

In this new world, then, consciousness is a power in human affairs, and human action central to the flow of history. In this the history plays are key; the actions of Richard III are linked, as Siegel so pithily argues, to gain and profit, and all morality subordinated to the pursuit of power. Human beings prostitute themselves to the 'universal whore' money; the individual confronts the world and in challenging the order, for good or ill, from conviction, error or greed, brings destruction in its wake. That is the tragedy of human intervention, but it is also the tragedy of the times; the logic of the new world was a logic of accumulation and profit, and its consequences invariably tragic. It is the past that enshrines the world of order and harmony – and it is lost; there is little sense of a future world though there are islands of gentleness and humanity among the ordinary people on the stage – the Fool, Flavius the steward, among others. But the logic of their world has yet to express itself in society, and there is no sense that Shakespeare can spring beyond the frame of his own class vision to see the future history of the emerging working class. And we cannot ask it of him.

Bringing it all back home

Yet time and again the words and sensitivities echo into our own day, and have a meaning for us. It is not that the language has some magical charismatic effect that spans the ages; in some sense or another, that meaning arises from an act of recognition. It is not the simple 'identification' that bad literary critics and teachers blithely assert – indeed the power of the figures and circumstances of the plays often originates in a sense of differentness, of strangeness. And yet in the symbolic landscapes that Shakespeare elects, and in the language whose effect is more often than not alienating, there is a familiarity which can be electrifying in its very unexpectedness. And that does not come from translation, but from the realisation that these so distant times were nevertheless besieged by dilemmas and pain that are still suffered in these times. Somehow those strange and distant times are our times.

That may seem to concede the argument to the advocates of eternal truths and great works. In fact, it does the opposite – for what is recognisable is not the universe of ideas from which Shakespeare spoke, where kings were bearers of a cosmic balance endlessly restored or where chaos came wherever human beings tried to direct the currents of history. Even in Shakespeare's time that belief belonged to a dying era. The drama lay in the shattering of that idea of a stable and unchanging order even as the stability of the Elizabethan state had proved to be a transient thing. Timon of Athens returns to nature in disgust at the corruptions of social life – but the conflicts he turned his back on continue. There can be no return to nature or the past, except as a metaphor, an act of imagination. The future belongs to those who mould the world, by any means necessary, to their ambitions; Henry V already belongs to the same lost past as John o' Gaunt's 'sceptred isle, the jewel in a silver sea'. Richard III, the conspirators against Caesar, the ruthless Coriolanus, are the figures of a modern world.

Shakespeare exposes and reveals that truth with enormous power, his yearning for what is past informing his insights with greater pathos and sense of tragedy. In *Hamlet* is enacted not simply the endless dynastic struggle for power, but the restless activity, the doing and undoing that is the mark of a history made by human action and decision. In the end,

Hamlet's decisions matter because they will shape the world. And from then until now, that endless and simultaneous act of destruction and reconstruction has marked the course of history.

For Shakespeare, the future was only disruption. At the end of his life, the rule of the Stuarts under James I brought what may have seemed like a new compromise. We know now that it was an interregnum, a prelude and a preparation for the bourgeois bid for power. When, in 1642, the Stuarts were removed by a new capitalist class, a new actor was present at the drama. The people for whom Shakespeare had so little regard, the spectators at the deeds of the mighty, were now beginning to evolve their own vision of the future informed by a sense of the past to which the Shakespearean vision of history, then as now, had contributed much. The dramatist could not supply that sense of the future, because the class to which he belonged had no other world to offer. The new, revolutionary class was the bourgeoisie – and as it grew, it too would produce contradictions and conflicts whose resolution was inconceivable without the transformation of society itself. That transformation would produce its visionaries and its artists – and act out the possibilities on a different stage.

The plays

What follows is a brief synopsis of the plays Siegel refers to in the book. The presumed date of writing of the plays are in brackets.

RICHARD III (1592-3)

Edward IV is dying, and his brother Richard, Duke of Gloucester, is determined to succeed him. Six people stand in his way; Edward's two sons, the young princes; Edward Prince of Wales and Duke of York, and his daughter Elizabeth; Richard's brother Clarence and his two children. He has Clarence drowned in a barrel of wine in the Tower of London, and then marries Lady Anne, who was to have married the Prince of Wales until Richard stabbed him to death at Tewkesbury, before the action of the play begins. When Edward finally dies, Richard attacks and murders several people riding with Queen Margaret and takes her two sons, the young princes, to imprisonment in the Tower. Buckingham then persuades the citizens of London to proclaim Richard king. As soon as he is crowned Richard kills the princes in the Tower, speeds the death of his wife Anne, and plans to marry Elizabeth.

Buckingham meanwhile baulks at the murder of the princes and tries to join Richard's sworn enemy Richmond. He is murdered before he reaches him; but Richmond rides on to meet Richard III in battle at Bosworth. On the eve of battle the ghosts of all those he has killed come back to haunt Richard and to predict his defeat. Horseless and undefended, Richard dies on Bosworth Field, and Richmond is proclaimed King Henry VII in his place.

Henry IV [part one and two] (1597-8)

The action covers the years 1403-13.
Hotspur and his father Northumberland join Worcester, Mortimer, Glendower and Douglas in rebellion against the king. At Shrewsbury, only Worcester and Douglas join Hotspur in battle. Hotspur is killed by Prince Harry, the Prince of Wales, Worcester executed and Douglas freed.
The young Prince Hal spends much of his time in the company of Falstaff, his boon companion, whom he joins in a robbery and later at the Boar's Head Tavern where they enact a parody of the interview beteen the Prince and his father the king. Later the meeting does occur and the wild young Prince promises to reform.
Falstaff is beside the prince at the Battle of Shrewsbury, where he expounds at length about honour and claims to have killed Hotspur.
Part 2 covers the period between the battle of Shrewsbury and Henry IV's death. Scrope, Hastings and Mowbray attempt rebellion in their turn but are tricked into disbanding their forces and are then executed. Pistol appears, and we see Falstaff with Mistress Quickly and Doll Tearsheet. Out in the English countryside, Falstaff goes recruiting for support and persuades Justice Swallow to lend him one thousand pounds on the strength of his special relationship with Prince Harry the future king. When he returns to London, however, he finds the prince crowned Henry V and very much reformed. Indeed he dismisses Falstaff and consigns him to prison.

Henry V (1598-9)

Encouraged in his ambitions by the Archbishop of Canterbury, Henry V sets out to take the Crown of France. Before taking ship, however, he discovers that Cambridge, Scrope and Grey are plotting to assassinate him at Southampton. He takes Harfleur and marches on to Calais; but the French army interrupts his advance at Agincourt, where Henry emerges victorious from battle. Now Henry marries the French king's daughter Katharine.

We learn of the death of Falstaff from Mistress Quickly who has married his companion Pistol. Pistol together with Bardolph and Nym go on campaign with Henry but the latter two are hanged for looting while Fluellen beats Pistol for insulting the Welsh. Fluellen is then drawn into more arguments by Henry himself, this time with the English soldier Williams.

Henry V represents the hero of English nationalism, a kingliness vindicated by his ability to act for a nation rather than for himself and to become the incarnation of every interest.

Julius Caesar (1599-1600)

Rome 44 B.C. With others, Cassius prepares a conspiracy against Julius Caesar whose power he both fears and envies. Once noble and unselfish, Caesar has become besotted by his own power. That is why the idealistic Brutus, once Caesar's friend and a wise and respected senator, is drawn into the conspiracy and agrees to strike the fatal blow against Caesar on the Ides of March. Brutus' argument is that he does what he does in defence of Rome against a tyranny which would destroy it. Mark Antony, much loved by Caesar and hitherto a boisterous young man without aspirations to power, seizes the time. Pronouncing the funeral oration over the dead Caesar, Mark Antony brilliantly turns the whole situation to his advantage, manipulating the citizens of Rome against the conspirators with his speech to 'Friends, Romans and Countrymen'. Thus the assassins are driven out and the triumvirate of Octavius, Lepidus and Antony takes power in

Rome. In exile, Brutus and Cassius quarrel, and Brutus accuses Cassius of greed and bribery. They are briefly reconciled. Then Brutus hears that his wife Portia is dead. Two years after Caesar's death, the armies led by Brutus meet the Roman legions under Antony at Philippi. Brutus and Cassius are defeated and kill themselves.

Timon of Athens (1604-5)

Timon is a wealthy ruler surrounded by sycophants and timeservers happy to share his riches. They flatter him and seduce him with worthless presents, and Timon seems unable to see how shallow is their respect and admiration for him, despite the warnings of his steward Flavius. When the money runs out, so does the admiration of his fairweather friends. When Timon turns to those he has helped, they reject him and ignore his appeals for help.

Timon summons them to a feast. They assume his wealth has been restored and arrive with their usual expressions of fawning flattery. When the dishes arrive, they are filled only with hot water and Timon throws the empty dishes at the 'smooth smiling parasites' and drives them out.

Timon then leaves the city for the woods, where he lives from what he can gather and refuses contact with any other human being. One day, while digging for roots he finds gold which he maliciously presents to any passing stranger. One of them, the rebellious general Alcibiades, takes the gold in exchange for a promise to Timon that he will lay waste to Athens. When Flavius finds him, Timon has to acknowledge that there is goodness in at least one other human being – yet he still sends him away. Meanwhile in Athens the besieged rulers plead with Timon to return and overcome the siege mounted by Alcibiades. His bitter retort is to suggest they kill themselves to escape the rebels' wrath. Later a poor soldier discovers Timon's grave by the sea, where his tombstone repeats his contempt for hypocritical mankind.

Antony and Cleopatra (1606-7)

Antony is in Egypt where he is fascinated – as Caesar had been before him – with the Egyptian queen Cleopatra. She is not only sensual and beautiful ('Age could not wither her, nor custom steal/her infinite variety') but also powerful and cunning in defence of her own state. While in Rome jealousies and rivalries break out, Antony remains with her and falls increasingly under her influence until he hears of the death of his wife Fulvia. In Rome internal wars are about to break out and his fellow consul Octavius is angry with Mark Antony's apparent disregard for matters of state, but is reconciled when Antony marries his sister Octavia and agreement is reached with Pompey.

But Octavius has other ambitions and getting rid of the third member of the triumvirate, Lepidus, turns against and defeats Pompey and 'speaks scantly' of Antony. Returning to Egypt, Antony prepares for the inevitable war with his erstwhile ally. Persuaded by Cleopatra, he embarks on a sea battle at Actium where Octavius Caesar triumphs, going on to defeat Antony finally at Alexandria. His friend Enobarbus deserts him – his errors the fruit of his internal confusions ('things outward/ Do draw the inward quality after them / To suffer all alike') – and rumours reach him that Cleopatra is dead. In despair he stabs himself and is carried to Cleopatra, who lives, in whose arms he dies. Cleopatra, distraught at Antony's death and unwilling to be paraded as the prisoner of Octavius Caesar, kills herself with the bite of an asp.

Coriolanus was a respected warrior in Rome and one known to be concerned above all with honour. He is the acknowledged leader of the city's armies but appears to disdain both the plaudits of his admirers and all possibility of gain or booty. But he is also an arrogant patrician with only contempt for the mass of the people.

Returning to Rome Caius Marcus (as he still is) after defeating the Volsce at Corioli, he is met with great popular acclaim, given the name of Coriolanus (victor over Corioli) and offered the consulship of Rome. The other tribunes, jealous of his power, conspire against him; but it is his own contempt for the common people that ultimately brings his downfall. He is banished from Rome, and in his rage he goes to join his old enemy Aufidius and appears again outside Rome, this time leading the Volscian armies. Old friends come to him and plead with him not to take the city; but it is eventually his mother Volumnia and his wife Virgilia who dissuade him from his purpose. He returns to Corioli but there he meets the smouldering envy of Aufidius, who murders him.

Shakespeare's English and Roman history plays : a *Marxist* analysis

Preface

The British Shakespearean scholar Kenneth Muir once wrote that he thought he could make a shrewd guess as to which of his American colleagues were Republicans and which were Democrats by the way in which they wrote about Shakespeare's English history plays: the Republicans, he suspected, emphasised his Tudor orthodoxy while the Democrats deprecated this emphasis. As a Marxist who regards literature historically, I do not see Shakespeare as either a Republican or a Democrat – or as a Marxist. It is all too easy to bend Shakespeare to make him fit into our own political position.

Yet if we understand the Shakespeare living in the world of nascent capitalism, we find that in some aspects he has a greater meaning for us, living in the world of late capitalism. His depiction of the decline of feudalism in his English history plays and of the rise and fall of Roman civilisation in his Roman history plays has significance for us in the period of the decline of capitalism. Shakespeare was not a Marxist. but just as Marx's reading of Timon of Athens helped him to crystallise his ideas about the workings of an acquisitive society[1], so a Marxist reading of Shakespeare's English and Roman history plays can help us to understand our own time. But this understanding can only be achieved if we are faithful to Shakespeare the Elizabethan. It is this belief that underlies this book.

I wish to thank the editors of Clio, English Language Notes, PMLA, Science & Society, Shakespeare Jahrbuch (Weimar), and Shakespeare Newsletter for granting me permission to use material published in their periodicals. I also wish to thank Dr Harry Keyishian, director of Fairleigh Dickinson University Press, for helpful suggestions that resulted in the improvement of the book.

Marxism and Shakespearean criticism

In my *Shakespearean Tragedy and the Elizabethan Compromise* (1957, re-issued with a new introduction in 1983) I sought to apply a Marxist analysis to Shakespeare's tragedies. In my *Shakespeare in His Time and Ours* (1968) I focused on his comedies. This book, then, concerned with his history plays, is in a sense the completion of over a quarter of a century's study of Shakespeare.

It may be well to begin by outlining its basic premises. What does Marxist criticism contribute to the understanding of Shakespeare? Before this question can be answered, the Marxist method of the study of literature must be defined – even if only in very concise form, for students of Shakespeare and others interested in him continue, despite the presentations of such Marxists as Terry Eagleton and Raymond Williams,[1] to have all too little knowledge of it.

Marxism holds that, just as coping with their environment leads in animals to the evolutionary development of natural organs, so in humankind it leads to the development of tools, human beings' artificial organs. The development of the means of production, the aggregate of tools socially organised, is the dynamic power of social development. Different social classes stand in different relationships to the mode of production. The class that owns the means of production determines within limits the distribution of the social product. Between this class and other classes there is a struggle over this distribution. The development of the means of production constantly transforms social relations, bringing about the rise of new classes and social revolution.

Each ruling class constructs an 'ideology', a system of ideas expressing its outlook on life, that dominates its age. Other classes have different interests and ideas, but until they become revolutionary they normally tend to accept the domi-
2 nant ideology.

In constructing an ideology, the ideologists of a class make frequent use of the ideas of the past in accordance with the same principle of economy of energy that distinguishes all production. The process, of course, is complex and is not a conscious one. An ideology acts as a rationalisation of a class's social position and material interests, but it is not mere hypocrisy: the rationalisation is to the class itself as well as to other classes. An example of this would be the Puritans among the bourgeoisie of Shakespeare's day, who were often denounced as hypocrites by their opponents, but who generally had the genuine strength of their belief that made it possible for them to gain adherents and make a revolution fifty years later. Ideology becomes a force in the class struggle, just as an individual's self-perception, even though mistaken, affects his or her actions.

On the 'economic foundations' or 'material base', the sum total of the relations into which people enter to carry on social production, there develops, then, an 'ideological superstructure' – the various systems of ideas and institutions of a society. 'Political, juridical, philosophical, religious, literary, artistic, etc., development is based on economic development,' noted Engels to Heinz Starkenburg. 'But all these react upon one another and also upon the economic base. It is not that the economic position is the *cause and alone active*, while everything else only has a passive effect. There is, rather, interaction on the basis of the economic necessity, which *ultimately* always asserts itself.'[2] The statement of Rene Wellek that 'Marx and the Marxists only admit the determining influence of economic and social conditions',[3] a hoary caricature that reduces Marxism to a crude economic determinism, is, therefore, indicative of general scholarly ignorance of Marxism.

In the different kinds of non-Marxist literary scholarship

(the study of literature in relation to the development of literary form, to intellectual history, to the history of science, to the history of religion, to myth and ritual, and so forth) the spheres of ideological activity are seen as independent 'factors', come from God knows where and each an 'influence' [3] on the others. Marxists, however, see all of these 'factors' as the different manifestations of a unified process of social development. They differ from the scholars studying 'the social and political background of literature', with whom they are often confused, in that they are not merely concerned with the influence of social institutions and political events upon literature. Seeing the class struggle as the motor force of history and the ruling ideas of an age as the ideas of the ruling class, they seek to analyse the living process of the interaction of literature with the other elements of the cultural superstructure and with the economic base upon which the superstructure is ultimately dependent.

Suggestions of the kind of questions Marxist analysis may lead one to ask of Shakespearean scholars of different schools may make these generalisations more meaningful. E M W Tillyard's *Elizabethan World Picture* is an important study in intellectual history that has deeply affected Shakespearean criticism. Marxists, however, ask what were the material and ideological forces that brought about the Renaissance modification of the mediaeval world picture and how the Elizabethan world picture is a rationalisation of the social position of the Elizabethan ruling class and an expression of its outlook.

They raise similar questions in considering the work of the literary historian tracing the development of a literary movement. Granted the significance of the morality tradition for Shakespeare and Elizabethan drama, what were the new social stimuli under whose influence the morality play developed into Elizabethan drama? What material and ideological forces caused the breakdown of the allegorical mode of apprehension in drama, literature, and other arts, but the persistence of many of its elements? And how did the class composition of the new theatre audience affect the drama?

Granted that, since writers economically make use of inherited materials, Falstaff is a marvellous compound of many literary traditions, how does the social psychology of the Elizabethan class of which he is a member affect his depiction?
4 What are the material roots of this social psychology?

And finally, Marxists ask students of 'the social and political background' like G B Harrison: granted that Essex's rebellion had the effect on the emotional climate you say it had, what were the class forces behind his rebellion? What were the developments in the economy that caused a 'climate of opinion' in which there was a rebellion and in which monarchy and parliament clashed? How did the developments in the economy, political events, and shifts in thought and feeling interact upon each other to produce what Patrick Cruttwell called 'the Shakespearean moment'?

Marxism does not pretend to have an easily used master key: there is no substitute for learning, judgment, and the critical insight that perceives the internal laws of a work of art. It does not offer an infallible 'party line'. It does not claim to overturn what has been established in 350 years of Shakespearean criticism: what could be offered by such a criticism could only be bizarre. But, seeking to unite the various kinds of historical scholarship into a single all-embracing system, it does offer the opportunity to attain a fuller understanding of Shakespearean drama by seeing it as the product of its society.

However, just as ideology is a force in the class struggle, so a literary work not only is a product of its society but acts upon that society. Indeed the great literary work also acts upon subsequent societies. It is able to do so, says Leon Trotsky, because, although societies differ, the different kinds of class society have common features. Basic human experiences are expressed in the great work of literature with such power that in expressing the ideology of its own age it throws into relief the common features of class society. Thus, for instance, the 'fear of death . . . in different ages, in different social milieus . . . has changed, that is to say, men have feared death in different ways. And nevertheless what was said on this score not only by Shakespeare, Byron, Goethe, but also by the Psalmist can move us.'[4]

'A work of art,' adds Trotsky, 'should, in the first place, be judged by its own law, that is, by the law of art.'[5] But the understanding of that law is enhanced by our study of how the ideological content of a work of art finds its form, without which there can be no art. The Marxist method, therefore, enables us to see Shakespearean drama in its fullest context.

That context includes contemporary society and how it has been shaped by the past. Just as, Frederic Jameson points out,[6] we read the parts of a literary work in the light of the entire work and yet cannot understand the work until we have read the parts of which it is composed, so we understand the past from the present and the present from the past. The historical study of Shakespeare is not, then, merely an exercise in antiquarianism. In the words of Robert Weimann, 'for literary history to study past significance makes no sense without an awareness of present meaning, and an awareness of present meaning is incoherent without the study of past significance.'[7]

The past with which Shakespeare's English and Roman history plays were concerned had meaning for his own day. So do these plays have meaning for the twentieth century. The critics of Shakespeare in closest touch with the reality of the present will find in the plays the truest 'present meaning' – provided that they understand their 'past significance'. Otherwise the 'present meaning' they find in them will be a superimposition that blurs Shakespeare's art. A Marxist understanding, however, will, as Jameson puts it, 'encourage us in a solidarity with the works and deeds of vanished or alien cultures and generations'[8] portrayed in the history plays and with the plays themselves.

6

Marx, Engels, and the historical criticism of Shakespeare

2

Marx and Engels not only provided an approach to literature that can be used by Shakespearean critics; they provided valuable hints concerning Shakespeare and his time. The foremost contemporary historian of seventeenth century England, Christopher Hill, has written of what Marx and Engels had to say about the English Civil War of that period: 'Marx and Engels were more right than the state of historical knowledge of their time could have led one to believe possible; their historical generalisations often anticipate the discoveries of much later researchers.'[1] The same can be said of their few pregnant remarks about the society of Shakespeare's time, the prevailing ideas of that society, and the way in which these ideas were used in Shakespeare's dramas.

'Absolute monarchy,' said Marx in one of his early essays, 'appeared in the period of transition, when the old feudal classes were decaying and the mediaeval burgher class was evolving into the modern bourgeois class, without either of the disputing parties being able to settle accounts with the other.'[2] In England a 'continuous alliance. . . united the middle class with the largest section of the great landowners. . . This class of large landowners, which had originated under Henry VIII,. . . did not find itself in conflict but rather in complete harmony with the conditions of life of the bourgeoisie. Its land-ownership, in fact, was not feudal, but middle class. On the one hand, it placed at the disposal of the middle class the necessary population to carry on manufactures, and on the other hand, it was able to impart to agriculture a development which corresponded to the state of industry and

commerce. Hence its common interests with the middle class, hence its alliance with the latter.'[3] This alliance, however, was carried on, it will be noted, by only a section of the great landowners, those who had commercialised their estates.
8 Consequently, when the civil war came, these landowners were split: 'the bourgeoisie was allied with the new nobility against the monarchy, against the feudal nobility, and against the established church.'[4]

R H Tawney fills in the meaning of 'feudal nobility', which, of course, was not the same as the feudal nobility of the Middle Ages. 'The wealth of some of the nobility, and especially of the older families,' was 'locked up in frozen assets – immobilised in sumptuous appurtenances, at once splendid and unrealisable. More important, the whole structure and organisation of their estates was often of a kind which, once a pillar of the social system, was now obsolescent. Side by side with more lucrative possessions, their properties included majestic but unremunerative franchises – hundreds, boroughs, fairs, and markets; a multitude of knights' fees, all honour and no profit.'[5]

Marx's distinction between the section of the landowners that was 'middle class' and that which was 'feudal' casts light on the celebrated 'gentry controversy' among the economic historians of our times. In the course of this ferocious polemic, in which Tawney and Lawrence Stone argued that the gentry rose relative to the aristocracy while H R Trevor-Roper denied it, it became clear to a careful reader that the participants were closer together than they admitted, agreeing, if only in passing, that both 'gentry' and 'aristocracy' were not homogeneous entities but rather that within each there were those who had been able to commercialise their holdings and those who had not. Thus Tawney, as seen above, at one point differentiated between the older and newer families in the aristocracy, and at another point he asserted that the 'frozen assets' that worked against the older aristocracy reorganising its estates likewise worked against the 'conservative landowners' who were 'commoners.'[6] So too

Stone interrupted his consideration of the aristocracy as an entity to admit: 'It is perhaps misleading, though convenient, to describe the Tudor aristocracy at the end of the reign of Elizabeth as a class' in view of its 'diversity of wealth, political ideas and heredity.'[7] Elsewhere he said, 'A great many of the older landed gentry were going under.'[8] And so too Trevor-Roper stated that very many of 'the older gentry, on their smaller scale, were in the same predicament as the older aristocracy' and that 'both classes were being transformed at an unequal rate'.[9]

In short, Marx's distinction between the 'new nobility' and the 'feudal nobility' ('aristocracy' might be a better term than 'nobility' so as not to exclude untitled members of the families of each and, instead of 'feudal', 'old' or 'feudalistic' might be better so as to avoid confusion with mediaeval feudalism) holds true, and the same distinction must be made between the 'enterprising' or 'improving' gentry and the 'unenterprising' or 'feudalistic' gentry. To the question of whether or not the gentry was rising, the answer would seem to be that part of it (the feudalistic gentry) was not rising and part of it (the enterprising gentry, producing for port towns and urban centres and having many links with the bourgeoisie) was rising. This is the conclusion to which Christopher Hill comes in his discussion of the controversy.[10]

The bourgeoisie, said Marx and Engels, served 'the absolute monarchy as a counterpoise against the nobility.'[11] Presumably, the 'new nobility', as a moderating senior partner of the bourgeoisie, was the great central support in the scale in which the monarchy balanced the bourgeoisie against the 'feudal nobility'. How, then, was this equipoise disturbed? Marx answers the question as follows: 'If the material conditions of life of society has so far developed that the transformation of their official political shape have become a vital necessity for it, the entire physiognomy of the old political power undergoes a transformation. . . Itself the product of the defeat of the feudal orders, and even taking the most active part in their destruction, it [absolute monarchy] tries now to

retain at least the semblance of feudal distinctions. Formerly favouring commerce and industry and also the rise of the burgher class, as being necessary conditions both of the national power and of its own brilliance, absolute power now
10 puts all kinds of obstacles in the way of commerce and industry, which have become more and more dangerous weapons in the hands of a powerful bourgeoisie.'[12] The growth in power of the bourgeoisie and its increasing weight in the political scale made it impossible for the monarchy to continue to use it as a 'counterpoise.'

In England this occurred when the war against Spain in 1588 mobilised the bourgeoisie, which was the leading force in pushing Elizabeth into the war and winning it.[13] The new spirit was expressed by clashes with the queen on matters –monopolies, taxes, church control, foreign affairs, the royal prerogative, and the rights of Parliament – that were also those on which the enterprising gentry and the bourgeoisie were to come into conflict with the Stuarts. 'The year 1588,' says A F Pollard, 'opened a new chapter in the political and constitutional development of England. . . Elizabeth. . . loses touch with her people; there is even a rebellion in London, and Protestants look forward to a change of sovereign. . . The Tudor period is dissolving into the Stuart.'[14]

Shakespearean scholars have been aware of a vital change in feeling during these years. 'The 1590s are the crucial years,' writes Patrick Cruttwell. 'In the Elizabethan *fin-de-siècle* there occurred a change, a shift of thought and feeling, which led directly to the greatest moment in English poetry: the 'Shakespearean moment' the opening years of the seventeenth century, in which were written all the supreme Shakespearean dramas.'[15] So, too, G B Harrison writes that 'a bitterness and disillusion' was very conspicuous in the last years of [Elizabeth's] reign. . . The causes of this pervading mood of melancholy are complex and difficult to analyse.'[16] The causes, which include lack of employment and patronage for university graduates, are undoubtedly complex and interacting, but underneath them all are the destruction of an equilibrium by the development of 'the material conditions of life of society.'[17]

As evidence that 'man's ideas, views, and conceptions, in one word, man's consciousness, change with every change in the conditions of his material existence, in his social relations, and in his social life', Marx and Engels point out that the history of ideas shows that 'the ruling ideas of each age have ever been the ideas of its ruling class.'[18] 'The class which is the ruling material force of society', they say in *The German Ideology*, 'is at the same time its ruling intellectual force. The class which has the means of material production at its disposal, has control at the same time over the means of mental production, so that thereby, generally speaking, the ideas of those who lack the means of mental production are subject to it.'[19]

How this statement holds for Shakespeare and the Elizabethan drama of the public theatre, whose audience was mixed but predominantly composed of apprentices, craftsmen, and small shopkeepers,[20] is indicated by Alfred Harbage: 'Combine the message of the Gospels, the conception of "laws and their several kinds" as codified in Hooker, the humane spirit of the circle of Colet, More, and Erasmus, and the moral emphasis of the Homilies, and one has the basic system of the popular drama in the time of Shakespeare.'[21]

This system of ideas, the system of ideas of Christian humanism, formulated by humanist scholars closely allied with the new aristocracy,[22] the conservative, specially privileged top sector of the enterprising landowners, was a modification of the mediaeval world view by classical learning. It retained the concept of hierarchy and degree as the basic principle of the universe, including the organisation of society, but altered the concept of the king, no longer a mere overlord, and of the aristocrat, in whom the virtues of the chivalric knight of the Middle Ages and those of the humanistic scholar of the Renaissance were now combined.[23] Christian humanism was the ideology of the new aristocracy, the dominant ideology of 'the period of transition' under absolute monarchy, and it received expression in the great literary works of the period as well as in the drama. That it lies behind the popular drama written for predominantly middle-class audiences illustrates the ideological subjection of which Marx and Engels speak.

12 Marx and Engels find, however, that the bourgeoisie that has become revolutionary has quite a different weltanschauung. 'The bourgeoisie, wherever it has got the upper hand, has put an end to all feudal, patriarchal, idyllic relations. It has pitilessly torn asunder the motley feudal ties that bound man to his 'natural superiors', and has left remaining no other nexus between man and man than naked self-interest, than callous 'cash payment'. It has drowned the most heavenly ecstasies of religious fervour, of chivalrous enthusiasm, of Philistine sentimentalism in the icy water of egoistical calculation. It has resolved personal worth into exchange value. . . For exploitation, veiled by religious and political illusions, it has substituted naked, shameless, brutal exploitation.' [24]

Written in the rhetoric of a manifesto, this statement, although it brings out well how the bourgeoisie shattered the inherited mediaeval notion of 'natural superiors', lacks the exactitude of a scientific treatise: the ideologists of any ruling class, including the capitalist class, weave new ideological concepts that veil exploitation, whether it is the concept that capital is the reward of enterprise and thrift or the concept that the 'survival of the fittest' is the law of human society. During the time of the Reformation, when 'the great international centre of feudalism was the Roman Catholic Church' and 'every struggle against feudalism. . . had to take on a religious disguise,' 'Calvin's creed was one fit for the boldest of the bourgeoisie of his time.' [25] Christopher Hill comments on this passage in Engels: 'All these ideas, of course, are familiar enough to historians today, thanks to the writings of Weber, Tawney and others. They have become almost commonplace. But they originally go back to Marx and Engels, and to no one else.' [26]

Just as the remarks of Marx and Engels on Renaissance society and ideology anticipate contemporary historians, so do some of their passing remarks on Shakespeare give insights unknown to the Shakespearean commentators of their own time, anticipate what has been written by contemporary critics, and are helpful even today. For these remarks arise out of their understanding of Shakespeare's time and of his plays.

In a passage in *Capital* in which Marx denounces the industrialists of his day, he refers to their 'Shylock-clinging to the letter of the law' regarding child labour and quotes *The Merchant of Venice*: 'The lynx eye of Capital discovered that the Act of 1844 did not allow 5 hours' work before mid-day without a pause of at least 30 minutes for refreshment, but prescribed nothing of the kind for work after mid-day. Therefore, it claimed and obtained the enjoyment of not only making children of 8 drudge without intermission from 2 to 8:30 p.m., but also of making them hunger during that time. "Ay, his heart, So says the bond".' [27] Thus, while some critics were arguing against the traditional interpretation of Shylock as an unmitigated villain, asserting that through him Shakespeare was presenting a plea for racial and religious tolerance (Marx's friend Heinrich Heine stated that in Shylock Shakespeare 'expressed the justification of an unfortunate sect'), [28] Marx stated that his most essential feature is not that he is a Jew but that he is typical of the capitalist who recognises 'no other nexus between man and man than naked self-interest.'

The comparison between Shylock and the nineteenth century industrialist is not fortuitous. Marx saw the mediaeval Jews as marginal traders and usurers who, unlike the capitalists of the Renaissance, did not bring a new mode of production but performed a necessary function in feudal society, as they did in the semifeudal society of nineteenth century Poland.[29] The modern Christian industrialist is, therefore, the consummation of the Jewish pre -capitalist trader and usurer: 'Judaism reaches its acme with the completion of bourgeois society, but bourgeois society first completes itself in the Christian world. Only under the reign of Christianity,. . . can bourgeois society. . . dissever all the generic ties of the individual, set egoism in the place of those ties, and dissolve the human world into a world of atomised, mutually hostile individuals.' [30]

Modern scholarship has shown that Shakespeare's contem-
14 poraries indeed saw their world as dissolving into 'a world of atomised, mutually hostile individuals' as a result of the activity of the most aggressive portion of the bourgeoisie, the money-lenders, who were subjugating both landowners impoverished by their dependence on fixed rents in a period of inflation and craftsmen needing credit now that they were producing within a more complex economic system, not merely for a local market whose requirements were readily discerned. [31] 'Throughout all England, not in London only,' lamented Thomas Wilson in 1572, 'men have altogether forgotten free lending,. . . making the loan of money a kind of merchandise, a thing directly against all law, against nature, and against God. And what should this mean, that, instead of charitable dealing,. . . greedy gain is chiefly followed and horrible extortion commonly used? I do verily believe the end of this world is nigh at hand.' [32] And, in fact, the half-mediaeval Elizabethan world would not too long after come to an end in the English Civil War.

Those who were most closely associated with money lending were the Puritans, the 'boldest of the bourgeoisie' who adhered most strongly to 'Calvin's creed'. 'The dissembling gospeller', says Wilson, 'under the colour of religion overthroweth all religion,. . . and for private gain undoeth the common welfare of man. And touching this sin of usury, none do more openly offend. . . than do these counterfeit professors of this pure religion.' [33] Engels's phrase about the 'religious disguise' of the bourgeoisie is here anticipated ('dissembling gospeller', 'under the colour of religion', 'counterfeit professors of this pure religion'), but Engels would not have so completely scored off Puritanism as mere hypocrisy: the function of ideology is precisely to rationalise the social position of a class to itself as well as to other classes.

The research of modern economic historians has to a

degree affected Shakespearean scholarship and criticism. It is now fairly much a commonplace among critics of *The Merchant of Venice* that, as the editor of the New Arden edition, John Russell Brown, said, 'in contrast to the "Jewish problem", the rights and wrongs of usury were a living issue to Elizabethans.' [34] Some critics have perceived that, in the words of E E Stoll, Shylock would have reminded Elizabethans of 'the precisians and Pharisees in their midst, who "put on gravity", were keen on money and, more than other Christians, addicted to usury.'[35] Others have perceived that there is an opposition of values between Portia's Belmont and Shylock's Rialto,[36] between 'the beneficence' that 'civilised wealth' gives 'to those who use it graciously to live together in a humanly knit group' and the 'ridiculous and pernicious consequences in anxiety and destructiveness' that 'the evil side of the power of money' brings,[37] between 'the life-value and the money-value.' [38] Still others have seen Antonio as 'the very embodiment of Christian love' and Shylock as 'the antithesis to it.' [39]

All of these positions are adumbrated by Marx and Engels, who saw Shylock as the representative of the capitalist ethic and Calvinism as the ideology of the incipiently revolutionary section of the bourgeoisie, which 'resolved personal worth into exchange value' and unknit the old feudal ties of a society whose exploitation was 'veiled' by 'religious illusions.' For what is Belmont, presided over by that great Renaissance lady, Portia, and won by Bassanio, a 'scholar and a soldier', (1.2. 111)[40] who conforms to the Renaissance ideal of the gentleman, if not the 'feudal, patriarchal, idyllic' picture of a Christian society that had been assimilated in modified form into the ideology of the new Tudor aristocracy?[41] To Belmont, where a gracious aristocracy appreciates him and his humour, comes Lancelot Gobbo, having left the service of the niggardly Shylock, who would have liked to have him working all of the time and eating none of the time (2.5.45-48), as did the industrial capitalists of Marx's day, to enter the service of the openhanded Bassanio, who possesses 'the grace of God'

(2.2.149) and gives freely.

Marx's view of capitalism as 'a world of atomised, mutually hostile individuals' in which there is 'no other nexus between man and man than naked self-interest' is derived from his reflections in *The Economic and Philosophical Manuscripts of 1844* on Timon's two apostrophes to gold (4.3.25-45 and 381-92), in which he hails gold as that which both 'sold'rest close impossibilities / And mak'st them kiss', which brings together seemingly irreconcilable things in close embrace and kiss, and severs the closest ties, as of 'son and sire.' Marx comments: 'Shakespeare portrays the essence of money excellently. . . If money is the bond that binds me to human life, that binds society to me and me to nature and men, is not money the bond of all bonds? Can it not tie and untie all bonds? Is it not, therefore, also the universal means of separation?. . . It is the universal whore, the pander between men and peoples.'[42]

Kenneth Muir makes an interesting observation about Marx's comment on Timon's speeches: 'Marx uses the quotations from *Timon of Athens* to support his criticisms of an acquisitive society. One might go further and say that some of these criticisms were suggested by Shakespeare, and that Shakespeare was one of the spiritual godfathers of *The Communist Manifesto.* Marx would doubtless have become a Communist even if he had never read *Timon of Athens,* but his reading of that play helped him to crystallise his ideas.' [43]

Be that as it may, it is indicative of Marx's sympathetic understanding of Shakespeare that he speaks of money as 'the universal whore', for Shakespeare twice uses 'usury', 'the means by which money multiplies, as synonymous with 'prostitution.' The fool in *Timon of Athens* tells the usurers' men that he, like they, serves a usurer, for his mistress is a whore (2.2.104–8), and the pimp Pompey says that the 'usury' of prostitution is superior to the usury through which wealth and dignity are acquired (*Measure for Measure*, 3.2.2, 6-11). So, too, Marx's characterisation of money as a 'pander' recalls the description by the Bastard (*King John,* 2.1.567-98) of 'Commodity', private profit, as 'this bawd, this broker', a word that meant both 'pawnbroker' (*OED*, 2,2) and 'procurer, pimp, bawd' (*OED*, 2,4).

Marx's comment is not merely an explication of Timon's speeches. It points to the very heart of the play. While his contemporaries were arguing against their predecessors that the early Timon is an ideal figure, not a depiction of foolishly ostentatious prodigality,[44] Marx went beyond them to suggest that Timon in his disillusioned idealism is reacting against what Shakespeare perceived was happening in Elizabethan society.

In this he anticipates what E C Pettet has said: 'As the Timon of the first Act is not an abstract type of the prodigal but an ideal feudal lord,[45] the representative of specific mediaeval values, a dispenser of feudal bounty, so the Timon of the last two Acts is. . . a man shattered and disillusioned to the point of madness by his discovery that the traditional beliefs he has lived by are no longer the beliefs of the world around him. . . Timon's acquaintances. . . are the children of the new world around him.. . . A dozen words of Lucullus. . . illuminate the change in a vivid lightning flash: "This is no time to lend money, *especially upon friendship without security.*" These words are the direct contradiction of mediaeval Christian morality, which had taught that money should be lent only as an act of friendship. . . All Timon's acquaintances. . . belong unmistakably to the Shylock world of the cash-nexus.' [46]

The contrast between the world of 'mediaeval Christian morality' and the 'Shylock world of the cash-nexus' is epitomised in Timon's imprecation against the brigands:

Love not yourselves; away,
Rob one another. There's more gold; cut throats,
All that you meet are thieves. To Athens, go,
Break open shops; nothing you can steal
But thieves do lose it.
(4.3.445-49)

The 'love not yourselves', which of course means 'love not each other', counterpoises with savage irony the 'love thy neighbour' ethic with the 'cut throat competition' of capitalist society, in which all property is theft. This is indeed, to repeat once more Marx's words, 'a world of atomised, mutually hostile individuals.' [47]

To Marx's statements about how Shakespeare presented in *The Merchant of Venice* and *Timon of Athens* the new world of the cash-nexus that was coming into being, we can add Engels's statement about the 'Falstaffian background' of 'impoverished hireling soldiers and adventurers of all sorts' in the 'period of the breakdown of feudalism' in his letter to Ferdinand Lassalle discussing Lassalle's historical drama *Franz von Sickingen*.[48] It is odd that in the vast amount that has been written on the character of Falstaff so little attention has been devoted to his relation to the London underworld of Shakespeare's day, drawn in large part from the declassed members of the declining feudal sector of society. Engels' remark about Falstaff, however, anticipates the observation by the British Marxist T A Jackson in a fine essay on Falstaff neglected by the world of Shakespearean scholarship: 'Shakespeare, in depicting Falstaff and his crew depicted from life, in vivid truth, the phenomena of *decadence*, the degeneration and decomposition of an absolute class – that of the dependents upon the feudal order.' [49]

Taken together, Marx's and Engels's statements point the way to the understanding of Shakespeare's historical position contained in this passage in an essay by A Smirnov: 'Living on the watershed of two epochs – between a feudalism which was already dying away and a capitalism which was still in the process of being born – Shakespeare was actively critical of both these orders.[50] On the one hand, he never wearies of exposing avarice and the power of gold, the cult of ready money: – in *Timon of Athens*;. . . in *King Lear* (where the old King, made wise by his misfortunes, cries out:. . . "Plate sin with gold, and the strong lance of justice breaks")[51]. . . in *The Merchant of Venice*. . . On the other hand, in his histories, Shakespeare shows how great was the evil and danger to the country as a whole represented by the wild, unruly feudal leaders,[52] ridicules aristocratic arrogance in the comedy *All's Well That*

Ends Well,[53] plays upon certain typical features of feudal parasitism in the image of Falstaff, etc.'[54]

Despite the excellence of this general statement, Smirnov's discussion of the individual plays in his *Shakespeare: A Marxist Interpretation* is abstract and schematic in its analysis and reductive in its description of the characters. Marx, however, was well aware of the dangers of making literary characters into mere spokesmen for ideas, as can be seen from his letter to Ferdinand Lassalle criticising the latter's *Franz von Sickingen*. The personae of the drama with some exceptions, he says, do not have 'characteristic traits' and indulge in 'much too much self-reflection'; Sickingen is 'drawn much too abstractly'; Maria is given a speech in which, contrary to her character as previously depicted, she presents 'a doctrine of rights'; Sickingen and Charles V in their confrontation sound too much 'like lawyers holding forth in court', there are lacking 'representatives of the peasantry' and 'the revolutionary elements in the cities', who would have provided 'an important and active background' and would have more appropriately voiced the 'modern ideas' assigned to Sickingen. If Lassalle had been more successful in these matters, Marx tells him, 'you would then have *Shakespearized* more; at present, there is too much *Schillerism*, which means making individuals into mere mouthpieces of the spirit of the times.' [55]

For Marx and Engels a literary work has its own dynamism that causes its characters to develop not in accordance with their creator's preconceived ideas but with the demands of the work. The demands of the work, in turn, are governed by the artist's perception of life, which may contradict his formally held ideas. Engels says of Balzac that, although *La Comédie Humaine* 'is a constant elegy on the irretrievable decay of good society' and its author's 'sympathies are all with the class doomed to extinction,' Balzac 'was compelled to go against his own class sympathies and political prejudices,' showing 'the necessity of the downfall of his favourite nobles' and portraying them 'as people deserving no better fate.' He therefore distinguishes between Balzac's reactionary ideology and the historical insight provided by his work, from which, he said, 'I have learned more than from all the professed historians, economists and statisticians of the period together.' [56]

This distinction is relevant to the study of Shakespeare's
20 history plays. Liberal-democratic critics object to the scholarship that finds Shakespeare's ideology to be that of a 'Tudor orthodoxy' that the critics boldly reject. They would like to make Shakespeare not an Elizabethan monarchist but a twentieth century democrat. But Shakespeare's ideology did not preclude his giving an insightful view of the past in which human beings – complex, living human beings representative of different social classes, not abstract ideas masquerading as human beings – clashed in struggles that not only had significance for his time but have significance for our own. In fact, it is precisely because of his ideology, which no one, I presume, would accept as providing answers to the ills of our society, that he is able to foreshadow those ills, the product of the destructive bourgeois individualism he witnessed in his own society. In doing so, he helps us to perceive how the capitalist content of bourgeois democracy is eating away at the democratic form and is threatening the destruction of the world.

The Marxist approach and Shakespearean studies today

3

Since the publication of *Shakespearean Tragedy and the Elizabethan Compromise*, in which I sought to develop the insights of Marx and Engels on Shakespeare and his time, making use at the same time of current scholarship, including my own, Shakespearean studies has become even more of an industry than it already was. The old capitalist slogan 'export or die' has its academic equivalent in the saying 'publish or perish' But Shakespearean studies is an industry of a peculiar sort: the crisis of overproduction does not cause the closing down of the factories but the piling up of the products in huge annual bibliographies consulted for special purposes by other producers. To attempt each year to go through the entire year's work on Shakespeare is a virtually impossible task. One would have time to read nothing else, not even Shakespeare's plays themselves.

It may be worthwhile, however, to try to stand back and to inspect insofar as one is able the results of these unceasing labours. In this a helpful guide through the vast warehouse is Richard Levin's *New Readings vs. Old Plays*, a book that has been widely and justly praised. Trained in the school of the so-called Chicago critics, who were concerned with the critique of literary criticism, Levin has a keen eye for the excesses of other critics concerned with English Renaissance drama, especially Shakespeare. He has industriously explored the warehouse and revealed the worthlessness of most of the goods contained in it.

However, Levin himself is not free of excesses in his evaluation of Shakespearean criticism. He has thus denigrated much that is of great value. It is as if one were to write slightingly of the neoclassical mechanical adherence to artificial rules without acknowledging the greatness of Johnson, of romantic effusions without acknowledging the greatness of Coleridge, and of Victorian moralising without acknowledging the greatness of Bradley.

What I propose to do, therefore, is to use the analysis of Levin in both its strengths and weaknesses as a convenient point of departure for a cursory discussion of contemporary Shakespearean criticism. Through this discussion I hope to indicate how Marxist Shakespeareans, while aware of the shortcomings of other kinds of Shakespearean criticism, can usefully assimilate the best of them.

Levin shrewdly traces the plethora of 'new readings' that allegedly reveal remarkably new insights hitherto undreamed of to the triumph of the New Criticism, with its use of 'close reading' techniques and its derogation of historical scholarship, and to the pressure to say something new. Contributors to the professional journals 'know that their interpretations are not likely to be published unless they say something about the work that has never been said before, which all too often means. . . that they must say something strange.' But this drive goes contrary to the 'most reasonable hypothesis about a play of this period', which is that, 'unless proven otherwise, it is in its primary aspect what it appears to be, and what it has been taken to be by the overwhelming majority of viewers and readers down to the present – namely, a literal representation of particular characters engaged in particular actions. . . If we begin by looking for the play's primary meaning in this experience [the "response" to "the contour of these actions"], then we will not assume that the literal representation which evokes it is a form of code or puzzle requiring some special lore to unlock.'[1]

In speaking of 'the most reasonable hypothesis', Levin is using the vocabulary of the Chicago critics, but one does not have to be a Chicago critic to agree with him. In fact, I have previously said something not unlike what he has to say: 'Shakespeare, a dramatist writing for a broad audience, used firm, bold strokes for the basic designs of his plays. . . If the critic, intent on the intricate internal patterns he sees or thinks he sees, does violence to the basic design, he has lost Shakespeare.'[2]

Within the firm outlines of these designs, however, there are manifold complexities. The new methods of analysis developed by each age in accordance with its own predilections reveal new things only dimly perceived before. It is to the complexities revealed by the best Shakespearean criticism of our time within what has been accepted by the overwhelming majority of viewers and readers of the past that Levin is insufficiently sensitive.

Levin's method is to divide the 'new readings' he examines into different categories. For each category he presents a series of anonymous quotations as illustrations of the fallacy inherent in that category of reading. Each critic parades, as it were, in the fancied gorgeous garment of his 'new reading', which, for the clear-eyed analyst and the reader enlightened by him, as for the innocent child in 'The Emperor's New Clothes', does not hide his actual nakedness.

The critics are unnamed because, Levin says, they were 'selected quite arbitrarily to exemplify a point and were no more 'guilty' than many others who could have been quoted for the same purpose' and because he did not wish to be 'gratuitously personal.'[3] At the end of the book, however, the authors and works cited for each category are given in alphabetical order. Thus, although the individuals in Levin's picture of naked critics are not given particular identification, the reader knows every one who is in the picture. Since Levin is not concerned with differentiating the critics from each other but rather with focusing on certain common anatomical features, there does not seem to be any good reason for forgoing the customary documentation. What does it matter if a given critic in the procession is not specifically named, if all are equally naked? On the other hand, the lack of documentation makes it almost impossible for the reader to check the quotations to see if in the context of their works some of the critics may not, after all, really be as naked as Levin believes. This is particularly troublesome when the list includes such respected and influential works as Robert B Heilman's *This Great Stage*, Northrop Frye's *Anatomy of Criticism*, and G Wilson Knight's *The Imperial Theme*.

By simply giving horrible examples and generalising about them instead of seeking to come to grips with critics worthy of his mettle, Levin presents abuses of method as the weaknesses of the method itself. 'The thematists', he says, '. . . assume that the play is not about what it appears to be about – the particular actions of particular characters – because it is really about a general idea. . . And since in the abstractness of that idea the specific structure or physiognomy of the play is inevitably lost, the tendency of this approach is to lead us away from our actual dramatic experience.'[4]

This is true of many of the disciples of the New Criticism, but is it true of their masters? In one of the revolutionary textbooks for undergraduates edited in the 1940s by Cleanth Brooks, Robert Penn Warren, and Robert B Heilman, the editors say: 'The most tempting account of the relation of the story to its theme is that which explains the story as merely an *illustration* of the theme. . .' But, they add, such an account 'neglects the fact that the organisation of the story, if it is valid, does much more than illustrate – it qualifies and modifies the theme. The form of the story states the theme so precisely that for an *exact* statement of it we must turn to the whole body of the story itself. The brief, condensed statements of the 'theme' which we use may serve well enough as a sort of shorthand account of a quite complicated matter. But they are not equivalent to the story itself. . . *even in terms of statement*.'[5]

Thus, when Brooks and Heilman explain to undergraduates the complexities of *King Lear* analysed in Heilman's *This Great Stage*, they inform them that its 'profound theme', which emerges from the 'remarkably skillful integration of its numerous parts in a controlled form,' 'cannot be simply set forth.' Nevertheless they find it useful to present the 'sort of shorthand account' that *Understanding Fiction* had emphasised was only an approximation: 'The play repudiates Gloucester's despair. . . What the play reaffirms, is, on the one hand, the tragic consequences of the human failure of understanding, and, on the other hand, the human ability to regain, or retain, understanding in the face of violent temptations to make bargains and save one's skin', an ability that rises from 'the capacity of man for a kind of spiritual rehabilitation.' [6]

The concept of theme has its limited use if one is aware that it serves as a crystallisation of critical analysis of the particularities of the play, not as what Levin calls a 'leap' from the particular to the general. In fact, such a crystallisation is often rather difficult to avoid even by those who reject the concept. Thus Levin includes Marvin Rosenberg's *The Masks of King Lear* in his 'honour roll' of 'voices. . . crying out in the thematic wilderness',[7] but Rosenberg, although interdicting all statements of 'a unifying thematic assertion' at the beginning of his book, emerged from his own critical analysis with the concluding statement: 'Only a tragic vision as vast as one of his own lines from *Lear* can suggest the whole implication of the play's world for our own: Edgar's "it is, / And my heart breaks at it." ' [8] He did not realise that the statement that the perception of ultimate reality must bring heartbreak is as much a 'unifying thematic assertion' as 'men learn by suffering' or 'the gods are just' or the others that he scorns.

It is true, however, that most of the 'thematists' Levin quotes do 'lead us away from our own actual dramatic experience', misusing a critical tool. So, too, Levin astutely demonstrates the arbitrariness of the 'ironic' readings he examines. *Irony* is a key term in the vocabulary of the New Criticism. Whereas, however, the best of the New Criticism uses this concept to show how the surface meaning is the text is qualified so that it is not negated but rendered more complex,[9] Levin's critics use it to destroy the surface meaning, making use of such techniques as what he aptly calls 'character assassination' – withholding information about a character's good points and emphasising whatever may possibly be construed to his disadvantage so that characters traditionally regarded as sympathetic are made to be unsympathetic – to make the play strangely 'new'. Thus Levin quotes the amusingly ridiculous statement of a critic about *Romeo and Juliet*: 'Sadly enough, most spectators have also taken at face value. . . [the] play's tragic sentimentality. . . They fail to see that as a hero Romeo lies midway between the surrealist horror of the homicidal Richard III, and the bathos of Pyramus. Like Richard, also, Romeo is a catalyst of disaster, and something close to a mass murderer.'[10]

Brooks and Heilman, on the other hand, in finding a number of ironic parallels between Falstaff and Hotspur, two outwardly dissimilar characters, do not deny the surface contrasts between them. Even though Falstaff is 'old in the ways of vice', he has a 'childlike quality' in his 'vitality' and 'thoroughgoing intellectual honesty', a 'kind of innocence' that contrasts with the 'pretence and hypocrisy' of 'the adult world.' So too Hotspur, even though he is in some respects 'an epitome of manliness', has in his impulsiveness and boyish love of adventure 'a kind of innocence which sets him apart from the more calculating of his fellow-conspirators.' His 'childish foolhardiness' in fighting before the arrival of reinforcements is as disastrous for the rebels as Falstaff's 'common sense' and selfish egoism, the egoism of the child who has not yet acquired responsibility, would be disastrous if practised by Hal, for whom he has acted as a father-substitute and tutor.[11]

Brooks and Heilman's recognition of these ironically incongruous similarities in the midst of dissimilarities illuminates the complexity of Shakespeare's character depiction. It is, moreover, useful for those who are concerned with Falstaff and Hotspur as expressions of Elizabethan ideology and as representatives of social classes, as they are not. Their analysis helps us to see them as being in different ways figures of disorder, although both are sympathetic characters, Falstaff a member of the decadent feudalistic aristocracy who exhibits the clown's irrepressible resilience and love of life and Hotspur a member of the feudalistic aristocracy at its best, with its chivalric virtues as well as its social defects.[12]

The fact is, that while the New Criticism may be deplored for looking upon literary works as self-sufficient objects apart from life, the New Critics gave the literary scholars of their day what might be called a much needed advanced course in remedial reading. It is not necessary to adopt their approach to make use of their lessons. As Leon Trotsky said of the Russian formalists, the precursors of the American New Critics, their methods have a 'subsidiary, serviceable and technical significance', but only 'the social and psychological approach. . . gives a meaning to the microscopic and statistical work done in connection with verbal material.'[13]

In the field of Shakespearean criticism Heilman's *This Great Stage*, in its study of the patterns of imagery in their relation to the interlinked themes of *King Lear*, represented a significant breakthrough that yielded many important insights. The study of imagery, initiated by Caroline Spurgeon in our time but anticipated by the eighteenth century William Whiter and by Dowden and Bradley, is one of the most distinctive contributions to the study of Shakespeare the twentieth century has made. Like other forms of analysis – the study of the characters in the plays, for example – it can easily be abused. By interweaving images arbitrarily plucked from the play the imagist can effect an artificially contrived pattern. What the imagist, like any other critic of Shakespeare, needs to do is to retain in his concentration on one element of the play a constant recollection of the total experience of the play. In Heilman's success in doing this lies the strength of *This Great Stage*.

As a consequence Heilman arrived through his study at some understanding of the way in which the play gives 'the sense of the passing of an era.' 'Lear, in one sense', he says, 'represents the old order, and the play becomes the tragedy of that order. . . Images of disease and injury and torture point the suffering of a world distracted by ripping out of old foundations. While some men are powerless and naked, others are overdressed, both in their hypocrisy and in their grasp of nine points of the law; as a sequence of images makes clear, clothes may protect, but they may also conceal; they signify the constant confusion of appearance and reality when standards are in flux.' [14]

This, however, is on a pretty high level of abstraction and needs to be reinforced by a concrete study of the historical crisis of Shakespeare's day that would in turn reinforce our understanding of the play. We may say of *This Great Stage* what Trotsky said of the formalists' study of folk art, 'You may count up the alliterations in popular proverbs, classify metaphors, count up the numbers of vowels and consonants in a wedding song. It will undoubtedly enrich our knowledge of folk art, in one way or another; but if you don't know the peasant system of sowing, and the life that is based on it,. . . you will have only understood the outer shell of folk art, but the kernel will not have been reached.' [15]

Just as Levin fails to give due credit to Heilman's *This Great Stage* for its contribution to the understanding of Shakespearean tragedy, so does he fail to give due credit to Frye's *Anatomy of Criticism* for its immense contribution to the understanding of Shakespearean comedy. The irrational law of society in Shakespeare's comedies, the passage through a 'green world' of woodland magic, the resolution of the problems caused by the irrational law as a result of this passage through the 'green world', the 'humours' character whose self-imposed bondage to his ruling passion corresponds to the irrational law of society, the magical power of the heroine whose return after her withdrawal through masculine disguise or presumed death brings about a new order – Frye's discussion of these and other features of Shakespearean comedy provides a chart that must serve as the basis for more detailed maps.

In dealing with the structural devices of the comedies, Frye is like a comparative anatomist. For most of us a bone is just a bone, but the comparative anatomist shows its function in the skeletal structure and compares it with the bones of animals of other genera and species that have the same function, pointing out the similarities. In doing so, the comparative anatomist provides a better understanding of how the organism works. So, too, with Frye in his *Anatomy of Criticism* and elsewhere.

But Frye is an anatomist without a theory that explains the course of evolution. For him each literary work is a 'self-contained unit' governed by its own 'dramatic postulate',[16] which is no more than a convenient gambit arbitrarily chosen. 'The author starts with a certain kind of story: this develops certain kinds of characters, occupying the strategic positions in that story, and each character owes his characteristic features, the things that make him what he is, to his place and function in the story. . . If one starts to tell a story about Tom Jones, one needs such a contrasting character as Blifil for structural reasons, not merely to symbolise the author's disapproval of hypocrisy.' [17] But surely Fielding's choice of hero in the first place, and accordingly his choice of his contrasting character, was an expression of his way of looking at life acquired from his class outlook. It is not just a matter of working out 'structural problems'; the structural problems arise from the artist's need to impose order on life in accordance with his ideology.

Frye accordingly does not see that the basic story of the romantic comedies, the 'certain kind of story' with which Shakespeare started, the winning by a simple gentleman (Valentine, Orlando, Sebastian, Bassanio) of the hand of a great lady, is a reflection of the rise of the new Tudor aristocracy. He does not see that the basic story of the satiric comedies, the rejection of a worthy gentlewoman (Helena, Mariana) by a proud lord representative of the nobility corrupted by Italianism (Bertram) or of the spirit of Puritanism (Angelo), is a reflection of the destruction of the balance of class forces. He does not see that the basic story of the romances, that of the lost royal child recovered after having been brought up in the renewing environment of nature (Thaisa in *Pericles*, Guiderius and Arviragus, Perdita,

Miranda), is an expression of faith that time will regenerate the present decadent society as it did with past decadent societies.[18] Frye has enabled us to understand better the structure of Shakespearean comedy, but he has not perceived how that structure was shaped by Shakespeare's changing climate of feeling.

Having come to the defence of Heilman and Frye against Levin (I shall reserve my comments on Knight for later), I shall do the same for myself. In his discussion of 'Fluellenism' Levin argues that Shakespearean critics who find Christ figures in Shakespeare are like Shakespeare's Fluellen in *Henry V* who, in the belief that there are 'figures in all things', found that Henry's life mirrored Alexander's 'indifferent well' (4.7.31-33), comically making use of some absurdly far-fetched parallels. Since 'any two objects in the universe, no matter how diverse they may seem, must have similarities', one can always work up a list of parallels. 'The examples we have been looking at', therefore, 'cannot be regarded as abuses of the method; they are the method itself.' [19]

Levin, it should be noted, is not the first discoverer of 'Fluellenism'. In my *Shakespearean Tragedy and the Elizabethan Compromise*, I said that in Fluellen's speech Shakespeare 'poked fun at straining for extended historical analogies' and that this should warn us against turning the plays into 'subtle and intricately constructed allegories.' [20] However, this does not mean that Shakespeare could not suggest analogies at all. The dramatist does not suggest analogies by a piling up of similarities but through an implicit or explicit comparison that is pointed up by diction, allusion, and reliance upon the audience's commonly held associations.

The critic's evidence for the analogies he finds is likewise not a matter of compiling a list of similarities. It is a matter of sensitivity to the implications of the dramatist's words. Of course, this means that there is often room for differences of opinion and that all kinds of extravagances are possible. This same distinction applies to the study of symbolism, and is revealed in the misguided attitude that regards symbols as literary chocolate chips sprinkled decoratively over the work instead of natural elements that arise organically out of it – an attitude exemplified by the student in the creative writing class who said, 'My instructor is going to go over my story with me and help me put in the symbols.' But, however far afield critics addicted to the game of hunt-the-symbol can go, this does not mean that the critical study of symbols is invalid or that there is no arguing specific instances.

Levin's objection to the idea that dramatists can suggest historical analogies would invalidate the statement of all the critics who have written on Arthur Miller's *The Crucible* that this play drew an analogy between the Salem witch hunts and the McCarthyism of its day. I am afraid that most of them would continue to do so even after reading Levin. They might point out in support of their position that the phrase 'witch hunt' was currently used to refer to McCarthyism, that in Miller's adaptation of Ibsen's *An Enemy of the People* the fomentors of mass hysteria against Tom Stockmann echo red-baiting clichés, and that Tom's wife, referring to their plan to emigrate to the United States, says: 'I'd hate to go half around the world, and find out we're in the same place.'

Levin, sticking to his argument, could retort that the reinforcement gained from *An Enemy of the People* is simply 'a self-sustained chain reaction' such as that in which 'a character's credentials for Christ figurehood' are 'established by comparing him to other alleged Christ figures.' [21] He could also retort that the belief that Miller's audience, alive to the issues of its time, must have been reminded of McCarthyism is a 'postulation of a special audience with special viewing habits' [22] similar to that invoked by those referring to the Elizabethans' habit of analogical thinking based on their belief that the universe is a divine pattern whose figures repeat each other. I think that most audiences and readers, however, would remain convinced, and rightly so, that *The Crucible* has reference to McCarthyism.

When I provided *The Crucible* as example in response to

an earlier published version of Levin's discussion of 'Fluellenism', he replied that the unanimity of the critics of *The Crucible* is itself evidence of the actual existence of the implied comparison and that in such comparisons the two things must be 'so close and so evident in their conformity' with each other (*PMLA* 90 [1975]: 192-93) that there is no doubting their existence, neither of which was true of the Christ figures referred to by Shakespearean critics. He apparently did not realise that he had shifted his ground. Whereas before he had argued that the method itself was defective and could not be used to assert the existence of implied historical analogies in any play, he now acknowledged it could properly be used for *The Crucible*. Whereas before he had argued that any one can draw up a seemingly impressive list of coincidences in pointing out alleged parallells, demonstrating the invalidity of the method of the 'Christ-figure hunters', he now demanded just such a list of overwhelming similarities, which, incidentally, cannot be found in *The Crucible*.

What it is relatively easy to see in a contemporary play is also true of Shakespearean drama. It is not only to parallels in events that some of the so-called Fluellenist critics point but to biblical echoes and allusions in the dialogue, such as the echoes and allusions in *An Enemy of the People*. This Levin entirely disregards. Let us look at a specific example that seems to me to be as certain as Miller's suggested comparison between the Salem witch hunts and McCarthyism.

The Bishop of Carlisle speaks of Richard II as 'the figure of God's majesty' – Fluellen is not the only Shakespearean character who speaks of 'figures' – and says that if he is deposed England will be called 'the field of Golgotha' (4.1.125,144). Since Carlisle's prediction of the devastation of the civil war to follow will prove to be, as Shakespeare's audience well knew, accurate, it is difficult to see him as other than a choric commentator whose expression of opinion one must accept. It is equally difficult to see how if the deposition is compared to the crucifixion one can avoid comparing Richard with Christ.

Richard himself speaks of the disloyalty of the nobility, some of whom, he says to them (4.1.239-42), show an 'outward pity' and 'with Pilate wash your hands' but cannot 'wash away your sin', and of the faithlessness of the officers of state, who had cried 'All hail' to him as 'Judas did to Christ' (4.1.169-70). He is here, as Kenneth Muir says in *The Complete Signet Classic Shakespeare* (p439), using 'the Elizabethan convention by which a character comments on his own situation. . . to guide the feelings of the audience.'

Finally, York's reference to Richard's 'sacred head' (5.2.30), on which the London crowd threw dust, would seem in the light of the preceding passages to suggest a comparison between him and Christ: just as Christ suffered humiliation at the hands of the Jews, so did Richard at the hands of the London crowd. Here, therefore, are two characters who explicitly compare Richard to Christ and a third who does so implicitly. Richard, as Levin rightly says, is very far from being free of blame, but, as I have previously written, 'at one moment in the drama the associations gathered about the figure of a king, the situation and the allusions make him take on the aspect of Christ.'[23] The tradition of comparing a king to God was so strong that the followers of Charles 1 also compared him to Christ in his martyrdom.[24]

It so happens that there is extremely strong external evidence for the Richard-Christ analogy. A French eyewitness account of Richard's deposition, quoted in the New Arden edition of the play, specifically compares Bolingbroke to Pilate and 'the rabble of London' to whom 'he gave up his rightful lord' to 'the multitude of the Jews.' [25] Whether or not one agrees with J Dover Wilson in the New Cambridge edition that Shakespeare necessarily knew this account, surely it is, as he says, 'most remarkable' that not only this account but all four contemporary French accounts of Richard's deposition 'compare his betrayal with that of Christ and his enemies with Pilate and Judas, much as the play itself does.' [26]

One may add that it is likewise remarkable that Holinshed, even though he is ambivalent about Richard (an ambivalence in which he is followed by Shakespeare), finding that Richard was punished for his sins but that he was 'most unthankfully used of his subjects', says of the Archbishop of Canterbury that, in giving false assurances to Richard, he spoke 'not as a

prelate but as a Pilate.' [27] It is clear that the concept of a king as the 'figure of God's majesty' and the situation of Richard's being betrayed, humiliated, and renounced led fifteenth and sixteenth century historians to compare him with Christ. To find that Shakespeare also did so is only to say that he was a man of his time.

Finally, we might take up Levin's argument that 'after more than forty years of searching' the Christ-figure critics 'have not found anything to suggest that any character in any play by Shakespeare. . . was ever regarded as a figure of Christ, or of any other biblical personage,[28] by anyone is his time. . . Yet this surely is the sort of thing one would expect to be recorded somewhere – for instance, in the spirited debate that was then being waged about the morality of the drama, where it would have been especially relevant.' [29] But Levin must know that practical dramatic criticism was not written in Elizabethan times. No Elizabethan critic speaks of Cordelia as one who in the greatness of her love is reminiscent of Christ – but then, no Elizabethan critic mentions her at all. As for the defenders of the stage, they did not engage in detailed analysis of dramatic method, and in any case such references to Christ figures would not have been effective arguments against their zealous Puritan antagonists, who thought that 'sacred matter' could only have been profaned by being 'mixt and interlaced with bawdry' in the playhouse temples of sin.[30]

Why am I as a Marxist critic insistent on the presence of Christ figures in Shakespeare? I can only repeat the words of Robert Weimann, already quoted in chapter one: through an understanding of 'past significance' we arrive at 'present meaning.' Thus I shall freely concede that it is impossible for a director to indicate to a modern audience that Cordelia is to be seen as a Christ figure, but a production governed by my interpretation would give her life and death a significance denied in Peter Brook's production of *King Lear*, governed by Jan Kott's existentialist interpretation, in which the audience sees a bleak, meaningless world. We need not believe in God for Cordelia's love to make us believe in humanity. The discoveries that Lear makes about himself and life through Cordelia engender an appreciation of what the extinction of humanity, whose possibility is envisaged in *King Lear* would mean after all its heartbreaking struggles, an extinction that is more than ever possible in the age of the hydrogen bomb.

The presence of Christ figures in Shakespeare's plays is only one feature in what has come misleadingly to be known as 'the Christian interpretation of Shakespeare', which is often taken to be an interpretation of Shakespeare advanced by Christians rather than an interpretation that sees him as expressing a Christian outlook on life. The 'Christian' interpretation has its origin in a fundamentally new understanding in our time of the English Renaissance and the drama it produced. This new understanding stresses both the basic mediaeval heritage of the Renaissance and its drama and the important humanist modifications of that heritage;[31] the underlying Elizabethan assumption of the universe as constituting a divinely created pattern, with figures repeating each other; the representation of characters as following the main patterns of human behaviour set by Lucifer, Adam, and Christ; the suggestions in the major tragedies of a Christian afterlife.[32]

Although Levin rightly warns against attributing to the Renaissance a uniformity of thought (p164), he attributes such uniformity to our time, speculating that the 'Christian' interpretation of Shakespeare stems from the tendency of 'the relativistic and skeptical "modern sensibility"' to seek in Shakespeare 'a kind of substitute scripture' for the 'religious and moral absolutes' that have been lost.[33] In reality the 'Christian' interpreters of Shakespeare can be divided into two camps, the theologisers and the historical scholars. The theologisers – Roy W Battenhouse, Peter Milward, Sister Miriam Joseph, and others – have concentrated on theological works and sought to apply them to the plays. Battenhouse, the chief figure among them, is enormously erudite in theology and enormously ingenious in applying this theology to Shakespeare. The trouble is that he is far more erudite and ingenious than were the Globe spectators. In general the theologisers regard the plays as if they were addressed to those learned in arcane texts rather than to spectators familiar with prevalent religious beliefs of their time.

The seminal works for the 'Christian' interpretation of Shakespeare by historical scholars were Theodore Spencer's *Shakespeare and the Nature of Man* (1942) and E M W Tillyard's *The Elizabethan World Picture* (1943). I know that I was influenced by them in seeking to show how Shakespearean drama is expressive of the Christian humanist ideology of the new Tudor aristocracy.[34] The essential novelty—despite much preliminary scholarship—of what these books had to say is indicated by Tillyard's prefatory statement: 'People still think of the Age of Elizabeth as a secular period between two outbreaks of Protestantism.' [35]

Their influence was aided by the work of G Wilson Knight, which actually antedated them. A neoromantic of penetrating insights despite his mystical leanings and often cloudy prose, Knight had nothing but scorn for historical scholarship; the wild and whirling words of his rhapsodies on the other hand, give offence to sober historical scholars. If one picks and chooses, however, from what is borne along on the torrent of his rhetoric, one finds much of great value that complements the work of the scholars.

Thus his perception of the two opposing sets of images throughout Shakespeare's drama, the 'tempest' images and the 'music' images,[36] anticipated Tillyard's presentation of the thought-idiom of the Tudor period. 'Tempest' images (furious storms, oceans engulfing the land, rivers flooding their banks, uncontrolled weeping), he pointed out, suggest disturbances in the universe, in society, and in individuals. 'Music' images (sweet music, soft breezes, rivers flowing quietly into the sea) suggest universal harmony, social harmony, well-integrated personalities, and love. These symbolic images are the poetic expression of the Elizabethan concepts that Tillyard explored, the concepts of interrelated cosmic, social, and psychological orders, of the universe as held together by God's love, of society as held together by human love, and of the universe and the well-ordered society as constituting beautiful harmonies.

Furthermore, although Knight was to deny his paternity of the 'Christian' interpretation of Shakespeare (he is too idiosyncratic for there to be 'a school of Knight'), the analogies with Christ and the biblical echoes he found influenced many 'Christian' interpretations, including my own. Here, too, his critical insight anticipated the findings of scholarship. Thus his expression 'miniature Christ',[37] used to refer to Shakespearean Christ figures, is similar to that of the anonymous seventeenth century writer who said that the Christian following the way of Christ is a 'microchristus'.[38] For this seventeenth century writer was merely echoing the idea repeatedly stated in the Elizabethan homilies[39] and going back to the mediaeval devotional manual *The Imitation of Christ* (which had many Protestant sixteenth century editions) that Christ left an example to be followed by all good Christians.

The controversy about the 'Christianness' of the tragedies has been perhaps the chief Shakespearean controversy of our time. Although the fighting is still going on (witness Levin), the 'Christians' seem to be winning. At any rate, the 'Christian' interpretation has entered the mainstream of Shakespearean criticism, having been absorbed by many prominent Shakespeareans not involved in the controversy.[40] While, however, the 'Christians' are winning in the discussion of the tragedies,[41] they are losing in the discussions of the history plays, an indication, it would seem, of the extreme specialisation in Shakespeare studies today. The sharpness of the reaction against Tillyard's once highly influential *Shakespeare's History Plays* may be judged from the fact that in *Shakespeare Studies VIII* (1975), of three reviewers discussing books dealing with the history plays, one asserted that the '"orthodox"

view of the histories' established by Tillyard was no longer orthodox, a second declared 'I no longer accept Tillyard's theory—no more, I suspect, than do most interpreters of Renaissance literature today', and the third assured his readers
38 that the book under review was not so unoriginal as to be merely 'another barrage against Tillyard's approach to Shakespeare's historical drama.'[42]

About forty years ago there was a similarly strong reaction against A C Bradley's *Shakespearean Tragedy* marked by L C Knights's celebrated *How Many Children Had Lady Macbeth?*, whose title is a parody of Bradley's questions in his appendix. At that time I published an essay answering Knights and Bradley's other critics ('In Defence of Bradley', *College English 9* [1948]: 250-56). Shortly after, the tide of critical fashion turned in favour of Bradley, whose greatness was now generally acknowledged, whatever qualifications one might wish to make concerning what he had to say. This was, however, not at all due to my essay, which remained buried until it was resurrected by Katherine Cooke's *A C Bradley and his Influence in Twentieth Century Shakespeare Criticism* (Oxford: Clarendon Press, 1972). I expect that there will be a similar turning of the tide in favour of Tillyard, although what he had to say will not be accepted in toto. In the change of critical opinion toward Tillyard, however, I hope that this book will be a factor.

Shakespeare's view of English history

4

Introduction: The concepts dominating Shakespeare's view of English history and their material basis

Beginning with E M W Tillyard's *Shakespeare's History Plays* in 1944, there have been no fewer than twenty seven books[1] and innumerable articles devoted to Shakespeare's dramas on English history. What is the Shakespearean overall view of English history that emerges from these studies? Some do not address themselves directly to this question; some deal with different aspects of Shakespeare's historical outlook; many disagree with each other in their discussions of this outlook. In this chapter I shall seek to analyse what seem to me to be the concepts dominating Shakespeare's view of English history, integrating the studies of various scholars, arbitrating between opposing opinions, and making use of my own study.

The origin of the discussion was Tillyard's book, which for a while had a very strong influence but then came under successive attacks on a scale and of a vigour perhaps exceeding even those of the Romantic critics on Samuel Johnson and of the symbolist and imagist critics on Bradley. As in the case of these critical reactions, the attacks have often gone too far. Tillyard's study of what he called 'the Tudor myth' and of Shakespeare's use of it needs to be modified and supplemented, but not discarded – it remains a useful point of departure.

The reaction against Tillyard extended beyond his depiction of the 'Tudor myth' in Shakespeare's historical drama to his presentation of the 'Elizabethan world-picture' and its importance for Shakespeare. But Tillyard's statement that the idea of cosmic order is 'one of the genuine ruling ideas of the age, and perhaps the most characteristic' [2] remains valid despite the attacks of his opponents. The ruling ideas of an age are the ideas of its ruling class, and I have endeavoured elsewhere to show how the idea of cosmic order served to rationalise the social position of the new aristocracy, the main support and beneficiary of Tudor absolutism.[3] In Shakespeare's history plays the idea of cosmic order enlarged the significance of the chaotic consequences of feudal particularism, which had to be overcome by Tudor absolutism for the national state to be supreme.

Tillyard not only failed to formulate the 'Tudor myth' correctly and to perceive the material basis of the 'Elizabethan world-picture'; he failed to see clearly how Shakespeare, in addition to expressing the myth, displayed in good measure the reality of which the myth was a rationalisation. The managing editor of *Foreign Affairs*, writing with considerable restraint of the process by which Americans wrested a country from its native inhabitants, whom they almost extirpated, seized large stretches of territory from its neighbour, and extended its influence first over a continent and finally over the world under the idea of a 'manifest destiny' to which it had been appointed by God, stated: 'American foreign policy, like American literature, has been nurtured on myths, though the darker side of the American dream has been more often manifested in our actions than our words.' [4] So, too, did Tudor policy, domestic and foreign, although nurtured on the myths that also nurtured Tudor literature, have its 'darker side', which Shakespeare saw and incorporated into his view of English history.

One Elizabethan commentary on the events of Shakespeare's history plays that I shall use frequently is the historical portion of John Davies of Hereford's philosophical poem, *Microcosmos.* This work was summarised by both Tillyard and M M Reese [5] as exemplifying 'the contemporary notion of order or degree which was never absent from Shakespeare's picture of disorder in the Histories.' [6] Tillyard stated that the poems of Davies, who there is very strong reason to believe was personally acquainted with Shakespeare, epitomise the commonplaces of the time's serious thought, all the better for being the product of a second-rate mind, 'and that in *Microcosmos* he gives a 'very Shakespearean version of English history.' [7] Indeed, Davies is even more Shakespearean than Tillyard recognised, for his compressed account of English history brings into high relief not only the concepts that divine providence rules history and that the social order is part of the divine order of the universe but the other Shakespearean concepts, insufficiently appreciated by Tillyard, that divine providence works ordinarily through secondary causes, with men's actions having natural consequences, and that governments need to be firm and even ruthless, politic and even devious, against both internal and external foes.

Of another Shakespearean concept, that the divinely ordained natural order does not preclude social change, Tillyard had some perception, pointing out that the world of Richard II is one of mediaeval ceremony and ritual in contrast to the businesslike efficiency of his successor, Henry IV. However, this concept needs to be more thoroughly explored so that the social changes depicted by Shakespeare and the manner in which these changes are reconciled with the idea of an enduring social order can be perceived more fully.

Shakespeare was unaware of the underlying economic movement that produced the conflicts within the nobility that he depicted in his two tetralogies, a movement described thus by G R Elton: 'The long-term effects of plague and agricultural depression [caused by the decline in population, the consequent rise in the value of labour, and the collapse of serfdom] were to assist the change from feudalism to bastard feudalism[8] which other developments in social and political life were producing. . . The lords. . . found their incomes decaying and their assets in land deteriorating, a fact which helps to explain their violent unrest, cut throat competition, and lawless and ruthless fight for advantages.' [9] Nevertheless, if Shakespeare was unaware of the economic movement that had altered the relationship between the monarchy, the aristocracy, and the rising middle class, affecting the evolution of each, he was very much aware of this evolution, however much he simplified and foreshortened it. In the history plays

it is seen in process. Because the process was continuing in Shakespeare's day, there are a number of analogies suggested with Shakespeare's own time, the Lancastrian plays, as Charles Barber says, 'managing to deal simultaneously with mediaeval and Elizabethan England.' [10]

Divine providence in history

Although the sense Tillyard attributed to the phrase 'the Tudor myth'[11] sometimes shifted, what he basically meant by it was the idea that Bolingbroke brought on himself and the English people a divine curse in deposing Richard II, a curse that was manifested in part during his uneasy reign as Henry IV, was temporarily suspended during the reign of the hero-king, Henry V, and came down in full force during the reign of the third-generation member of his house to hold the throne, Henry VI. The Wars of the Roses that raged under Henry VI and his Yorkist successors were mercifully brought to an end when God, relenting, sent his chosen agent, Richmond, who defeated Richard III and ascended the throne, reuniting England by marrying a member of the house of York. This Tudor myth, Tillyard believed, was widely accepted and was expressed in Shakespeare's two tetralogies, which, even though the *Henry VI-Richard III* tetralogy was written before the *Richard II-Henry V* tetralogy, constitute when arranged in the order of history a great epic cycle, with *King John* acting as a kind of prologue and *Henry VIII* a kind of epilogue to it.

Scholars, notably Henry A Kelly, have, however, shown that the really pervasive Tudor myth was the narrower meaning of it that Tillyard sometimes used – the belief that Richmond, who as Henry VII was the founder of the Tudor line, was God's instrument in ending the dynastic struggle and the horrors of civil war.[12] Although Hall, whom Tillyard believed to be the main influence on Shakespeare, traced the inception of the dynastic struggle to Henry IV's deposition of Richard, he did not categorically state that there was a consequent hereditary curse and left the matter in doubt.[13] Holinshed, in discussing Richard II's reign, said that Henry IV 'and his lineal race were scourged afterwards as a dire punishment unto rebellious subjects',[14] but he did not refer to this statement or follow it up in any way in discussing the Wars of the Roses.

The fact is that Tudor historians were much less inclined to refer to divine providence than Tillyard indicates. Both Samuel Daniel in the introductory stanzas of his *Civil Wars* and Sir Walter Raleigh in his preface to *The History of the World* set forth in large terms a providential plan but subsequently failed to trace the pattern in detail. For humanist historiographers agreed that while everything is ultimately the work of God's providence, this providence normally operates through natural law, which is what the historian should study.[15] As Raleigh said, 'It is God that only disposeth of all things according to his own will. . . It is Nature that is obedient to all. It is God that doth good unto all. . . It is Nature that secondarily doth also good, but it neither knoweth nor loveth the good it doth.' [16] Nature operates in human affairs through 'the medium of men's affections [passions] and natural appetites.' [17]

The mediaeval analysts, who attributed everything directly to God, merely recorded isolated events as instances of God's judgments, not seeking to determine the causes of things. This, says Edmund Bolton in his notes on historiography in the early seventeenth century, is the weakness of Christian historians: 'The part of heavenly providence in the actions of men is generally left out by most of the Ethnics [pagans] in their histories. . . On the other side Christian authors, while for their ease they shuffled up the reasons of events in briefly referring all causes immediately to the will of God, have generally neglected to inform their readers in the ordinary means of carriage in human affairs.' [18] To explain everything as providential without seeking to explore 'the reasons of events' is the easy way for the historian.

It is this kind of perception of history that made possible Shakespeare's historical drama, which is concerned with human actors on the stage of history impelled by 'men's affections and natural appetites' and participating in a great series of events in which each of their actions has its necessary effects. That these events are understood to be part of a divine scheme of things gives a sense of historic inevitability, of human beings doing things to gain goals they wish to attain but unable to alter for their benefits the course of events, which proceeds in its own prescribed direction toward an end they cannot fathom. In the words of Raleigh, 'The corrupted affections of men, impugning the revealed will of God, accomplish, nevertheless, his hidden purpose and without miraculous means confound themselves in the seeming wise devices of their own folly.' [19]

Shakespeare more than once refers to the mystery of God's plan. In *Richard II*, York, with Gaunt, one of the two old men who, speaking with the wisdom of age, act as choric commentators, in describing Richard's gentle patience in the face of the crowd's jeering, states (5.2.34-38): 'Had not God, for some strong purpose, steeled / The hearts of men, they must perforce have melted, / And barbarism itself have pitied him. / But Heaven hath a hand in these events, / To whose high will we bound our calm contents.' So, too, the three choric citizens in *Richard III*, expressing their misgivings on hearing of Edward's death, comment on the inscrutability of God's purpose. 'All may be well', says one uncertainly (2.3.36-37), 'but if God sort it so'/ 'Tis more than we deserve, or I expect.' Another states that their very misgivings come from a 'divine instinct', a divinely inspired sense of approaching dangers, but concludes with the pious acceptance of God's will (41-45), 'But leave it all to God.' Each case presents a sense of a divine plan that includes calamities but has an ultimately beneficent purpose. So Daniel found that the fury of civil war that England had suffered was recompensed by 'the bliss of thee, Eliza, happy gain / For all our loss',[20] a kind of repetition of the paradox of the fortunate fall. For, as Raleigh said, God 'doth good unto all.'

Tillyard, then, makes too clear and distinct in its omnipresence the mystery of God's plan. His error is like that the 'Christian' interpreters of Shakespearean tragedy who place the Christian afterlife in the foreground rather than in the distant background, which can only result in nullifying the suffering already witnessed, robbing it of tragic significance. So also would too constant an insistence on divine providence cause the actions of the characters in the drama of history to lose their significance for the determination of the lives of future generations, the characters becoming mere puppets in the hands of a higher power.

Yet, as in the controversy on the 'Christianness' of Shakespearean tragedy, many have gone to the other extreme. Although the two tetralogies do not constitute the single unified organism animated by the governing theme of the consequences of Bolinbroke's original sin that Tillyard thought them to be (the references to Richard's deposition in the three parts of *Henry VI* are simply historic justifications made by the Yorkists in claiming the throne, without a hint of any kind that divine retribution is at work), providence is shown in operation at the culmination of the first tetralogy and at the inception of the second one. These are such exceptional moments as when, in the words of Francis Bacon, although God's 'secret will' is usually obscure, that will is written 'in such text and capital letters, that, as the prophet said, "He that runneth by may read it." '[21]

In the second and third parts of *Henry VI* one death is piled on top of another, as the members of each side seek vengeance on those of the other side, the feudal nobility regarding such vengeance as a matter of aristocratic honour. The Elizabethan audience, however, would have remembered the frequent attacks on personal vengeance by Tudor moralists and homilists intent on strengthening the national state against feudal particularism. The biblical quotation they cited,

'Vengeance is mine, sayeth the Lord', was taken to refer to
divine vengeance either through the justice of his ministers,
the rulers of the state, or through unexpected death, seeming
accidents, and the like, dramatically appropriate in their man-
46 ner of occurrence. In *Richard III* the violent deaths of the
criminals reaches its height and is now clearly seen to be
divine vengeance.

Moody Prior, however, argues in his erudite and judicious book that the murder of Clarence is not to be regarded as divine retribution and that Margaret in her curses is not to be regarded as calling down the vengeance of God.[22] He cites the exchange between Clarence and the murderers, in which Clarence, reminded of his guilt in killing young Prince Edward, responds (1.4.221-25), 'If God will be revenged for this deed, / Oh, know you yet, He doth it publicly. / Take not the quarrel from His powerful arm; / He needs no indirect or lawless course / To cut off those that have offended Him.' Clarence, then, is alleging that the murderers would not be doing the divine will in killing him. Pleading for his life, he forgets, however, as does Prior, the oft-voiced Elizabethan idea that God uses evil men for his own purpose.[23] The revenger accomplishes the will of God, but, unless, like Macduff, he takes 'no indirect or lawless course' but meets his enemy on the field of battle as the public representative of God, he damns himself in doing so. Clarence, therefore, is entirely correct in telling the murderers that they themselves are incurring God's vengeance but incorrect in saying that they cannot be doing God's work.

This impression is heightened by Clarence's recital of his dream immediately before the murderers' entrance. In this dream he and his brother Richard are on board a ship, from which he is knocked into the ocean when Richard accidentally, as it seems, stumbles into him. He is transported to Hades, where the ghost of Prince Edward calls upon a 'legion of foul fiends' (1.6.58) to assail him. Obviously, the dream is premonitory, Clarence shortly afterward dying at the secret instigation of Richard, drowning not in the ocean but in the barrel of wine into which the murderer throws him. His vision of Hades thus seems also to be a prefiguration of hell – or, perhaps, purgatory in view of his expression of repentance and his prayers.

Nor does Margaret's virulent malevolence prevent her curses from being heard by heaven. She herself is told by Richard, Queen Elizabeth and her kinsmen, Hastings, and Buckingham that the curses of York 'are all fall'n upon thee, / And God, not we, hath plagued thy bloody deed' (1.3.180-81). She exclaims:

Did York's dread curse prevail so much with Heaven
That Henry's death, my lovely Edward's death,
Their kingdom's loss, my woeful banishment,
Could all but answer for that peevish brat?
Can curses pierce the clouds and enter Heaven?
Why then, give way, dull clouds, to my quick curses!
(191-96)

Although her malevolence is not assuaged by the thought that all her sorrows are a punishment for her own ruthless cruelty, she accepts the idea and calls upon heaven to hear her curses, as it did York's. That her curses on Queen Elizabeth, Rivers, Hastings, Buckingham, and Richard all come true in precise detail is surely indication that they are indeed heard. Evil is punished even if it is at the solicitation of an evil person herself suffering punishment for her crimes. If God responds to such solicitation, it is to effect His own purpose, for which he may make use of evil persons.

Prior, however, cannot believe that the death of Queen Elizabeth's Edward, called for by Margaret so that Elizabeth may grieve as she grieves for her Edward, is to be regarded as part of the scheme of divine retribution, the death of an innocent child seeming to be irreconcilable with the idea of retribution by a divine providence.[24] But those who are committed to finding the will of God present in everything must find a justification for whatever occurs. Davies of Hereford comments that although Edward IV tried to ensure his son's succession, 'Yet could no skill or human providence / Protect his sons from their Protector's [Richard III's] spite: / Who as he serv'd King Henry, serv'd them right. / The blood of innocents on innocents/With heavy vengeance mixed, amain doth light:/Thus, innocents are plagu'd for the nocents [innocents]/Such are the Highst's inscrutable judgments.'[25] Davies drives the point home even more in two footnotes: 'God's judgments are inscrutable but none unjust' and 'Justice equal in quality and quantity, for Henry VI and his son were murdered, etc.' Here, one may say, is poetic justice with a vengeance!

48

Shakespeare, to be sure, is subtler than Davies. Although Margaret's words contribute to the total effect, she is not the spokesperson for the dramatist. At the same time that she is thanking 'upright, just, and true-disposing God' (4.4.55) for justice equal in quantity although not in quality, matching Edward with Edward, with 'young York' thrown in as an extra but unable, together with Elizabeth's Edward, to outweigh her Edward, the pathos of the death of the two young princes is emphasised. Obviously, the audience is not expected to exult with her or to tick off the names complacently as instances of an exquisitely appropriate divine justice, but the deaths, horrifying and shocking as they may be, are nevertheless presented as necessary in the divine scheme of things. Blood is paid for with blood, but the death of the princes is not only retribution but the sacrifice that makes it possible for the deadly process that has claimed as victims York's child Rutland and Henry VI's child Edward to come to an end. As Tillyard aptly says, 'Whereas the sins of other men had merely bred more sins, Richard's are so vast that they are absorptive, not contagious. He is the great ulcer of the body politic into which all its impurity is drained and against which all the members of the body politic are united.' [26] This reaction of all of England against Richard begins with the death of the princes, which brings to an end the strife between the houses of York and Lancaster.[27] The princes are like Romeo and Juliet, who are, as Capulet says at the conclusion, the 'poor sacrifices' of the 'enmity' of the rival houses (5.3.305).

Another factor that enables one to accept their deaths as the working of divine providence is the reminder – though it is Richard who says it with his usual sardonic humour – that now they 'sleep in Abraham's bosom' (4.3.38). They have escaped from the cruel world of dynastic struggle, in which – the principle of hereditary succession being incarnated in children – it is inevitable that children be killed, and in escaping from it they have enabled a new world of peace and concord to come into being.

The other time that Shakespeare showed divine providence in 'such text and capital letters' that it could be clearly read, as the scroll of history unrolled before the eyes of the Globe audience, was in *Richard II* when the Bishop of Carlisle predicts (4.1.125–29) 'tumultuous wars' in 'future ages' that 'shall kin with kin and kind with kind confound'[28] if Bolingbroke deposes Richard. However, Kelly, while agreeing that the speech looks forward to the War of the Roses, denies that Carlisle is speaking of divine retribution: 'The bishop is not speaking in terms of divine punishment here, but in terms of a human situation – if they raise one house against the other, a terrible division will result. . . There is no suggestion that the sufferings of the future will be undergone in expiation of or as a punishment for the sins of the present.'[29]

But the Bishop of Carlisle is here the voice of religion. He says of himself that he is moved by the divine spirit, speaking as one 'stirred up by God' (133). The deposing of a king, 'the figure of God's majesty, / His captain, steward, deputy elect', is a deed 'so heinous, black, obscene' that it is incompatible with the behaviour of 'souls' in a 'Christian climate.' (124-31). It is a violation of the natural order ordained by God. As such, it must naturally have disastrous consequences. 'Oh, if you raise this house against this house, / It will the woefullest division prove / That ever fell upon this cursed earth' (145-47). But operating through the natural law that decrees that the setting up of opposing claims to the throne must eventuate in civil war is divine providence. The significance of Carlisle's statement that England will be called 'the field of

Golgotha' (143) as a prophecy of divine retribution has already been discussed.

Kelly believes, however, that such a prophecy of divine retribution would be contrary to the practice of the chronicles
50 and the Elizabethan literary works dealing with history. He states at the conclusion of his book that 'the concept of divine wrath extending for generations over a whole people for a crime committed in the remote past presupposes the kind of avenging God completely foreign to the piety of the historiographers of mediaeval and Renaissance England.' [30] He forgets, however, that he stated in his introduction that 'Christianity contains many disparate elements', that 'the second commandment of the decalogue contains this statement of divine justice: "For I, Yahweh your God, am a jealous God and I punish the fathers' fault in the sons, the grandsons, and the great-grandsons of those who hate me,"' and that 'the notion of original sin. . . involved. . . all generations until the end of time' in 'the guilt and punishment of Adam's sins.' [31]

Actually, his observation that the Tudor historians and poets speaking of hereditary retribution confined this retribution to 'the immediate family circle' of the guilty king is not entirely true. Holinshed not only stated that Bolingbroke's 'lineal race was scourged afterwards, as a dire punishment unto rebellious subjects'; he stated that both the nobility and the commons were also 'rebellious subjects' who were punished for their rebellion after Bolingbroke became king: 'Worthy were his subjects to taste of that bitter cup [the taxes Henry IV imposed on the commons and the punishments he inflicted on the nobles] sithens they were so ready to join and clap hands with him, for the deposing of their rightful and natural prince King Richard.'[33] If the people suffered a justified punishment together with Henry IV, it might be inferred they also suffered it together with his descendants. Daniel went even further, speculating that there must have been at least some members of the parliament that deposed Richard who realised that their action in deposing him was even more sinful than his misrule and said to themselves that it must usher in an age of calamities sent by God: 'But yet in this, the heavens, we fear, prepare / Confusion for our sins as well as his; / And his calamity beginneth our: / For he his own, and we abus'd his power.'[34] He had Carlisle, moreover, tell the parliament that imprisoned Richard after Henry's assumption of the crown that this action will have accumulating consequences and will be punished in the future by 'the hand of vengeance': 'Have you not done enough, with what is done? / Must needs disorder grow, from bad to worse?'[35]

Shakespeare, therefore, was not alone in having Carlisle predict divine retribution. He has Carlisle make this prediction, it should be noted, to an assemblage of noblemen on their way to parliament, whose commons representatives, we are told (4.1.226–27, 272), insist that Richard make a humiliating confession of misdeeds in order that his deposition may be justified. All classes of England share the guilt of Richard's deposition.

But Shakespeare, like Holinshed and Daniel, after asserting the providential plan at the outset does not keep it to the forefront in his dramatisation of the reigns of Henry IV and Henry V even though the dying Henry IV refers to his guilt and Henry V prays to God before Agincourt not to think of his father's sin on that day. It is with the history that human beings make, the consequences of their actions, that Shakespeare is primarily concerned.

The monarchy and the social order

The king, Tillyard has shown, was regarded by Elizabethans as an integral part of the social hierarchy, which in turn was an integral part of the universal hierarchy. *The locus classicus* in Elizabethan literature for the all-pervasive doctrine of 'order and degree' is the 'Homily of Obedience'; the *locus classicus* for the doctrine in Shakespearean drama is Ulysses' famous speech in *Troilus and Cressida*.

The Elizabethan world picture does not merely enable us to recognise allusions; it enables us to perceive themes through symbolic images. Society as a harmony emanating from the inner harmony of the king (or a discord emanating from his inner discord);[36] society as an organism, the body politic, whose health reflects the spiritual health of the king;[37] the king as the sun preeminent among the planets in times of order[38] – these images express the importance of the monarchy as the source of order and stability.

So, too, does Tillyard's discussion of the doctrine of passive obedience due even to evil kings remain useful. It has to be modified, however, for Tillyard, seeking to smooth out the self-contradictions and opposing views in Tudor political theory into a monolithic doctrine by which Shakespeare's self-contradictions could be explained, goes wrong. 'Richard II, however', he writes, summarising *A Mirror for Magistrates*, 'was not the worst kind of king. His deeds were bad, but his heart was not utterly corrupted. Thus it was a sin to rebel against him. But if a king is quite bad, and especially if he has attained the crown by violence, then rebellion is justified. The words constantly used to describe the quite bad king are *tyrant* and *tyranny*. . . Such was Richard III. . . As well as being a tyrant Richard had got the crown by force and could thus not command loyalty. This exception to loyalty is made quite clear. . . [in *A Mirror for Magistrates*]: 'Whatsoever man, woman or child is by the consent of the whole realm established in the royal seat, *so it have not been injuriously procured by rigour of sword and open force*, but quietly by title either of inheritance, succession, lawful bequest, common consent or election, is undoubtedly chosen by God to be his deputy.'[39]

Tillyard, however, forgets that he just before (p 84) quoted another passage in *A Mirror for Magistrates*: 'Who that resisteth his dread sovereign lord / Doth damn his soul by God's own very word. / A Christian subject should with honour due / Obey his sovereign though he were a Jew.' Clearly, 'Jew' here means 'the worst kind of king' and clearly, too, a Jew could not have come to the throne by 'inheritance, succession, lawful bequest, common consent or election'! – but it is now said that he must be obeyed in any event.

The truth is that the dominant though not unanimous sixteenth century opinion was that rebellion was sinful even against the worst of kings. So it was roundly stated in the most authoritative of the statements of absolutist doctrine, 'An Homily Against Disobedience and Willful Rebellion: 'A rebel is worse than the worst prince, and rebellion worse than the worst government of the worst prince.'[40] This was the basis of Tudor absolutism, coming after the Wars of the Roses: the belief that 'civil war is far worse than tyranny.'[41]

The paradox was that Henry VII, the founder of the Tudor line, had gained the crown from Richard III with slight hereditary claim to it and in consequence of leading a rebellion. Moreover, he had come to power through French support, having received money from Charles VIII and 'permission to raise 3000 men in Normandy, who turned out to be mainly ragamuffins', with the charge made against him that the rebellion in his favour was being instigated by 'our ancient enemies of France.'[42] But if Henry's claim was weak, his assertion that he was God's agent was strong. 'He told his first parliament that he had come to the crown by inheritance (leaving the details studiously vague) and by the proof of God's will expressed in his victory.'[43] The 'Tudor myth' came straight from the horse's mouth.

Hall, writing under Henry VIII and regarding his king's father as the instrument of divine providence, did not speak of the doctrine that rebellion is sinful in dealing with the deposition of Richard II. Exalting Henry VII, who was not only a Lancastrian like Henry IV but came to the kingship by leading a rebellion, he would have found it difficult to do so. 'In the house of the hanged, one does not speak of rope.' Shakespeare, using Hall as his primary source,[44] does not in his first tetralogy make specific mention of the doctrine, although, of course, he condemns the strife for the crown. Even when Henry VI contends with York as to who has the better claim to the crown, instead of asserting, as Hal does (*2 Henry IV* 4.4.221-23), that the de facto possessor of the crown is the rightful king, who must be obeyed, Henry accepts the Yorkist line of argument that legitimacy is derived not from the oath of allegiance but through direct succession in an unbroken descent, and is forced to admit in an aside: 'My title's weak' (*3 Henry VI*, 1.1.134).

Holinshed, Shakespeare's primary source in his second tetralogy,[45] does, however, speak of the sinfulness of rebellion in dealing with Richard's deposition, for at the time he was writing the circumstances of Henry VII's assumption of the kingship were less fresh and, with Elizabeth threatened by the papal bull releasing her subjects from allegiance to her and by the hostility of France and Spain, a greater emphasis was put on the doctrine that a prince, no matter what his faults, is God's deputy.[46] Shakespeare, therefore, makes Bolingbroke's deposition of Richard sinful, but, once Bolingbroke has himself become Henry IV, rebellion against him becomes in turn a sin. Actual possession of the crown and not genealogical tables is what determines who is the rightful king.

Shakespeare's Richmond, however, is not in the paradoxical position of his Henry IV of possessing a rightfully held though sinfully acquired crown, for Shakespeare in *Richard III* tacitly accepts not the official Tudor doctrine of obedience even to tyrants but the minority doctrine of the extreme Protestants – the Marian exiles, the Scotch Protestants under Mary Stuart, the French Huguenots after St Bartholomew's Eve – who proclaimed the right to rise up against tyrants.[47] For the first of the Tudors, the Tudor doctrine does not apply. Tillyard was right in seeing Richard III as an exception to the doctrine of passive obedience but wrong in thinking that this kind of exception was provided for in the orthodox doctrine.

Some critics, however, are uneasy about the entire attempt to see Shakespeare's historical dramas in relation to Tudor political theory. For S C Sen Gupta, Tillyard's approach is 'essentially homiletic.'[48] So, too, Robert Ornstein asks, 'Can we believe. . . that Shakespeare. . . wrote play after play to persuade his audiences of the need for order and obedience?'[49]

This is a wrongheaded way of putting the matter. One may as well ask: can we believe that Spenser, even in leaving his task only half-done, wrote six books of twelve cantos each to give instruction in how to be a gentleman? Despite Spenser's announced didactic intention and the standard Elizabethan didactic justification for historical drama, both Spenser and Shakespeare were of course writing imaginative literature, not conduct books or homilies. Shakespeare was not preaching a platitudinous sermon to the already converted; he was revivifying the past and in so doing making the commonplaces about history come thrillingly alive. His audiences did not have to be persuaded of the need for order and obedience; they had to be made to feel with every fibre of their beings what they already accepted.

Although Shakespeare's history plays are shaped by the dominant ideology of the age, this does not mean that they merely teach a simple lesson. The seeming paradox that Ornstein presents – 'Embodied in *Richard II*, we are told, is the orthodox view that the deposition of Richard was a heinous sin that brought down on England God's wrath and the curse of civil war. Yet on the eve of Essex's rebellion, his adherents paid a bonus to Shakespeare's company to play *Richard II*, presumably in hope that it would stir the audience to sympathy for the uprising'[50] – is not really so difficult to understand. Whatever might have happened if Essex had gained the support of London, the cry of his men as they paraded through the streets was; 'For the Queen!' His attempted display of strength was, at least ostensibly, not aimed at rebellion but at rescuing Elizabeth from bad advisers and from plots by some of them in behalf of the Infanta of Spain.[51] The dramatisation of the sinfulness of Richard's deposition would, therefore, not have been contrary to his purpose.

The performance of *Richard II* would, however, have called attention to the harm poorly advised monarchs do themselves and their country in provoking their subjects beyond endurance. It would have raised the same kind of uncomfortable questions about the irresponsibility of kings who wrong their subjects that the authorities feared were raised by Sir John Hayward, who was tried for his description of the deposition of Richard in his history of Henry IV. Yet Hayward had stated the 'orthodox view' that the fate of Henry IV, whose reign was one of 'great discontentment and disquiet', and whose grandson lost the crown, proved that 'God in his secret judgment doth. . . provide. . . revenge [for] our injuries and harms.'[52]

Even though deposition is a heinous sin, the king who is deposed, it was said even in orthodox places, must have been guilty of misrule. 'Whosoever rebelleth against any ruler either good or bad', states *A Mirror for Magistrates*, 'rebelleth against God. . . Yet this I note by the way concerning rebels and rebellions. Although the devil raise them, yet God alwayes useth them to his glory as a part of his justice. For when kings. . . will not hear nor remedy their people's wrongs when they complain, then suffreth God the rebel to rage and to execute that part of his justice which the partial prince would not.'[53] So, too, Davies of Hereford says: 'And where Vice reigns, rebellion oft doth rule.'[54] Thus Davies finds that Richard II's deposition was a divine punishment for the sin of his grandfather, Edward III, in deposing and murdering his own father and that Henry IV's deposition of Richard II was in turn avenged by his grandson Henry VI's loss of the crown. However, Richard II, since God 'ordinarily works by a concatenation of means', depriving 'governors of understanding when he intends evil to the multitude,' [55] himself encouraged rebellion through his poor judgment: 'But, if this king had not so childish been / When Mowbray preached [impeached] th' Usurper of treason, / He might have been secure from all his Kin: / But blinded judgment is the heir of Sin. / Thus fares it with weak kings and cousins strong.'[56]

Shakespeare's Richard also brings his deposition upon himself. The dying Gaunt tells him that if his grandfather had been able to foresee his follies he would have deposed Richard before he acquired the crown, Richard, now that he has the crown, being 'possessed. . . to depose thyself ' (2.1.108). In farming out England to his favourites, he continues, Richard has already in some sense deposed himself: 'Landlord of England art thou now, not King' (113). Indeed, Richard, intoxicated by a false sense of security, drives unwittingly along the road to deposition. Immediately after Gaunt's death, he seizes, despite Gaunt's warning, the estate that should have gone to Gaunt's son Bolingbroke. York, aghast, remonstrates that he is taking from 'Time' his 'customary rights', violating the natural law that makes the son the inheritor of his father's possessions, and exclaims (2.1.198–99): 'Be not thyself, for how art thou a king / But by fair sequence and succession?' Richard, in disinheriting Bolingbroke, is paving the way to his own deposition.

Through Bolingbroke's disinheritance Richard shows the other nobles the arbitrary despotism that can at any time turn against them and that, as Northumberland says (2.1.245), threatens 'our lives, our children, and our heirs.' In order to maintain his extravagant court Richard has already alienated them by fines and the commons by his taxes. The disinheritance of Bolingbroke is the displacement of the rock which starts the avalanche that, gathering momentum, buries Richard with breathtaking rapidity. The nobles proclaim their support for Bolingbroke, returned from abroad in violation of the exile to which he was sentenced to claim his estate. He and they swear that this is the sole purpose for which they have gathered their forces, but the deference with which Northumberland speaks to Bolingbroke and the graciousness Bolingbroke shows him is a tacit indication of the new relationship of king and noble counsellor toward which they are headed. Whether or not Bolingbroke was actually thinking of the crown at this time is left uncertain – in *2 Henry IV* (3.1.72-74) he says it had not been his intent, but it was the necessity of the time, which weighed down upon the country, that forced him to take it – but, however much or little he was reluctant, the time did not permit the continued existence of a vacuum in the place of power. Richard's forces drift away,

Bolingbroke's forces grow – 'Both young and old rebel'(3.2 119) – and Bolingbroke wins without a battle.

Richard at first continues to live in the dream world in which he is inviolate. For every man Bolingbroke has, he says (3.2.60–62), 'God for His Richard hath in heavenly pay / A glorious angel. Then, if angels fight, / Weak men must fall, for Heaven still guards the right.' John C Bromley believes that 'Shakespeare uses the sacramental tradition [that was "part of the legend that had grown round Richard's deposition"] simply to render the king's pretensions yet more pretentious; the angels, after all, do not appear.'[57] But it is Carlisle, the most powerful voice for the sacramental tradition, who urges Richard to take action in his own behalf. God, as Raleigh says, does not accomplish his purposes through 'miraculous means.'[58] Richard also forgets that God raises 'rebels and rebellions' as 'a part of his justice'[59] and that his vengeance, although it does not sleep, is often long delayed. Richard himself is prophetic in stating (3.3.88-90) that God will strike 'Your children yet unborn and unbegot, / That lift your vassal hands against my head / And threat the glory of my precious crown.' Shakespeare does not use the sacramental tradition 'simply': it serves to give ironically false assurance to Richard, but it is also intended to emphasise the sanctity of the crown.

Plunged into an ecstasy of despair, Richard virtually thrusts his crown upon a Bolingbroke who is still protesting (3.3.196), 'My gracious lord, I come but for my own.' As he himself says later (4.1.248), he has been 'a traitor with the rest' in submitting to his own deposition, tamely participating in a ritual that reverses the ritual in which he was crowned. But this counter-ritual is only the completion of the process by which he has long been deposing himself.

The effect of *Richard II*, then, is much more complex than the adjuration: 'Rebellion, a heinous crime, does not pay.' The sense of inevitability gained from the whole course of events does not diminish the guilt of Bolingbroke and England, but it does affect the reader's response, by making that guilt a part of the great scheme of things. All of the links of the chain of history must be accepted in order to reach the ultimately beneficent end to which that chain leads.

Because effects follow from their causes, history can be seen not only as inevitable but as predictable. Richard predicts that Northumberland, who enabled Bolingbroke to gain a throne, will feel inadequately recompensed and that Bolingbroke will fear that Northumberland, who learned how to make kings, will do so for someone else. So it comes to pass. Each side is suspicious and fearful of the other, although each regards the other as blameful. 'The King will always think him in our debt', says Worcester (*1 Henry IV* 1.3.286-88), 'And think we think ourselves unsatisfied, / Till he hath found a time to pay us home.' Warwick, on the other hand, tells Henry IV (*2 Henry IV* 3.1.88-92) that Richard was able to make his prediction because he saw that Northumberland, false to him, would grow in falseness. But, above all, Bolingbroke, in revolting against Richard, showed the way for others to revolt against him after he became king,[60] just as Richard showed others the way to violate 'fair sequence and succession' when he seized Bolingbroke's inheritance. When the mystique of kingship and of 'order and degree' is not maintained, power becomes a game in which the 'king of the hill' sits insecure on his precarious perch, liable to be assaulted and dethroned from any side.

This game becomes more and more deadly and its players more and more unscrupulous and ruthless as it goes on. Thus the wily papal legate, Cardinal Pandulph, a master of power politics, is able to foresee that John will be driven to kill his young nephew, Prince Arthur, whom he has superseded:

A sceptre snatch'd with an unruly hand
Must be as boisterously maintain'd as gain'd;
And he that stands upon a slipp'ry place
Makes nice of no vild hold to stay him up:
That John may stand, then, Arthur must needs fall;
So be it, for it cannot but be so.
(*King John*, 3.3.135-40)

It is this 'grand mechanism'[61] that enters into play when the natural laws of the social order are violated that Tillyard, intent on expounding the providential view of history, neglects. Nevertheless, his exposition of 'order and degree'
60 points the way to an understanding of it.

The force and craft of strong kings To prevent the struggle for power in the kingdom, with all of its evil consequences, a king has to be strong. The Protestant reformer William Tyndale, writing in 1528, goes so far as to say, 'It is better to have a tyrant unto thy king than a shadow, a passive king that doth nought himself but suffreth others to do with him what they will and to lead him whither they list.'[62] This was also the lesson taught by Davies of Hereford. Edward II, Richard II, Henry VI, and Edward V were, he said, weak kings, 'childish, frail, improvident', and 'mirrors for kings negligent.'[63] Kings should not only be virtuous themselves but should see to it that their subjects are virtuous. 'Lysander was no less to blame, for he / Allow'd those vices in the multitude / From which himself refrain'd religiously; / For if by princes vices be allowed, / It is as one as if they vice ensued.'[64] This is readily applicable to Shakespeare's *Henry VI*, who, it might be said, as Davies said of the historical *Henry VI*, was a 'saint'[65] but permitted envy, contentiousness, and hatred to grow among his noblemen until their quarrels brought England to devastation.[66] So, too, the comment of Davies about weak kings, with its sun imagery and its distinction between 'show' and substance, applies to Shakespeare's *Richard II*: 'The subjects' strength which Sov'reigns' weakness brings, / A fatal potion made for king and realm, /. . . Kings must be kings indeed and not in show, / Like as the Sun is active with his beam; / For if they suffer subjects kings to grow, / Kings must be slaves and to their subjects bow.'[67]

On the other hand, Davies lists as strong kings who ruled well Edward III, despite his coming to the throne as a result of the deposition and murder of his father; Henry IV, despite his deposition and murder of his cousin; Henry V, despite the curse on his house; Edward IV, despite the murder of his brother Clarence, which Davies attributes to him rather than to Richard III. 'These princes were of Fortune ne'er forsook, / Because they governed with due regard' and 'made their subjects' loving fear their guard.'[68] The murders are presented as crimes for which England must pay – and yet, paradoxically, the kings themselves are said to have served England well. His ambivalence is such that, after condemning Edward IV's murder of Clarence as 'Turkish', he more than half condones it as a necessity of power politics: 'Besides, a sliding and newfangled nation / Full of rebellion and disloyalty / May cause a prince for his securer station / To stand upon the like extremity / Where virtue hath no place of certainty. / What prince (if provident) will stick to strain / Both law and conscience in secrecy / To cut one Member off, that lets his reign, / Which the state's body doth in health maintaine? /. . . Then must we lose a part the whole to save.' Davies adds in a footnote: 'The law itself will rather admit a mischief than inconvenience',[69] that is, will permit a misdeed if it is necessary. The murder of Clarence is thus what Machiavelli called a 'ragione di stato' and what English political observers in later ages called a 'raison d'etat' and 'Realpolitik' – foreign phrases used to refer to what the English preferred to regard as un-English.

This is the 'dualism' that Felix Raab finds characteristic of the Tudor attitude toward Machiavelli. 'He horrified them, instructed them, entertained them – in fact he affected them over the whole attraction/repulsion spectrum through which basically new concepts are often seen in times of rapid social change. . . Particularly was this so near the end of the century.'[70] The effect of this 'dualism' was that, as Michael Manheim puts it, 'political leaders were victims of a kind of double-think whereby they sincerely believed themselves true and devout Christians at the same time that they felt increasingly justified in ignoring Christian precepts in political dealings.'[71] Elizabeth herself, it should be noted, torn between her need to get Mary of Scotland out of the way and her fear of the political consequences abroad if she executed the anointed queen, instructed Mary's keeper, Sir Amias Paulet, to have her assassinated in such a way that the death would appear to be natural.[72]

62 What has often been said to be Shakespeare's impartiality is really his 'dualism', which, to be sure, is not as schizoid as is Davies's. There is no doubt, for instance, that he is not impartial but on Henry IV's side against the rebels, who threaten the unity and order of England. Moreover, he presents Henry sympathetically as a king intensely concerned about his country and as a father intensely concerned about his son. But although the historical pressures that pushed him first to depose Richard and then – as living persons surrounded by the mystique of kingship are ever a focus for rebellion by such as Aumerle – to have him assassinated assume a prominent part in the play, his guilt in the deposition and death of Richard can never be forgotten. For this stern, lonely, dedicated man, who had the generosity to pardon Aumerle and Carlisle, himself does not forget it. Power politics makes demands for which one must pay.

Shakespeare's feelings about the realities of power politics are expressed by Philip, the bastard son of Richard Coeur de Lion, in *King John*. A humorously cynical commentator on the action, the Bastard exclaims concerning the politic peace made by John and Philip of France, a betrayal of principle on both sides: 'Since kings break faith upon commodity, / Gain, be my lord, for I will worship thee!' (2.1.597-98). But, unlike another bastard, Edmund, whose 'Thou, Nature, art my goddess' (*King Lear*,1.2.1) echoes these words, he does not act on them. His ironic vow is only his sardonic humour. In reality, he is concerned solely with the welfare of England, remaining true to John, who, whatever his faults and misdeeds, represents England against the Pope, France, and Austria. Knowing that kings all too often are not what they should be, he is a practical idealist.

Tillyard was aware of the Machiavellian element in Shakespeare's view of history,[73] but he did not explore it in any depth. Shakespeare believed, he says, alluding to Machiavelli's comment that the prince should possess both the strength of the lion and the cunning of the fox, that the good king should have the characteristics of the lion, the fox, and the pelican, which Elizabethans believed nourished its young with its blood and hence was representative of devotion and self-sacrifice.[74]

However, what little Tillyard has to say on this Machiavellian element is objected to by Herbert Howarth. The duping of the rebels by Prince John, who swears to redress their grievances but after they have dispersed their army orders them executed for high treason, asserting that he will do as he swore but that it was no part of his oath that they would go unpunished, Howarth alleges, is poorly dealt with by Tillyard because of his 'order-disorder thesis': 'Cold Lancaster inherits his father's treacherous statecraft. Tillyard's discrimination tells him that Shakespeare intended to condemn Lancaster; and he writes a sentence: "The justice of John of Lancaster in his cold-blooded treatment of the rebels verges on rigour." But that is a pulled punch. . . Any full examination of the '"justice" of the case must have dented the world-picture. The royal forces (the forces of "order"!) stand convicted.'[75]

For Howarth, Shakespeare is equally condemnatory of the politician Worcester and the politician Lancaster. But Shakespeare, as Paul Jorgensen has shown, was not thus impartial. Jorgensen sees the scene in the light of the disheartening war against the Irish, which continued to drag on, a war in which both sides accused each other of not keeping the intermittent truces. The English defended their actions as being necessary against treacherous rebels. Thus Edmund Spenser in his *View of the Present State of Ireland*[76] justified the Smerwick Massacre, 'the most shocking example of English breach of faith – perhaps like the Lancaster incident a heartlessly legalistic interpretation of a truce', in which 'five or six hundred filibusters helping the Irish' were slaughtered after they surrendered. Elizabeth herself in 'private governmental advices' made 'sufficiently clear her convictions about the ethical responsibilities of a prince in honouring a disagreeable truce, observing that "neither is a Prince bound by his contract, when for just cause the contract turneth to the public detriment." Elizabeth and her government were, moreover, adept at translating political expediency into religious terms.'[77]

Perhaps even closer in some respects to the Lancaster incident than the incidents in the Irish war cited by Jorgensen is the Pilgrimage of Grace under Henry VIII, which was probably remembered even though it took place seventy five years earlier. G R Elton says of it: 'Neither Norfolk [Henry's commander] nor Henry thought themselves bound by promises made to rebellious subjects. . . Norfolk promised vaguely to adhere to some of the demands and offered a full and free pardon. There upon Aske [the rebel leader]. . . declared himself the king's faithful subject and with great difficulty prevailed upon his followers to disperse. . . The leaders of the late rising were separately executed. It was made possible only by a wholesale breaking of promises.'[78]

This historical background seems to justify Jorgensen's conclusion: 'In both parts of *Henry IV* Shakespeare wished to present a complete and up-to-date picture of Elizabethan warfare. . . And because the members of the audience were becoming increasingly aware of the political necessity and reality of this picture, I do not believe that they would have been so obdurately embittered by the play as later critics have been. . . I do not, however, go so far as to believe that there was any applause for John. . . Prince John, like Machiavelli, was the type of person to be used rather than to be applauded.'[79] The Elizabethan reaction may be better understood by a comparison with the hard-boiled spy thrillers popular during the Cold War. In these the intelligence agent engages with cold-blooded cynicism in all sorts of 'dirty tricks', which, it is suggested, are regrettably necessary. The fact that it is done by 'our side' makes it, if not exactly savoury, at least capable of being swallowed.

Even more strongly denied than Shakespeare's acceptance

of the cunning of the fox in the Lancaster oath incident is his acceptance of the strength of the lion in *Henry V*. Many critics have found Shakespeare to be sharply critical of Henry. They find that he cynically goes to war with France to divert his subjects' minds from the illegitimacy of his kingship, that his war, despite his ostensible concern that it be a just one, is concerned with acquiring booty, that his threats of rapine and devastation if the besieged town of Harfleur does not submit are horrifying, and that his order at Agincourt to kill the prisoners of war is brutal.[80] But Henry is undoubtedly to be seen as 'the mirror of all Christian kings' (Act 2, Prologue, line 6) that the Chorus says he is. Shakespeare was not subtly criticising the national hero. If Henry takes harsh measures in time of war, they are the measures that necessity dictates even to Christian kings.

Concerning Henry IV's advice to his son to 'busy giddy minds / With foreign quarrels' (*2 Henry IV* 4.5.214-5), frequently regarded as shockingly cynical, Prior points out, 'The idea of a foreign war as a way of removing the threat of civil war was fairly common during the fifteenth and sixteenth centuries, and in that age not very shocking', and goes on to quote Garrett Mattingly's *Renaissance Diplomacy* by way of explanation: 'Outside Italy, all Europe was saddled with a class in possession of most of the landed wealth, most of the local power, and most of the permanent high offices of state, who had no business except war and few peacetime diversions as attractive as conspiracy. Before it attained its zenith, the territorial state had no way of ensuring the allegiance of this class so effective as giving them some foreign enemy to fight.'[81] So Davies of Hereford comments on the Wars of the Roses: 'The effects of civil war: for look how much peace is better than war, so much is foreign invasion better than civil dissension.'[82] Henry IV's advice is to be seen, then, as an attempt to stave off what could not be staved off indefinitely, the Wars of the Roses.

In *Henry V* however, where the unity of England under its great king is emphasised, there is no such prudential need shown for the war. Instead, the war is made to be a matter of national honour to regain England's rights in France and to reply to the Dauphin's insult, which reflects on the national dignity. Henry's concern with the justice of the war is very real and deep, expressed in his weighty and solemn appeal to the Archbishop of Canterbury to remember the blood that will be shed in the war and to consider well whether, if he counsels that it is a just war, he is speaking in 'conscience washed / As pure as sin with baptism' (1.2.31-32).

Nor are the Archbishop of Canterbury and the Bishop of Ely wily churchmen who are enacting a cynical charade with Henry in which they tell him what he wants in return for his not supporting a proposed tax on the church. Shakespeare retains the matter of the tax from Holinshed, who, following the strongly Protestant Hall, uses it to attack the motives of the archbishop, but Shakespeare makes Canterbury speak not as another Pandulph but in the spirit of a good Anglican clergyman devoted to the king. In his conversation with Ely there is not a hint by either that Henry is implicitly threatening them in order to gain their support for the war or that they are gulling him by vouching for the justice of the war only as a way to get out of paying the tax. On the contrary, they extol him as a consummate theologian, statesman, and soldier and as 'a true lover of the Holy Church' (1.1.23). If Canterbury is spurred by the tax urged by the commons to suggest the war as a means of gaining a greater sum than could be gained from the church, this does not mean that either he or Henry is dishonest in what he says and does.[83]

Although national honour is the reason for the war, however, the Chorus indicates that in the service of this national honour not only the king but the gentry, the aristocracy, and even the armourers will profit from it:

Now all the youth of England are on fire,
And silken dalliance in the wardrobe lies.
Now thrive the armourers, and honour's thought
Reigns solely in the breast of every man.
They sell the pasture now to buy the horse.

For now sits Expectation in the air,
And hides a sword from hilts unto the point
With crowns imperial, crowns and coronets
Promised to Harry and his followers.
(Act 2, Prologue, lines 1-11)

The phrase 'crowns and coronets' refers to the crown of France for Henry as well as to the coronets of nobility for the gentry and the aristocracy it is hoped the war will bring, but 'crowns' possibly refers also to coins, to money. If so, this is not a cynical comment but a realistic detail, the money being accepted as a concomitant of the honour gained in war. The real basis of the myth of national honour is glimpsed here, but the myth is presented in all its power, the Chorus speaking in an intoxication of patriotism. The irony, recognised by modern historians although not by Shakespeare, is that the unity in the pursuit of honour here celebrated would be lost through 'the quarrels of a baronial party debauched by foreign spoil'[84] gained in a war that Shakespeare's Henry IV and the historical Henry V intended as a diversion for the powerful feudal magnates.

Pistol's words to his friends, 'Let us to France, like horse-leeches, my boys, / To suck, to suck, the very blood to suck!' (2.3.57-58) is not Shakespeare's satiric comment on the rapacity of Henry's expedition, just as Bardolph's 'On, on, on, on! To the breach, to the breach' (3.2.1), followed by his hanging back, does not undercut Henry's rousing summons, 'Once more unto the breach, dear friends, once more' (3.1.1), but is a comically contemptible burlesque of it. Petty looting is as despicable as cowardice. Pistol and Bardolph are realistic reminders of the rag-tag element that attends an army, even so heroic a one as that which fought at Agincourt. Henry, who has Bardolph hanged for the sacrilegious pilfering of a religious plate from a church, orders that nothing should be exacted from the French villagers and that they should be well treated. To be sure, one reason for his command is to gain the villagers' support against the French king: 'For when lenity and cruelty play for a kingdom, the gentler gamester is the soonest winner' (3.7.118-20). Shakespeare shows Henry as both a shrewd statesman and an honourable soldier.

Henry not only serves the national honour; he serves God. It has been said that he confuses the Christian God with Mars.[85] But Shakespeare's Henry V in his horrible threats before Harfleur is merely speaking in the vein of the historical Henry V, who, says Kelly, referring to the contemporary chronicles, 'invoked against the city the ultimatum that God dictated to the Israelites for their use against enemy cities (in a city that refuses to surrender peacefully, they are to put all the male adults to the sword.)'[86] The mediaeval and Renaissance Christian God bore varied aspects. One of these aspects was that of the 'God of Battles' prayed to by Henry (4.1.306), who supported his chosen people against its enemies and his, wreaking havoc upon these enemies, just as He wreaked havoc upon his chosen people itself when it yielded to its propensity to backsliding.[87] Henry's statement (4.1.177) that 'War is His beadle, war is His Vengeance', that war is the scourge, the parish beadle whipping offenders, by which God punishes an offending people, was a truism of the time.[88]

Talbot, another Shakespearean military hero, who is addressed by the French general commanding Bordeaux as 'our nation's terror and their bloody scourge' (*1 Henry VI*, act 4), tells him (lines 9-11), as Henry tells the citizens of Harfleur, if not with the same amplitude of imagery: 'But if you frown upon this proffered peace, / You tempt the fury of my three attendants – / Lean famine, quartering steel, and climbing fire.'[89] Indeed, the codified rules of war prescribed that a city that created unnecessary bloodshed by useless resistance was subject to devastation, and it was customary for the commander to disclaim responsibility for what would happen in giving his last warning.[90] Thus in *King John* Philip of France offers (2.1.257) to 'leave your children, wives and you in peace' if the citizens of Angiers will accept him as their ruler, continuing (263-66), 'Then tell us, shall your city call us lord. . . ? / Or shall we give the signal to our rage / And stalk in blood to our possession?'

Henry, then, is following conventional practice in his threats and in his disavowal of responsibility for the fulfilment of these threats. If the city is devastated, he tells the citizens, 'you yourselves are the cause', and he calls upon them to 'take pity of your town and of your people' (3.3.19, and 28). He is trying to hold in leash, he says, the terrors he must loose in the stern necessity of war if they do not submit. If his men get out of hand and commit the crimes he describes in vivid detail, it will not be his fault. The lack of discipline of the English army that he presents as inevitable, which goes contrary to the rules of war he has had them observe, may be a realistic recognition of what happens in the heat of battle or may be a strategic bluff to effect his purpose. When the citizens of Harfleur do surrender, he commands, 'Use mercy to them all' (3.3.54).

It is the French who violate the rules of war during the battle of Agincourt by wantonly killing the boys guarding the baggage of the army. ' 'Tis expressly against the law of arms', says Fluellen (4.7.1-2). Henry's order to kill the prisoners, on the other hand, is a military necessity, for the French are making new preparations to attack, re-grouping and reinforcing their routed forces, and the prisoners, the adequate guarding of whom would divert men from answering this attack, are a source of danger, for they may turn on their captors if there is not proper guard. Moreover, it is presented as justified retaliation for the killing of the boys, one of whom, the boy with Pistol and his crew, just before appeared on the stage and engaged the audience's sympathy with his pertly perceptive comments addressed directly to it about these pusillanimous swashbucklers. ' 'Tis certain there's not a boy left alive', indignantly exclaims the Scotch captain Gower (4.7.5-11), 'and the cowardly rascals that ran from the battle ha' done this slaughter. . . Wherefore the King, most worthily, hath caused every soldier to cut his prisoner's throat. Oh, 'tis a gallant King!'

To many this throat cutting will not appear to be the epitome of gallantry. However, to try to recapture the Elizabethan audience's reaction, we may recall a contemporary audience's reaction during World War II to a scene in the film *China* in which the hero, played by Alan Ladd, is guarding a group of Japanese prisoners. He meets again some Chinese girls whose youthful charm and innocence were captivating in an earlier scene. They are utterly bereft, having recently been raped by the Japanese soldiers he is guarding. Ladd, an actor whose frozen handsome face seemed incapable of expressing any emotion, looks at them and then at the Japanese, grinning gloatingly and arrogantly, secure in their status as prisoners of war, and turning his automatic rifle at them shoots them dead without the flicker of an eyelash. War does not arouse the prettiest emotions at any time.

The Henry V who is capable of such measures as the killing of the prisoners is Shakespeare's representation of a strong and good king, a contrast to all of his weak or bad kings. Malcolm in Macbeth describes the ideal king with different emphases, listing as the 'king-becoming graces': 'justice, verity, temperance, stableness, / Bounty, perseverance, mercy, lowliness, / Devotion, patience, courage, fortitude' (4.3.91-94). These attributes Henry has too, in addition to fiercer ones not mentioned, but one would not put courage and fortitude at the end of the list. But then Malcolm is presenting the portrait of a king who would be appropriate for a 'time' that is 'free' (5.8.55) from the tyrant Macbeth, a time when Scotland is at peace with itself and its neighbours. Henry, however, is a king in time of war, and, as he himself says (3.1.3-6), 'In peace there's nothing so becomes a man / As modest stillness and humility. / But when the blast of war blows in our ears, / Then imitate the action of the tiger.'

Henry is strong not only in waging war but in subduing conspiracy. Critics have attacked him for the cat-and-mouse game by which he has Scroop, Cambridge, and Grey condemn themselves to death, before he reveals his knowledge of their conspiracy, by urging the need for severity in the case of a drunken man arrested for railing at the king. However, Henry in this is like God, who watches with an all-seeing eye while malefactors perform their evil deeds thinking they are unobserved and then visits a poetically appropriate punishment upon them. 'The King hath note of all that they intend', says Bedford (2.2.6-7), 'By interception which they dream not of', and later Scroop exclaims (151), 'Our purposes God justly hath discovered.' The conspirators themselves, overwhelmed by their sense of guilt and by the appropriateness of their having pronounced their own just punishment, ask for death but forgiveness for their crime, and Henry, imposing the death they request, expresses his forgiveness, praying that God will do the same.

This severity, through which he serves the interest of the kingdom despite the commiseration he feels, is the way in which the ideal king rules. The regard his subjects have for this ideal king is best expressed by Cambridge even while he is trying to deceive Henry (25-26). 'Never was monarch better feared and loved / Than is your Majesty.' 'Loving fear', we may remember, was Davies of Hereford's description of the emotion evoked by strong kings.[91] The ideal king, it was often said by Renaissance political theorists, has the virtues of God[92] – and the subjects of the ideal king look upon him as they do upon God: as a stern but loving father who is feared as well as adored.

Monarchy, aristocracy, and bourgeoisie in changing times

Although the king is God's image and substitute on earth, the earth, unlike heaven, is subject to time, and so is the king and his kingdom. 'Shakespeare's idea and image of "time"', says the Marxist scholar Zdenek Stribrny in an important article that I believe is too little known to Western scholars, is 'by its dynamism. . . directly antithetical to the static idea of "order" ' of Tillyard's recreation of the Elizabethan world picture, which did not do 'full justice to Shakespeare's infinitely varied vision of all the ways of the world and its history.'[93]

From the very beginning of his history plays Shakespeare conceived of history as being an organic process – germinating, growing, decaying, renewing itself. In *1 Henry VI*,

Richard of York exclaims (2.4.99) that he will confound Somerset if 'growing time once ripened to my will', if time will develop as he wishes it would. Richmond at the conclusion of *Richard III* delivers the prophetic prayer (5.5.19-34) that, as a result of the 'fair conjunction' of 'the white rose and the red', his wedding with Elizabeth of York, 'their heirs' may 'enrich the time to come' with 'smiling plenty', the fair harvest of this planting. In *Richard II*, York accepts, now that it has come, 'this new spring of time' (5.2.50), the reign of Henry IV. Worcester in *1 Henry IV* seeks to curb Hotspur until 'time is ripe' (1.3.294). Exeter asserts that Henry V, having gone far beyond 'the promise of his greener days', now 'weighs time / Even to the utmost grain' (2.4.136–38). 'Grain', as Stribrny explains, refers not only to the most minute weight used by the apothecaries and to the sand in an hourglass but 'may suggest grains of corn which grow into a rich harvest, if planted and cultivated with due care', as it means in Banquo's exhortation to the witches (1.3.58–61): 'If you can look into the seeds of time / And say which grain will grow and which will not, / Speak then to me.'

Stribrny, however, is mistaken in believing that Shakespeare's idea of time is 'antithetical' to the idea of order described by Tillyard. Organic growth, the law of time's development, is part of the order of the world. 'The earth, trees, seeds, plants, herbs, and corn . . .' says the 'Homily of Obedience', 'keep them in their order.'[94] So Nature in Spenser's 'Cantoes of Mutabilitie' says in response to Mutability that although all things are constantly changing they are doing so in accordance with the principles of their beings, fulfilling themselves and maintaining universal order:

I well consider all that ye have sayd,
And find that all things stedfastnes doe hate
And changed be: yet being rightly wayd,
They are not changed from their first estate;
But by their change their being doe dilate:
And turning to themselves at length again,
Doe worke their owne perfection so by fate:

Then over them Change doth not rule and raigne;
But they raigne over Change, and doe their states maintaine.
(Canto 58)

The dominant symbolic image of the history plays, England as a garden,[95] is emblematic of both growth and order. In the allegorical gardener's scene in *Richard II*, the importance of degree is maintained in the midst of growth, and 'too-fast-growing sprays' are trimmed, as upstart courtiers like Bushy, Bagot, and Green should have had their rise checked while overluxurious fruit trees have their excess sap drained so that they might not become 'overproud', as 'great and growing' noblemen like Bolingbroke should not have been allowed to become too mighty (3.4.34, 59, 61). The gardener in properly doing his work is performing his function in the order of things, as Richard should have performed his.

If, however, the proper functioning of gardeners and kings produces orderly growth, it is true that weeds, 'things rank and gross in nature' (*Hamlet*, 1.2.136), can readily overrun a garden. A continual tension exists between the decay of nature, which set in with the fall of Adam and Eve, and the order of things established by God. 'There is the everpresent glory of God's creation, the perpetual pressure of his Providence. Yet disorder or chaos, the product of sin, is perpetually striving to come again'.[96] The fair soil of England is too frequently drenched by the blood of its sons or bruised by the hooves of opposing armies in civil war. Time brings not only orderly growth but disorder and death. 'Oh God!' exclaims Henry IV, using 'disorder' imagery to refer to the things future history has in store,

that one might read the book of fate,
And see the revolution of the times
Make mountains level, and the continent,
Weary of solid firmness, melt itself
Into the sea!
(*2 Henry IV* 3.1.45-49)

Yet, although mountains are eroded and coastlines altered, mountains and coasts remain. In 'the revolution of the times' Jack Cade may lead a mob of handicraftsmen and peasants that commits such unheard -of violations of the social order as

killing noblemen and threatening London and the royal court, but order is restored. Moreover, Cade, who tells his followers that 'all the realm shall be in common' (*2 Henry VI*, 4.2.69-70) and that everyone will wear one uniform, without distinction of rank, absurdly proclaims himself the king of England, thus recognising, however perversely, the principle of degree, which reasserts itself despite everything.

Although Stribrny is wrong in counterposing Shakespeare's idea of time to his idea of order, he does reveal Shakespeare's acute awareness of the changing times he depicted. These changing times are 'constantly evoked in such images as "that hapless time" of Henry VI (repeated four times in the trilogy), "the fearfulls't time" of Richard III, "the perilous time" of King John, the "wasted time" of Richard II, or the "justling time" of Henry IV (Part 1), which finally becomes utterly "misordered" (Part 2) for the old lords temporal and spiritual' [97]

The times are seen to change with the reign of each king.[98] The changes inaugurated by each new reign are often, it may be added, expressed in musical terms. Edward IV's reign, coming after the wars of Henry VI's reign, is in Richard's contemptuous phrase a 'weak piping time of peace' (*Richard III*, 1.1.24). 'For the concord of my state and time', says Richard II (5.5.47–48), he did not have 'an ear to hear my true time broke.' 'And now my death', says Henry IV (*2 Henry IV* 4.5.199-200), 'changes the mood', a pun on 'mode' or musical key. The musical key characteristic of his disturbed reign will be succeeded by that of the triumphant reign of a son who has gained his crown from his father, not wrested it from another king. English history is like a great symphony, with each new movement being conducted by a new king.

Although the quality of the king's conducting will affect

the music of his state, he is constrained by the score. He, like everyone else, is a child of his time[99] and subject to its necessities, the natural consequences of all that has gone before, which impose constraints on the actors in the drama of history. 'Oh, my good Lord Mowbray', says Henry IV's emissary Westmoreland to one of the rebels (*2 Henry IV* 4.1.101–4), 'Construe the times to their necessities, / And you shall say indeed, it is the time, / And not the King, that doth you injuries.' This is, of course, a diplomatic disclaimer of Henry's responsibility for Mowbray's grievances; yet, strong as Henry is, he is in large measure at the mercy of events. Although he is in many ways an admirable king, his reign is an unquiet one, for in violating degree by revolting against Richard he showed others how to revolt against him after he had gained the throne – and yet the historical pressures causing him to revolt against Richard, who had himself violated natural law in depriving him of his inheritance, were well nigh irresistible.

Nevertheless, Henry does not give himself up to 'the rough torrent of occasion' (4.1.72), the compulsive current of circumstances, as another rebel, the archbishop of York, calls it in making a similar disclaimer of responsibility to Westmoreland. 'Are these things then necessities?' Henry exclaims, immediately after his statement of despair about the 'revolution of the times', on hearing from Warwick that Northumberland's rebellion grew inevitably from the development of both Northumberland's character and the historical situation. 'Then let us meet them like necessities.' It is the difference between him and Richard II.

The world of *Richard II* is, as Tillyard and others have shown, an older world in its mediaeval ceremony and ritual, with knights meeting in the pageantry of trial by combat, than the 'new world' (4.1.78) of Bolingbroke. It is, however, also a world of the decadence of a mediaeval royalty derived from a still older mediaeval past, of a court whose king learns each 'vanity – / So be it new, there's no respect how vile' (2.1.24-25) that is initiated abroad by 'proud Italy'. Richard is, then, a devotee of that Italianism which Elizabethans felt was weakening the moral fibre of its old aristocracy.[100] 'Time-honored' Gaunt, so addressed in the first line of the play, is the representative of the distant mediaeval past, of the time when the 'royal kings' of England were renowned as far away as Palestine 'for Christian service and true chivalry' (2.1.51-54), the time of the Crusades. Richard in the decadence of his late mediaeval court is doing away with the memory of this early past and clearing the stage for the world of Bolingbroke.

Richard, with feudal aristocratic contempt for the lower classes, speaks disparagingly of Bolingbroke's 'courtship to the common people' (1.4.24), of his doffing his bonnet to oyster wenches and draymen. Bolingbroke not only foreshadows Elizabeth's courting of popular approval but, 'wooing poor craftsmen with the craft of smiles' (1.4.28), even the modern politician, grinning and waving to the man in the street.

Himself a feudal noble, Bolingbroke heads a rebellion of the nobility against the king, but he becomes a new kind of monarch who is indebted also to the commons and seeks to stamp out the feudal power of those who were his fellow nobles. His suppression of the rebellion of Northumberland and Hotspur would have undoubtedly reminded Elizabethans of Elizabeth's suppression early in her reign of the Northern Rebellion led by the Percies of her day.[101]

As Henry IV, he is concerned about the similarity he thinks he sees between his son Hal and Richard II, who like Hal associated with low company. With Richard, however, this association meant the neglect of kingship and the giving of himself to frivolous pleasures. With Hal, it is not merely a prelude to his reformation, making it shine more brightly; there seems to be a suggestion that it is a part of his education for kingship, a means by which he acquires a rapport with his people that he retains after assuming the royal dignity. At Agincourt he moves easily among his soldiers, able to maintain his disguise, talking to them in their own language and inspiring them to battle. This is something that Richard could not have done. The war, moreover, is presented as a national war, not a war of feudal lords concerned only with their family rights and family honour and contemptuous of their soldiers, as the French are. The patriotic character of the war is symbolised by the four captains – English, Welsh, Scots, and Irish – constituting between them the Great Britain that the Stuart monarchy would seek to weld together. The parallel with the Tudors is reinforced by the references to Henry's Welsh ancestry, their supposed derivation from the legendary King Arthur being part of the Tudor myth.

With Henry VI we are back in the world of feudalism. Richard of York, with the feudal nobility's contempt for learning, speaks disparagingly of Henry's 'bookish rule' (*2 Henry VI*, 1.1.257). Henry's bookishness is, however, not the same as the humanistic study of which the Archbishop of Canterbury says Henry V's discourse on theology, statesmanship, and war shows evidence. His monkish study, befitting one whose 'hand is made to grasp a palmer's staff, / And not to grace an awful princely sceptre' (*2 Henry VI*, 5.1.97-98), is evidently of manuals of devotion. His is the spirit of the mediaeval saint, not of the Renaissance monarch. He is, consequently, overshadowed by his nobles.

Richard III, however, is more like a Renaissance Borgia than a feudal king or nobleman. He is of a different epoch than his father, Richard of York, who is jealous of his family honour. Richard, however, does not scruple to have Buckingham suggest to the citizens that his brother Edward was a bastard, Richard's mother having been unfaithful to his father. Absolute power is his sole concern.

The court of Henry VIII is the court of a Renaissance absolute monarch. Although great nobles like Norfolk, Suffolk, and Surrey are discontented by the immense power of the Lord Chancellor of England, Cardinal Wolsey, a butcher's son, they dare say or do nothing until the king's wrath has turned against his counsellor. Humanistic scholars, Wolsey, Cromwell, Cranmer, men of humble origin, have great influence as administrators in a new society.

Wolsey's fall is the fall of one of those rapid social climbers whom Elizabethans distrusted. Other Shakespearean examples are Richard II's courtiers, Bushy, Bagot, and Green – simple gentlemen as against the earls and dukes whose enmity they incur – and the newly ennobled kinsmen of obscure gentry origin of Queen Elizabeth in *Richard III*. Wolsey is arrogant

and greedy, Richard's courtiers selfish and grasping, Elizabeth's kinsmen touchy and insecure. The characteristic vices of the feudal nobility, on the other hand, are pride, contentiousness, vengefulness.

The ideal aristocrat is Talbot, who wins nobility not through intrigue but through valorous deeds on the field of battle, in contrast to York and Somerset, who in their emulous rivalry, forgetful of their country, bring about his defeat. His is that service to the state which the Renaissance courtesy books spoke of as the goal of the training of the gentleman. Talbot, to be sure, is a mediaeval chivalric warrior rather than a Renaissance gentleman, but the new Tudor aristocracy of Shakespeare's day, which, recruited from the gentry, merchants, and lawyers, had been given a territorial basis by Henry VIII's expropriation of the monasteries and had been ennobled and married into noble families, liked to relate itself to the past.

The contrast in Tudor times between the old feudalistic aristocracy and the new aristocracy is best exemplified by the opposition between Hotspur and Hal. To repeat partially what I have said elsewhere,

'Hotspur is a figure representative of the Elizabethan period as well as of the feudal past. . . Hotspur's concept of honour. . . is. . . that of the devotees of the neo-chivalric cult of honour [the most dedicated of whom were members of the old aristocracy in Elizabeth's court] who argued, according to Bryskett, that ". . . a man for cause of honour may arm himself against his country." Full of the sense of his family's "nobility and power" he feels that Henry has disgraced it and seeks to avenge the family honour, urging his father and uncle to "redeem / your banished honours" and "revenge the jeering and disdained contempt / Of this proud king" (I, iii, 170–82). . . Hotspur has the old feudal contempt of the humanistic virtues of the gentleman. . . [He] is not the man for what he calls "mincing poetry" (III, i, 34). Hunting and war are his pursuits. . . In killing Hotspur, Hal, who has "a truant been to chivalry," (V i 94) takes over Hotspur's chivalric virtues, but he purges them of their accompanying faults. He is not concerned as is Hotspur, who could brook no "corrival" (I, iii, 205), with a reputation of preeminent valour, but is rather concerned with the honour that comes from doing public service, an honour that in his speech before Agincourt he calls upon the commonest soldier to share with him.'[102]

The bourgeoisie, whom Hotspur regards with contempt (3.1.251-54), is an intermittently perceived force throughout the plays. The significance of its support of Bolingbroke has already been examined. To Green's statement that the king's favourites are hated by those who 'love not the King', Bagot replies (2.2.128-130), 'And that is the wavering commons, for their love / Lies in their purses, and who so empties them / By so much fills their hearts with deadly hate.' The 'wavering commons' often is decisive, at least for the moment, in the struggle of the rival houses. 'Trust me, my lord', says Warwick, the 'kingmaker' (*3 Henry VI*, 4.2.1-2), after having switched from Edward IV to Henry VI, 'all hitherto goes well; / The common people by numbers swarm to us.'

The bourgeoisie is primarily concerned with two things: the relief from taxes of which Bagot speaks and the maintenance of a strong central government that would put down disorders and protect the flow of trade. The Bishop of Winchester, the great uncle of the king, vying with Humphrey of Gloucester, uncle of the king and Protector of the realm, seeks to incite the Lord Mayor of London against him by saying (*1 Henry VI*, 1.3.62-4), 'Here's Gloucester, a foe to citizens, / One that still motions war and never peace, / O'ercharging your free purses with large fines.' The Lord Mayor's attitude toward these mighty ones, whose retainers have engaged in an altercation that has raised an uproar, is one of a 'plague on both your houses': 'Fie, lords! that you, being supreme magistrates / Thus contumeliously should

break the peace!' (57-58). He proclaims that all those who have engaged in this disturbance 'against God's peace and the king's' (75) must disperse immediately and henceforth not wear weapons, threatening to call out the apprentices from
80 their shops to assist the city officers if the combatants do not leave the scene. The strength of the bourgeoisie here apparent is even more clearly seen in the fact that Richard III feels that he needs the support of the Lord Mayor and the leading citizens, the commercial oligarchy of London, before he can be crowned king.

Shakespeare, then, does more than show the changing relationship between monarchy, aristocracy, and bourgeoisie and the evolution of each in the historical period he is depicting. He shows the changes in his own time and even foreshadows the time when the bourgeoisie and its allies will overthrow a Stuart king.

Conclusion: Shakespeare's view of English history and our own time

Not many in the twentieth century believe in such notions as the operation of divine providence in history or kings being the deputies of God. But to understand Shakespeare's historical plays we must understand the concepts that govern his view of history. It is not, however, a matter of undertaking the impossible task of becoming an Elizabethan. It is a matter of understanding the Elizabethan Shakespeare in order that he may take on meaning for the twentieth century. That does not mean that there will not rise tensions between 'past significance' and 'present meaning'. Thus for anti-imperialists the glorification in *Henry V* of the birth of the national state in a patriotic war is affected by the perception of the destructiveness of the national state in its twentieth century apotheosis. Henry's concern with the justness of his war recalls all the diplomatic manoeuverings of our time to place the onus of the war on the enemy; his assurance that God is on his side recalls the Kaiser's 'Gott und mich' and Rupert Brooke's 'For God,

King, and Country' in the senseless carnage of World War I; his talk of national honour recalls how national honour was invoked in the fighting of such a dishonourable war as that in Vietnam; his statement before Harfleur that he has no choice but to release the horrors of war if the city does not submit recalls all the generals who have agreed with Sherman that 'war is hell' and proceeded with their devastation. The anti-imperialist's attitude, then, will tend to be the attitude of detached admiration mixed with irony of Hazlitt, who, after some scathing comments on military conquerors and their 'pleasure of destroying thousands of other lives', says that 'in the play', where 'no dead men's bodies are found piled on heaps and festering the next morning', if not in life, Henry is 'a very amiable monster', 'a panther or a young lion in their cages', from whom we 'catch a pleasing horror from their glistening eyes, their velvet paws, and dreadless roar.'[103] To be sure, there are other things in the play, such as its picture of the courage and camaraderie with which men face a common danger, to which one can respond more wholeheartedly.

If, however, intervening history, particularly the history of our own time, may qualify our appreciation of Shakespeare's history plays, it may also evoke a deeper response to what they have to offer to this age of wars and revolutions. They create a heightened awareness of the drama of history. In our time of television news broadcasts, events are images on a screen that appear in random sequence and then are lost in Orwellian 'memory holes' of oblivion. Shakespeare's history plays, however, provide a renewed appreciation of the momentousness of events that determine the destiny of peoples. Through them comes the perception that the luxury of escaping into the cultivation of one's own garden while occasionally looking at the images of the screen is no longer possible, for the private gardens are part of a larger garden whose weeds must spread into each individual plot.

History in Shakespeare's plays is not a series of disconnected happenings, as it is in the mediaeval annals or in the nightly television news of modern times. It is a chain of cause and effect. The historical past therefore imposes constraints on all men and women seeking to affect their time. Yet what individuals do within the range of possibilities that history permits them may have a crucial effect. Henry IV's acceptance of the necessities of the times but his resolution to act within the limits permitted by these necessities is in the spirit of Marx's 'men make their own history, but they do not make it just as they please; they do not make it under circumstances chosen by themselves, but under circumstances directly encountered, given, and transmitted from the past.'[104] Although the characters in Shakespeare's drama of history are not completely free, history in Shakespeare – except for intermittent intimations of a divine plan – is not characterised by the fatalism often wrongly attributed to Marxism (human beings are not the puppets of a historical geist but 'make their own history'). In freeing his readers from the sense of fatalism, Shakespeare's history plays serve to free them from the sense of powerlessness.

At the same time, they suggest the harsh choices that history demands and the great problems involved in striving to form a new kind of government that will wipe out the evil inherited from previous times. The difficulties Henry IV has in suppressing the power of the feudal nobles and the reversion of England to an intensified feudal strife in the reign of Henry VI are reminders that social revolution may be the only way to defeat the powers of destruction but that it demands struggle and is not easily effected.

These powers of destruction are unforgettably dramatised. The blind drives and passions of the contending nobles – hungry wolves tearing at each other's throats – that bring havoc recall the blind drives and passions of twentieth century rulers, who strike out against their rivals in the capitalist world and their victims in the colonial world. The feudal wars are a thing of the past, but if a war between York and Lancaster in present day England would seen absurd, so will war between France and Germany or the United States and Japan seem absurd in the future if we are able to construct an international socialist order in place of capitalist national states. The possibility that such a future can be realised is indicated by Shakespeare's living picture of a dead past in which people went to die for York and Lancaster as a matter of course.

Richard III and the spirit of capitalism

5

It may seem strange to regard Richard III, a member of the feudal house of York, whose conflict with the rival house of Lancaster marked the waning of the Middle Ages in England, as representative of the spirit of capitalism. However, as seen in chapter two, Shakespeare regarded the Tudor order as threatened by the rampant individualism of both the old nobility, with its tradition of feudal prerogatives that superseded the national state, and the most aggressive section of the bourgeoisie, which was already in the 1590s beginning to challenge the monarchy. He more than once identified the individualism of the one with that of the other, in the same way that the American capitalists of the late nineteenth century are called 'the robber barons.'

Thus *King Lear* although its social setting is that of an early, primitive feudalism and its characters are members of either royal or feudal families, reflects the conflict in Shakespeare's time between the mediaeval and the modern worlds. The evil members of the younger generation are of the new capitalist world. The language of Goneril and Regan, says Wolfgang Clemen, citing the research of one of his students, Lotte Schmerz, has 'frequent occurrence of quantitative and mercantile terms as well as the use of calculating comparatives.'[1] The words of Edmund, 'Let me, if not by birth, have lands by wit' (1.2.187), might have served as a motto for the acquisitive bourgeoisie, which was buying up estates from the older landowners.

Richard is very much of the new capitalist world. He uses the language of business and displays its attitudes throughout.

Much attention has been paid to the stylisation of the play's dialogue, with its stichomythia in the wooing scene of Anne, its ritualistic curses of Margaret, its chorused laments of the three queens, but little notice has been taken of what Charles Lamb called the 'sprightly colloquial' language of Richard,[2] which acts as a counterpoint to this stylisation. It is a colloquial language that often recalls the contemporary turns of phrase expressing the values of our own business civilisation.

We might begin by looking at a line of images that can be called that of 'the peddler and his pack horse.' In his soliloquy at the end of the first scene of the play, Richard says that Edward 'must not die/ Until George be packed with post horse up to heaven' (1.1.145-46). He regards Clarence as a bale of goods that he will sling over a horse's back and ship express from the kingdom of England to the kingdom of heaven. Richard's quick mind then leaps ahead to his plans after Clarence and Edward are dead, but he stops himself with the jocular reminder: 'But yet I run before my horse to market / Clarence still breathes, Edward still lives and reigns; / When they are gone, then must I count my gains' (1.1. 160-62). 'I run before my horse to market' was a proverbial phrase meaning 'I'm running ahead of myself in my eagerness' or, as Kittredge glosses it, 'I count my chickens before they're hatched.'[3] The pack horse has to take one's goods to the market before one can make his profit. Only then, when one has carried out his plans, can he sit down to total up what he has made. The image of the peddler and his pack horse is used again when Richard says to Queen Elizabeth of his labours on behalf of her husband Edward, 'I was a pack horse in his great affairs' (1.3.121) and also, a little later, when he says in disclaiming any desire to be king, 'I had rather be a peddler' (1.3.148). It is an image that seems to spring naturally to his lips.

Richard also frequently uses financial and monetary terms. 'Repaired with double riches of content' (4.4.319), 'advantaging their loan with interest / Of ten times double gain of happiness' (4.4.323-24), 'go current from suspicion' (2.1.96) – that is, pass as genuine currency without being suspected of being counterfeit – these are but a few examples. In addition to these and subsequently cited examples, I have counted eight others.[4]

Although he may possibly use more such terms than any Shakespearean character with the exception of Shylock, what is most important is not the frequency with which Richard uses them but their effect in a number of instances. This effect may be contrasted with that of the recurring Shakespearean image of the lover as a merchant and his mistress as a treasure of great price for which he is venturing forth on an ocean journey.[5] The image of the lover as a merchant suggests the romance of foreign commerce, the exotic appeal of strange lands in new worlds, with great fortunes to be won through high risks in ventures in which aristocrats could partake.[6] Such are the ventures of Antonio, the aristocratic merchant prince who stands in opposition to the niggardly usurer Shylock and finances Bassanio on his romantic overseas quest to gain Portia, the 'golden fleece' (1.1.170).[7] Richard's financial and monetary language, on the other hand, undercuts the romanticism of mediaeval chivalry and its ideal of aristocratic honour.[8]

A noteworthy instance of Richard's use of monetary terms occurs when he says in disparagement of the queen's kindred, who are of obscure gentry origin but have been ennobled by the king, 'Great promotions / Are daily given to ennoble those / That scarce, some two days since, were worth a noble' (1.3.79-81). 'Worth a noble' refers to a coin of the time. Richard measures nobility by money, not by blood, in direct opposition to Bassanio, who tells Portia, 'When I did first impart my love to you, / I freely told you all the wealth I had / Ran in my veins. I was a gentleman' (3.2.253–55). The words 'gentle' and 'noble' had long had moral connotations as well as referring to social classes, the suggestion being that members of the aristocracy had a fineness of character and sensibility peculiar to them. For Richard, however, 'noble' refers to money. 'Money talks.' Just so Shylock, who in his insistence on the supremacy of the bond, the sacred business contract, over the claims of humanity is the representative of the capitalist ethic, is not referring to Antonio's moral character, as Bassanio thinks, when he says 'Antonio is a good man' (1.3.12), but means that he is a good business risk. The bourgeoisie, said Marx and Engels in *The Communist Manifesto*, 'has resolved personal worth into exchange value.'[9] The idea of personal worth as exchange value lies behind both Richard's and Shylock's lines, as it does behind our own expressions 'that man is worth a million dollars' and 'he is good for the money.'

Other monetary terms Richard makes use of are also indicative. 'My dukedom to a beggarly denier', he exclaims (1.2.251), when he wishes to express a certainty. His dukedom is for him a source of wealth and power, which he will wager against a denier, a small French coin; it is not a heritage of honour that he must jealously protect. His concept of it is worlds apart from that of his father, who had said, 'And for these wrongs, those bitter injuries, / Which Somerset hath offered to my house, / I doubt not but with honour to redress' (*1 Henry VI*, 2.5.124-26). But Richard had said of himself, 'I have no brother, I am like no brother; / And this word `love,' which greybeards call divine, / Be resident in men like one another / And not in me: I am myself alone' (*3 Henry VI*, 5.6.80-83). The bourgeoisie, to quote *The Communist Manifesto* again, with its 'egotistical calculation', 'reduced the family relation to a mere money relation.'[10] The notion of family honour and family devotion is alien to Richard, who has Buckingham suggest to the citizens that his brother Edward was the illegitimate issue of an affair of his mother's. He is indeed motivated only by 'egotistical calculation.'

When Richard wishes to propose to Buckingham that he murder the two young princes, he tells him, 'Ah, Buckingham, now do I play the touch / To try if thou be current gold indeed' (4.2.8-9). Personal worth is again spoken of in terms of money. Richard is to be the touchstone that will measure the genuineness of Buckingham's gold. If Buckingham is really 'as good as gold', he will murder the two children.

When Richard wishes to entice Elizabeth to marry her daughter to him, he tells her that, after having conquered Buckingham, he will to her daughter 'retail my conquest won, / And she shall be sole victoress' (4.4.335-36). 'Retail,' derived from the earlier meaning (*OED* 1) 'to sell (goods, etc.) in small quantities,' signifies (*OED* 2) 'to recount or tell over again', suggesting not only relating in detail but counting and recounting money. Richard is, therefore, promising Elizabeth's daughter the joys of gaining all of England, which he represents as something to be counted out bit by bit.

Richard uses not only monetary terms but business language. He greets the men he has hired to kill Clarence with 'How now, my hardy stout-resolved mates! / Are you now going to dispatch this thing?' and sends them off with 'about your business straight./Go, go, dispatch.' (1.3.339-40, 353–54). 'Dispatch' was a word with business connotations. One of its meanings was (*OED* 1, 3) 'to dismiss (a person) after attending to him or his business; to settle the business and send away.' This was easily extended to (*OED* 1, 4) 'to get rid of or dispose of (anyone) by putting to death; to make away with, kill.' Richard is playing on the word: the murder of Clarence is just a little business matter to be speedily taken care of. Clarence may try to talk them out of it, but the professional killers, enterprising freelance forerunners of Murder Incorporated, know their jobs (after all, 'business is business') and will not allow themselves to be diverted. The word 'business' in 'about your business straight' suggests the same coldbloodedness as in Edmund's words in calculating his course, 'A credulous father, and a brother noble. . . I see the business' (1.2.183-86).

Richard is twice referred to by other characters as a business agent. Buckingham, urging him before the citizens to rule in his own stead, not as the lord protector of the boy king, tells him to take on 'the charge and kingly government of this your land; / Not as protector, steward, substitute, / Or lowly factor for another's gain' (3.7.130-33). 'Steward' meant, of course, the business manager of an estate, and 'factor' meant the business agent acting in behalf of his principal. Richard, despite his public professions, was really not content to be either, but the irony is that in the last analysis a business agent is all that he is: Margaret, reciting the many deaths of guilty persons that have already occurred, says, 'Richard yet lives, hell's black intelligence, / Only reserved their factor to buy souls / And send them thither' (4.4.71-73). He is the business agent of hell, buying souls and shipping them off to it.

As a businessman, Richard is, to use the language of Babbitt, a 'real hustler', a 'go-getter'. He displays enormous energy from the time he says, in *3 Henry VI*, that he is as one 'lost in a thorny wood' from which he will 'hew' his 'way out with a bloody axe' (3.2.174–81) until the time of his last battle when he dashes frantically about calling 'A horse! A horse! My kingdom for a horse!' (5.4.7). Hustle and bustle characterise his behaviour throughout. 'Delay leads impotent and snail-paced beggary, – (4.3.53) – inactivity is invariably followed by bankruptcy – he exclaims, calling forth to combat. On the eve of his last battle, he says, in an attempt to regain his old zest, 'Tomorrow is a busy day' (5.3.18). And before entering the final fray he cries out, 'Come, bustle, bustle. Caparison my horse' (5.3.290). His underlings in their way speak his language. 'Tut, tut, my lord, we will not stand to prate / Talkers are no good doers', says the First Murderer (1.3.349-50), assuring him that they will not allow Clarence to engage them in conversation and move their pity. 'Talk is cheap' and 'time is money'.

Richard's energy is the energy of the bourgeoisie. 'The bourgeoisie', says *The Communist Manifesto*, 'has disclosed how it came to pass that the brutal display of vigour in the Middle Ages, which reactionaries so much admire, found its fitting complement in the most slothful indolence. It has been the first to show what man's activity can bring about . . . Constant revolutionising of production, uninterrupted disturbance of all social conditions, everlasting uncertainty and agitation distinguish the bourgeois epoch from all earlier ones.'[11] The word 'business', it may be pointed out, is derived from 'busyness'.

With Clarence dead, says Richard, 'God take King Edward to his mercy / And leave the world for me to bustle in!' (1.1.151-52). The world that had been rejected by mediaeval otherworldliness as one of the three great temptations – 'the world, the flesh, and the devil' – he welcomes as his sphere of activity, gladly relinquishing an alleged heaven to Edward. In response to Gratiano's attempt to joke away Antonio's melancholy by telling him that he has too great care for the things of this world, Antonio replies, 'I hold the world but as the world, Gratiano – / A stage, where every man must play a part' (1.1.77-78) – a theatre with the ephemerality of the theatre in contradistinction to the eternity of heaven. But for Richard this world is all. The bourgeoisie, says *The Communist Manifesto*, 'has drowned the most heavenly ecstasies of religious fervour . . . in the icy water of egotistical calculation.'[12]

In his disdain for religion, in his contempt for the generality of men, to whom he regards himself as far superior, in his ruthlessness, cunning, and dissimulation, Richard is, as has often been noted, the greatest Machiavellian villain of Elizabethan drama. In the drama the Machiavellian villain is generally a powerful nobleman or a usurper of a throne or a dukedom, often that of a corrupt Italian court, with the great exception being Marlowe's Jew of Malta, the precursor of Shylock. But in Elizabethan satiric literature Machiavellians are either 'Italianate' members of the old aristocracy or Puritan members of the bourgeoisie, the two threats, from the right and the left, to the Tudor order.[13] Robert Greene's satiric portrait of Gorinus the usurer, who on his deathbed advises his sons to devote all their energies to amassing money and advancing in this world by following the precepts of Machiavelli on trickery and dissimulation, is an example of the Machiavellian under the guise of bourgeois respectability: 'Wise he was, for he bore office in his fox-furred gown, as if he had been a very upright-dealing burgess. He was religious, too, never without a book at his belt and a bolt in his mouth, ready to shoot through his sinful neighbour.'[14] So Richard, when approached by the mayor and other city dignitaries whom Buckingham has persuaded to petition him to become king, presents himself with a bishop on each side of him and a Bible in his hand, supposedly not ready to receive any 'worldly suits' (3.7.62), but he has had Buckingham make some aspersions about the lustfulness of Edward and the legitimacy of his sons.

Richard, like the other Machiavellian villains produced by the Elizabethan imagination contemplating the new world coming into existence, is governed by the principle that the entire world may be destroyed as long as he achieves his will. This is the principle that has governed the ruling bourgeoisie of the advanced capitalist countries and plunged the world into two great wars, costing the lives of millions. Shakespeare, incarnating in the monstrous form of Richard III the spirit of the bourgeoisie at the time of its menacing approach to power, was able to anticipate the bourgeoisie's behaviour when it gained world domination. For that spirit did not die at Bosworth Field.

Falstaff and his social milieu

6

Falstaff, the great comic character of the English history plays, is, as has not sufficiently been recognised, drawn from the life of Shakespeare's London. His meaning for our time is better understood by seeing him in his social milieu.

Shakespearean scholars have found that entering into Falstaff's making were such literary traditions as the braggart soldier and the clever parasite of classical comedy, the Vice of the morality play, the Devil of the miracle play, the Riot of the interlude, the Lord of Misrule, and the privileged court jester.[1] All of these traditions did indeed enter into Shakespeare's rich comic creation, but Falstaff is something different from any of them or the sum total of them. John W Draper, Lily B Campbell, and Paul Jorgensen have shown him to follow the corrupt practices of accepting bribes for not pressing men into service and of padding the muster rolls to receive more money, which went into his pocket, practices of which Elizabethan army officers were frequently accused.[2] But while Falstaff's occupation after Hal has got for him the command of an infantry company is that of an officer and he uses the practices associated with army officers, he is not merely the member of an occupation but of a social class.

T A Jackson, in the essay referred to in chapter two, wrote of Falstaff as follows: 'In form Falstaff's company is a quasi-feudal military company headed by a knight. In substance and in fact they are a crew of degenerate thieves, parasites, and spongers, foot-pads, tavern bullies, souteneurs and tricksters. Their lives and their ends follow closely the line followed in actual fact by François Villon in Paris, a century before

Shakespeare's birth, while as more or less amusing scoundrels they form one of the earliest examples of the *picaresque* – the line. . . which is, as Maxim Gorky has pointed out, the nearest to an heroic line, persisting all through bourgeois literature

from its beginnings.'[3]

By the end of the sixteenth century, London, the leading commercial city of Europe and the centre of wealth in England, had swelled to twice the size it had been in the time of Henry VIII. It sucked into itself from all parts of the country a motley crew of fortune seekers, including impoverished feudalistic gentry, whose fixed rents for their peasant tenants were reduced in value during this time of capitalistic expansion and inflation, feudal retainers and servingmen who had been laid off, and professional soldiers, drawn in large part from these classes, who were out of service between foreign wars. Jackson's reference to Villon came close to Elizabethan reality in ways other than he realised. The graduates of the expanded universities were, as an academic dramatic trilogy, *The Pilgrimage to Parnassus*, makes clear, unable to find jobs sufficient for their numbers. Literary patronage was also partly breaking down, and the literary marketplace accommodated only penurious hacks. Representative of these hacks was Robert Greene, a Bohemian like Villon, although, unlike him, untrue to his Bohemianism, he produced on his deathbed (perhaps for money, perhaps for salvation), not a mocking self-epitaph but a fervent, even fevered, pamphlet proclaiming his repentance. The sensational manner in which Greene regaled his readers with the sins of thought and action he had committed shows how shocked citizens regarded these dangerous elements in their midst.

Down-and-out university men, down-and-out former soldiers, down-and-out outcasts of the declining feudal sector of society, assorted riff-raff pretending to be soldiers returned from the wars, travellers returned from abroad, and gentlemen of ancient lineage – all of these were the declassed members of the London underworld. The way of life of Falstaff and his crew is theirs. As Jackson points out, Pistol's 'Base is the soul that pays!' expresses 'the innermost soul of "Bohemianism" from François Villon, jesting before the gallows, down to this day.'[4] But it is not only in his way of life that Falstaff resembles Greene, but in his rejection of conventional belief. Falstaff, to be sure, parades his religion, although it is only lip service, amusingly contrasted with his actions, while Greene and Marlowe, the great Elizabethan rebel who had his being in this Bohemian milieu, were charged with privately flouting it, but Falstaff in his catechism on honour rejects conventional belief as they do. So, Robert Louis Stevenson with an artist's perception has Villon contemptuously refute the notion of aristocratic honour in his 'A Lodging for the Night.'

Of all the Elizabethan descriptions of the members of the underworld, the closest in a number of ways to Falstaff is the burlesque description of another tavern knight, 'The Melancholy Knight', by the Elizabethan versifier Samuel Rowlands. The melancholy knight, speaking in the tavern that is his haunt, tells of how his wife spends more than the rents he receives from his estate. His melancholy is very definitely connected with his economic situation: 'The Golden Age and Silver is decayed: / oh, now comes on a melancholy fit, / To write of gold and not possess a whit.'[5] He bewails the fact that a cobbler can buy more for cash than he for credit and, while proudly proclaiming his knightliness, will not fight even if this means permitting others to call him a liar, 'knowing that I often lie when none perceives it.'[6]

So, too, Falstaff, full of comic exuberance and enormous vitality though he be, is vain of his knighthood and sometimes mournfully deplores his comedown and his way of life. The waiters at the tavern think of him as a 'proud Jack' (*1 Henry IV*, 2.4.11); Mistress Quickly tells of how, on promising her marriage, he advised her to leave off her familiarity with her friends, for before long they would call her 'madam' (*2 Henry IV*, 2.1.97–100); and Poins, reading Falstaff's impudent letter to the Prince, exclaims at the first words: '"John Falstaff, knight," – very man must know that, as oft as he has occasion to name himself. Even like those that are kin to the king, for they never prick their finger but they say, "There's some of the king's blood spilt."' (*2 Henry VI*, 2.2.108-12). In *Henry IV Part 1* he is continually voicing repentance for living in a manner unbecoming a gentleman. 'If I do grow great', he says, having claimed the reward for valour in having 'killed' Hotspur, 'I'll grow less; for I'll purge, and leave sack, and live cleanly as a nobleman should do' (*1 Henry IV*, 5.4.161-163).

Repentance and melancholy go together: 'The devil was sick, the devil a monk would be.' 'Sblood', sighs Falstaff, put in mind of the gallows that awaits highwaymen by the Prince's persistent jokes, 'I am as melancholy as a gib-cat or a lugged bear', and goes on, 'Hal, I prithee trouble me no more with vanity' (*1 Henry IV*, 1.2.73–74, 82–83). His melancholy, like that of Rowlands's melancholy knight, is partly affectation, for melancholy was the Byronic prose of disaffected gentlemen or pretended gentlemen of the time, but Falstaff's melancholy is his very own. It is as deep and long-lived as his repentance; he bounds from it with his characteristic resilience. It serves his humour, however, to reverse the truth by speaking of himself as a melancholiac, just as it does to speak of himself as an innocent misled by a wicked Prince of Wales: 'A plague of sighing and grief, it blows a man up like a bladder' (*1 Henry IV*, 2.4.334–36). Like Villon, although he engages in lamentation, he is really distinguished by his vitality.

In *Henry IV Part 2*, however, having, like so many other Elizabethan sham soldiers, acquired a bogus military reputation on which for a time he can get credit, he speaks no more of repenting. He has given up the dangerous profession of highwayman for swindling. He continues, however, to maintain his pretence as a young blood. Whereas before he had valiantly assaulted the peaceful travellers on the highway with the cry, 'What, ye knaves, young men must live' (*1 Henry IV*, 2.2.92–93), he now inveighs against the age that cannot appreciate and make use of such gallants as he: 'You that are old consider not the capacities of us that are young' (*2 Henry*

IV, 1.1.2.75–76). For in 'these costermongers' times' (*2 Henry IV*, 1.2.170–71), in this commercial age of successful tradesmen, all that valiant men can find to do is the ignominious taking charge of the bears used in bear-baiting, and all that clever men can find to do is adding up the bills for drinks in acting as waiters in taverns. Why, things are come to such a sorry pass that merchants lead gentlemen on into debt and then demand security before giving them credit.

Thus in his disdain for the commercialism and the degeneracy of the age, in his pride in his lineage, in his sometimes assumed melancholy, and in his lying and cowardice – these last two traits certainly do not need illustration (I regard as settled the famous controversy about Falstaff's cowardice) – Falstaff resembles Rowlands's melancholy knight. This is probably not because Rowlands, who wrote his poem after the Falstaff plays, recalled Falstaff. It is because both Falstaff and the melancholy knight are representatives of the same social class.

The Falstaff of *The Merry Wives of Windsor* is often said to be another fat knight with the same name. This is, however, rather exaggerated. The Falstaff of *The Merry Wives of Windsor* remains his old self in his referring to himself as a young blood, in his talking about repenting, and in his continuing to make use of his ingenious and blustering form of argumentation in speaking to Pistol. He has degenerated more than ever, but this degeneration is a logical progression, a progression also exhibited in *Henry V*, where Shakespeare, with relentless artistic honesty, has Bardolph die on the gallows for robbing French churches, where Pistol becomes a pimp and a cutpurse, and where Dame Quickly dies of syphilis. In Falstaff's first appearance in *The Merry Wives of Windsor* he is turning away his retainers, Bardolph, Pistol, and Nym, whom he can no longer keep up, and announcing his need to live by the worst kind of thievery and trickery. Whereas in *Henry IV Part 1* he had followed the tradition of the robber barons in robbing travellers on the highway and in *Henry IV Part 2* had followed the custom of the impoverished

gallant of not paying his debts to the tradesmen, he now accepts a share of the petty loot of his followers, who have degenerated into pickpockets, swearing in their behalf that they are honest, soldierly servingmen. More than this, he
98 thinks to be paid by Mrs Ford and Mrs Page for honouring them with his love and plays the part of a pimp toward the supposed Master Brook, although this is only the game of a confidence man who does not plan to come across with the goods.

It is true, however, that in *The Merry Wives of Windsor* Falstaff is an easy butt, having lost the mental agility that had enabled him to escape from his previous predicaments, although not without some laughter at his expense. The quick witted scoundrel has become a ridiculous old lecher at the mercy of the clever middle-class wives. Karl Kautsky in his *Thomas More and His Utopia* says that *The Merry Wives of Windsor*, which pictures the 'struggle between decrepit knighthood and the upward striving capitalist class', is 'the exuberant shout of joy of the advancing bourgeoisie.'[7] However, the tradition dating from the eighteenth century that *The Merry Wives of Windsor* is a court play gains strong evidence, as has been pointed out by William Green, from the allusions in the play to Queen Elizabeth, Windsor Castle, and the Order of the Garter.[8] The mishaps in love and the final exposure of the degenerate old knight, so proud of his lineage and so unknightly in his behavior, who had stooped to two citizens' wives and stumbled as he stooped, would have tickled a court audience, as had the ludicrous love for a country wench and the final exposure of the pretender to gentility, Don Armado, in *Love's Labour's Lost.* Falstaff's flattery is unable to turn the heads of the merry but honest wives, who in their bourgeois country-town milieu know their place in society, scoffing at the notion that they were meant to be court ladies. So, too, Page objects to his daughter marrying Master Fenton not only because that gentleman had squandered his fortune but because Page is suspicious about marrying outside of one's class: 'He is of too high a region'

(3.2.69). These bourgeois are from a conservative sector of the bourgeoisie, not at all upward striving.

'If it were not for one trifling respect', says Mrs Ford ironically, 'I could come to such honour. . . If I would but go to hell for an eternal moment or so, I could be knighted' (2.1.43–48). For Falstaff, however, 'honour', here as in *Henry IV Part 1*, is but an empty word, and since it is that for a knight such as he, it must, he thinks, be so for everyone. When Pistol demurs at acting as Falstaff's pander, Falstaff indignantly asks him how dare he speak of his honour when Sir John Falstaff himself is at times constrained to forget his.

What is the secret of the power and attraction of this old scoundrel, especially in the *Henry* plays? One answer, I should say, lies in his questioning of conventional values, even though that questioning springs from an absence of all values except those of mere egoism. It is a reminder that the conventional call to duty may be destructive if unthinkingly obeyed. If Falstaff's rejection of honour, a rationalisation for his cowardice, is amusingly contemptible, in addition to being amusingly adroit, Hotspur's devotion to honour causes him to be manipulated by the crafty politician Worcester and to bring havoc to England, just as appeals to national honour today are used to justify the worst crimes against humanity. The juxtaposition of Hotspur's comments on honour and Falstaff's comments on it is, as has been frequently pointed out, certainly significant.

But it is not only Hotspur and the feudal nobility whose values are questioned by Falstaff. The language in which he addresses the travellers whom he and his companions rob questions the values of another class. The travellers consist of a group of franklins. Franklins were prosperous landowners below the gentry in social position, who, as the description of Chaucer's franklin indicates, had a reputation for good living off the fat of the land.[9] Falstaff, as he and his companions dash out at them, cries out: 'Strike! Down with them! Cut the villains' throats! Ah, whoreson caterpillars! Bacon-fed knaves! They hate us youth. Down with them! Fleece them!' (*1*

Henry IV, 2.2.84-87). The travellers exclaim in fear, 'O, we are undone, both we and ours for ever!' and Falstaff responds, 'Hang ye, gorbellied knaves, are ye undone? No, ye fat chuffs; I would your store were here!'

100 Of course, part of the humour lies in the fact that Falstaff, the greatest of parasites, calls the franklins 'caterpillars', the current term for parasites, that he, who is by his own admission close to sixty, presents himself as youth confronting age, that he, whose girth undoubtedly surpasses theirs, great as theirs undoubtedly is, calls them 'gorbellied'. Part of the humour also lies, however, in the suggestion that they are fat rogues of another kind and that in some sense there is little to choose between Falstaff and them as they stand quaking in fear before the hectoring of one who, unknown to them, is as great a coward as they. For commercial farmers had long been denounced for applying the screws to the peasantry, accumulating the pelf that Falstaff wishes were there so that he might deprive them of it and really ruin them. Handy-dandy, which is the thief?

Even more important than Falstaff as a questioner of conventional values in explaining his enduring attraction is Falstaff as the possessor of a zest for life that is unaffected by his circumstances. Robert Burns in his 'The Jolly Beggars' drew an unforgettable picture of humanity in the midst of misery and degradation snatching some gaiety from existence. Falstaff and his crew do the same in their tavern. They are a tribute to the thirst for life and the human solidarity that persist despite squalor. 'Would I were with him', says the much abused Bardolph of the dead Falstaff, 'wheresome'er he is, either in heaven or in hell!' (*Henry V*, 2.3.7–8).

Falstaff, subtly drawn though he be, is based on the tradition of the clown or buffoon, the comic figure who throughout theatrical history has acted as the expression of man's irrepressible spirit. 'The buffoon,' says Susanne K Langer, 'is essentially a folk character, that has persisted through the more sophisticated and literary stages of comedy, as Harlequin, Pierrot, the Persian Karaguez, the Elizabethan jester or fool, the *Vidusaka* of Sanskrit drama; but in the humbler theatrical forms that entertained the poor and especially the peasantry before the movies came, the buffoon had a more vigorous existence as Hans Wurst, as Punch of the puppet show, the clown of pantomime, the Turkish Karagoz (borrowed from the Persian tradition) who belongs to the shadow play. These anciently popular personages show what the buffoon really is: the indomitable living creature fending for itself, tumbling and stumbling (as the clown physically illustrates) from one situation into another, getting into scrape after scrape and getting out again, with or without a thrashing.'[10] The great clown of today, of course, is Charlie Chaplin's tramp, always being chased away by the cop, but always returning after the cop has gone, and always maintaining his shabby elegance through everything.

So Falstaff, too, is a comic figure outside of the confines of the regular social order. Combining the highest reaches of wit and the horseplay of farce, he always finds ways of talking himself out of uncomfortable situations, even though he often has to endure some twitting, and, on being physically attacked by Hal and Poins, manages to run away, roaring as the clown does in his mishaps, and pricked on by a thrust at his rear. That the fat knight, heavy of body but nimble of mind, old in years but youthful in élan, is thus representative of the enduring spirit of ordinary humanity coping through the ages with the knocks of a rough world is his final triumphant paradox.

The American revolutionists and the political ideology of Shakespeare's English and Roman history plays

7

The Tudor political ideas that lie behind Shakespeare's English history plays also lie behind his Roman history plays. They were still being cited by the most reactionary of the American loyalists at the time of the revolutionary turmoil more than a century and a half later. For literature is expressive of ideology, and human beings are economical in their use of ideologies, clinging stubbornly to them as long as they can. The Tudor political ideas, which had served a progressive purpose in their time, were now, with some modifications,[1] the very ideas that the American revolutionists were engaged in combating. But if Shakespeare's political ideas were reactionary in the time of the American revolution, he was able to see that the bourgeois individualism that was to be justified by the revolutionary theory of natural rights was a destructive force with ultimately pernicious consequences.

The ideas of the Declaration of Independence – that 'all men are created equal, that they are endowed by their creator with certain unalienable rights;. . . that to secure these rights governments are instituted among men, deriving their just powers from the consent of the governed; that whenever any form of government becomes destructive of these ends, it is the right of the people to alter or to abolish it' – these ideas, as Bernard Bailyn has shown in *The Ideological Origins of the American Revolution*, were derived from the theory of the common law of the seventeenth century lawyers, notably Sir Edward Coke, the chief defender of the supremacy of common law over the royal prerogative; from the covenant theology of the New England Puritans; from the social and political thought of the revolutionists of the English Civil War and of their successors, the coffee house radicals and the anti-Court politicians of the early eighteenth century; and from Enlightenment rationalism, notably the 'original compact' concept of John Locke's justification for the Revolution of 1688.[2] They were at the opposite pole from the Tudor-Stuart ideas drawn upon by the reactionary loyalists.

'Their warnings, full of nostalgia for ancient certainties,' says Bailyn of these reactionaries, 'were largely ignored. But in the very extremism of their reaction to the events of the time there lies a measure of the distance revolutionary thought had moved from an old to a very new world.'[3] A glance at what one of these worthies had to say will make clear the oldness of this world, the world of Shakespeare's time.

Jonathan Boucher's sermon 'On Civil Liberty, Passive Obedience, and Nonresistance,' delivered in 1775, quoted Lancelot Andrewes, the Anglican bishop and dean of the royal chapel under James I, to the effect that 'princes receive their power only from God, and are by him constituted and entrusted with government chiefly for his own glory and honour, as his deputies and vicegerents upon earth.' The concept of the equality of all men, says Boucher, is a 'particularly loose and dangerous' one, for 'without some relative inferiority and superiority' there can be only chaos. 'A musical instrument composed of chords, keys, or pipes all perfectly equal in size and power might as well be expected to produce harmony as a society composed of members all perfectly equal to be productive of order and peace.' Similarly dangerous is the idea of a contract based on the consent of the governed. 'So far from deriving their authority from any supposed consent or suffrage of men, ["kings and princes"] receive their commission from Heaven; they receive it from God, the source and original of all power.' 'Obedience to government' is, therefore, 'enjoined by the positive commands of God,' and the duty of the subject is '(in the phraseology of a prophet) *to be quiet, and to sit still.*'[4]

Others spoke and wrote in the same vein. Isaac Hunt, for instance, in his *Political Family*, which carries forward

Boucher's argument that 'the first father was the first king: and . . . it was thus that all government originated,'[5] states that 'in the *body politic*. . . a due subordination of the less parts to the greater is . . . necessary to the *existence* of both.'[6]

These ideas – the king as vicegerent of God; the need for social hierarchy; society as a musical harmony (in the well-known words of Ulysses, 'Take but degree away, untune that string, / And, hark, what discord follows' [*Troilus and Cressida* (1.3.109–10]); the king not only as the deputy of God but as the symbol and image of God, who is his 'original'; the subjects' duty of obedience; the king as father of his people; society as a body, some parts of which are inferior to others (a concept most fully expressed by Menenius in *Coriolanus* (1.1.7–15) – these ideas, as we have seen, are the ideas of Shakespeare's age called attention to by Tillyard in his *The Elizabethan World Picture* and *Shakespeare's History Plays.*

The reaction against Tillyard has made it fashionable to say that his Shakespeare is a mere simple-minded propagandist of Tudor orthodoxy. But Shakespeare, of course, as Tillyard was well aware, was neither simple-minded nor a propagandist in the sense of one who oversimplifies for partisan purposes. He was a great playwright who made dramatic use of the ideas of his time. His history plays have the complexity of great art, but they are shaped by his age's view of history.

Thus in *Richard II*, his drama of the deposition of a king, Richard is by no means a character who calls forth the audience's full and unambivalent sympathy, the kind of sympathy a zealous propagandist demands for the leader of his cause. He is frivolous, extravagant, and self indulgent and is governed by corrupt favourites, the 'caterpillars' who swarm over England's 'wholesome herbs' (3.4.47,46) in the Gardener's allegorical scene. Yet, despite his previously shown shortcomings, Richard develops in dignity and takes on the aspect of a sacrificial martyr. As J Dover Wilson says, 'Shakespeare's genius succeeded in fusing' two 'originally contradictory conceptions,' the conception of Richard of his supporters, 'which represented him as a saint and a martyr, comparing his sufferings and death with those of Christ himself,' and the conception of him of the Lancastrians, 'which depicted him as a weak, cowardly, moody man who surrendered himself and abdicated of his own free will.' From the fusion of these two opposing conceptions comes Shakespeare's unified, complex Richard, 'one of the most living of his characters.'[7] But regardless of the character of Richard, there can be no doubt that his deposition is to be regarded as a heinous sin for which all England will have to pay for years to come.

In language reminiscent of Richard's own description of his 'liberal largess' toward 'too great a court,' which had forced him to 'farm our royal realm' (1.4.43–5) to his favourites, that is, grant them profits from the collection of taxes, and of Bolingbroke's description of these favourites as 'caterpillars of the commonwealth' (2.3.165), the American revolutionary pamphleteer John Allen referred to George's favourites as 'this junto of courtiers and state-jobbers,' these 'court-locusts'.[8] But there was no question in his mind about the justice of rebelling against a king under the domination of such a crew. Indeed one of the charges he made against these 'court-locusts' was that they 'instil in the King's mind a divine right of authority to command his subjects.'[9] For between the time of Shakespeare and that of George III was the time of Milton, whose political polemics were an important influence on the American revolutionists and who in his *Second Defense* scornfully rejected the notions that 'tyrants' are 'viceroys, forsooth, and vicars of Christ' and that those who supported the execution of Charles were, as the royalists characterised them, in language similar to that of the followers of Richard II, 'parricides' and 'deicides.'[10] In this view it was absurd to call a king the father of his people and an image of God.

In addition to the Civil War and Commonwealth periods the American revolutionists looked for their inspiration to Republican Rome, whose sturdy virtues and love of liberty they contrasted with the decadence and despotism of the Empire. 'They found their ideal selves, and to some extent their voices,' says Bailyn, 'in Brutus, in Cassius, and in

Cicero.'[11] Britain was to America, wrote John Adams, 'what Caesar was to Rome.'[12]

Although the Elizabethans also glorified the virtues of the early Roman republic, they asserted that the supplanting of the later corrupted Roman republic by the imperial power of Augustus was necessary for Rome's wellbeing.[13] They were in this closer to the view of the loyalist John Chalmers, who wrote, 'If we examine the republics of Greece and Rome, we ever find them in a state of war, domestic and foreign,'[14] than to that of the American revolutionists. Chalmers's words, in fact, are reminiscent of the titles of two Elizabethan books, William Fulbecke's *An Historical Collection of the Continual Factions, Tumults, and Massacres of the Romans and Italians during the Space of One Hundred and Twenty Years next before the Peaceable Empire of Augustus Caesar*, and of the 1578 translation of Appian, *An Ancient History and Exquisite Chronicle of the Romans' Wars, Both Civil and Foreign,* whose translator described it as teaching that 'people's rule must give place, and prince's power prevail.'[15]

Shakespeare's republican Rome is certainly not the idealised state of the American revolutionists. *Coriolanus* presents a strife filled, class-divided society, whose leading figure, though possessing many admirable traits, lacks the necessary *noblesse oblige*, whose plebeians, fickle though fundamentally good-natured, are easily manipulated by their power-seeking tribunes, and whose pusillanimous patricians acquiesce in the unjust banishment of the saviour of the city.

Nor does *Julius Caesar* present the conspirators as the idealised republican heroes in whom the American revolutionists saw themselves. Cassius is guided by bitter envy of Caesar; Cicero is vain and unwilling to follow the lead of other men; Brutus, the one member of the conspiracy solely motivated by concern for the public good, is a misguided idealist who only succeeds in bringing disaster to Rome. The erroneousness of his republicanism and the futility of his resistance to Caesarism is ironically illustrated when a member of the unthinking populace to which he expresses his political sentiments in his post-assassination address exclaims in admiration: 'Let him be Caesar!' (3.2.51). 'Caesar had his Brutus,' said Patrick Henry in his famous words, 'Charles I had his Cromwell, and George III may well profit from their example,' but it is would-be

Brutuses of the future who have to draw a lesson from Shakespeare's play.

To be sure, *Julius Caesar*, like *Richard II*, is not a simplistic propaganda tract. Many critics have found it to be enigmatic, being unsure with whom our sympathies are to lie. Not only does Brutus, a noble, kind person, join in the assassination of one who is his 'best lover' (3.2.44–5), but Cassius, despite his envy of Caesar, has a genuinely deep affection for Brutus and is ruled by him against his better judgment. Most complex of all is Julius Caesar, who has accomplished remarkable feats, whose greatness and force of character are acknowledged by Brutus, who is loved by the common people, and who has generosity of spirit, as proved by his feeling for Brutus and Antony and by the fortune he leaves to the citizens of Rome, but who, carried away by ambition and intoxicated by his pre-eminence, is vainglorious, pompous, and boastful. Here Shakespeare, instead of welding together two disparate traditions, as in his depiction of Richard, draws upon a long-standing tradition of Caesar as a man in whom good and bad qualities were strongly intermixed. 'In the literary treatment of Julius Caesar before Shakespeare,' says Geoffrey Bullough, there was 'a weighing of pros and cons, a representation of good and bad characteristics. . . The English [Renaissance] attitude to Julius Caesar preserved its mediaeval ambivalence.'[16]

Yet, as in the case of *Richard II*, the play's language, imagery, and course of action indicate clearly enough how the fall of its title character should be regarded: Caesar is representative of the monarchical principle necessary for the wellbeing of Rome. Just before Caesar's assassination there are earthquakes, fearful storms, and other prodigies, as at the murder of Duncan, the 'civil strife in heaven' (1.3.11) prefiguring the civil wars to come on earth. Brutus is 'with himself at war'

(1.2.46), his 'little kingdom' suffering in itself 'an insurrection' (2.1.68, 69), as Macbeth in doing what is unnatural has to fight against himself. The disagreement between the conspirators (2.1.101–11), like the disagreement between Glendower and Hotspur in *Henry IV Part 1*, indicates the lack of unity and the discord to follow among the perpetrators of disorder. The disease imagery used in reference to Brutus and Caius Ligarius (2.1.235–68, 310–24) suggests the sickness of the enterprise, as does the sickness of Northumberland in *Henry IV Part 1*. Caesar's invitation to the conspirators to 'taste some wine with me' and then, 'like friends' (2.2.126–27), go with him to the Senate House brings home that they, like Timon's friends at his banquet and Macbeth at the banquet for Duncan, are violating the communion of fellowship.

The panic of the people on hearing of the assassination, responding to the news 'as it were doomsday' (3.1.98), is reminiscent of the doomsday imagery betokening the horrors of the deaths of Duncan and Lear. The ritual bathing of the conspirators in the blood of Caesar at the suggestion of Brutus, who would have it that they are 'sacrificers,' not 'butchers' (2.1.166), is dramatically ironic: the 'lofty scene' that Cassius prophesies 'shall be acted over / In states unborn and accents yet unknown' (3.1.112-13) was at the very moment being re-enacted in English before an audience aware that this ceremony was really the 'savage spectacle' (3.1.223) Brutus denied it to be and would inaugurate the savage butchery of civil war.

Antony's soliloquy prophesying this 'domestic fury and fierce civil strife' (3.1.263) is, as Brents Stirling says, 'similar in utterance, function, and dramatic placement to Carlisle's prophecy on the deposition of Richard II, and for that reason it is to be taken seriously as a choric interpretation of Caesar's death.'[17] Indeed the action that follows fulfils this prophecy that 'Caesar's spirit, ranging for revenge,' will, 'with a monarch's voice / Cry havoc and let slip the dogs of war' (3.1.270–73). The triumphant spirit of Caesar is really the principle of Caesarism, reincarnated in Octavius Caesar, the man of destiny who is to win out over his fellow triumvirs and establish the empire that will bring peace to all the known world.[18]

There is one other historical event on which Shakespeare and the American revolutionists differed significantly, the signing of Magna Carta. For the American revolutionists this was a reduction to writing of the 'original compact' that has always existed between governments and the governed. Magna Carta is, said John Dickinson, 'but a constrained declaration. . . in the name of Kings, Lords, and Commons of the sense the latter had of their original, inherent, indefeasible, natural rights.'[19] Shakespeare in *King John* has, however, not a single reference to Magna Carta, for before Coke's famous exposition no great significance was attached to it.

The political thinking of Shakespeare's history plays is, then, diametrically opposed to that of the American revolutionists. Yet the Tudor expropriation of the monasteries and the building up of a new aristocracy based on a more businesslike agriculture than that of the old feudal nobility was the first stage of a revolution that culminated in the English Civil War, to which the American revolutionists owed their inspiration. The 'Homily Against Disobedience and Wilful Rebellion' attacked as a sin against God the Northern rebellion of the powerful nobles protesting the rise to power of the newly made peers of the queen and the suppression of the old religion.[20] Seventy years later the descendants of these nobles and their tenants and dependents in the still half-feudal 'North Parts' were a mainstay of Charles's army. Such are the dialectics of history.

Tudor absolutism, based on a balance of classes but ultimately dependent on the dominant new aristocracy, was opposed to both feudal decentralisation and the individualism of the most aggressive section of the bourgeoisie. Shakespeare exposed the dangers in both of these forces. The bourgeois individualism of which he was critical came to be expressed in the theory of natural rights, preminently the right to the unrestricted use of one's private property, to preserve which men entered into a contract with the government they instituted.[21]

'The sale and purchase of labour-power . . .' said Marx, 'is in fact a very Eden of the innate rights of man. There alone rules Freedom, Equality, Property. . . Freedom, because both buyer and seller of a commodity, say of labour-power, are constrained only by their own free will. They contract as free agents . . . Equality, because . . . they exchange equivalent for equivalent. Property, because each disposes only of what is his own. The only force that brings them together. . . is the selfishness, the gain and the private interests of each.'[22]

'The only force,' 'the selfishness, the gain and the private interests of each,' that brought men together under capitalism Marx called elsewhere 'the cash nexus'. It was this force that Shakespeare portrayed in *The Merchant of Venice* and *Timon of Athens* as working against the sense of humanity. But the naked rapaciousness of the new acquisitive society was often cloaked in religious garb. The money-lender Shylock thinks of himself as belonging to a 'sacred nation' (1.3.45), just as the Puritan usurers of Shakespeare's day regarded themselves as the elect of God whose prosperity in this world was a sign of God's favour. So, too, did the New England Puritans regard themselves as having entered into a covenant with God by which they were to build the American 'New Eden' that was God's purpose. In the nineteenth century secularised version this covenant became the 'manifest destiny' of American imperialist expansionism.[23]

If, then, Shakespeare's political ideology was by the time of the American Revolution a reactionary doctrine that had to be swept away if the American colonies were to be free, his view of bourgeois individualism as characterised by egotism, self-seeking, and alienation was prescient. Although the ideals of equality and freedom can be less and less realised under monopoly capitalism, their proclamation during the revolutionary upsurge was a great step forward. Yet that monopoly capitalism grew out of the 'New Eden' itself, with its insistence on the right to accumulate private property in the means of production.

Shakespeare's view of Roman history

8

The material basis for Roman history and the idea of Rome

Roman history, the subject of three of Shakespeare's mature tragedies, had, because of the emphasis on the classics in the grammar schools of his day, a much greater imaginative appeal than it does today. Shakespeare wrote his Roman plays in accordance with a coherent conception of Rome's history that he had inherited. This conception can be more readily examined if the plays are arranged not in the order in which they were written but in the order of the historical events they depict. To *Coriolanus*, *Julius Caesar*, and *Antony and Cleopatra*, *Cymbeline* and *Titus Andronicus* must be added. In the last two plays, a romance and a revenge tragedy with fictitious characters, Shakespeare was not concerned with the kind of accuracy (in essentials, if not in detail) with which he was concerned in the history plays, but they are set in Roman times and share the concept of Roman history of the three Roman tragedies. From *Coriolanus* to *Titus Andronicus* – from the early city-state to the disintegration of the empire – there is a representation of the rise, decline, and slide to collapse of what was regarded as the greatest civilisation humanity had seen.

Shakespeare's concept of Roman history has been studied by a number of scholars in this century. M W MacCallum in his *Shakespeare's Roman Plays and Their Background* (1910) emphasised the importance in *Julius Caesar* and *Antony and Cleopatra* of the idea that monarchy was essential if Rome was to survive. James Emerson Phillips Jr, in *The State in*

Shakespeare's Greek and Roman Plays (1940) pointed to the importance of the Elizabethan concept of hierarchical order and degree for the monarchic principle. J Dover Wilson in his New Cambridge edition of *Julius Caesar* (1949), on the other hand, showed that there was a significant Renaissance exaltation of republican Rome. T J B Spencer in *Shakespeare and the Elizabethan Romans* (1957) held that Shakespeare, despite some anachronisms in details, made a deliberate effort to give a consistent and authentic picture of the Roman world and succeeded better than his learned contemporary Ben Jonson in doing so. J Leeds Barroll in *Shakespeare and Roman History* (1958) called attention to the Elizabethan idea that Rome served a purpose in the divine scheme of things.

The last twenty years have seen further refinements and extensions. Ernest Schanzer in *The Problem Plays of Shakespeare* (1963), taking issue with both the pro-Caesarists and the anti-Caesarists, demonstrated that there was a tradition extending from Julius Caesar's own time to that of Shakespeare in which Caesar was regarded in an ambivalent manner and concluded that Shakespeare deliberately left the nature of the 'real' Caesar and the justifiability of his murder a puzzle. Geoffrey Bullough in reprinting the sources and analogues of the Roman tragedies (*Narrative and Dramatic Sources of Shakespeare*, vol 5, 1964) concurred with Schanzer concerning the tradition of the ambivalent response to Caesar and Antony but reiterated the importance of the monarchic principle for Elizabethans. Joseph L Simmons in *Shakespeare's Pagan World* (1973) found that Shakespeare viewed Rome as a pagan society whose characters necessarily operate with no reference to St Augustine's City of God and are therefore viewed with a cosmic irony. Paul A Cantor in *Shakespeare's Rome: Republic and Empire* (1976) contrasted the Rome of *Coriolanus*, austere, disciplined, and unspoiled, and the Rome of Antony, sophisticated, corrupt, and decadent. Robert S Miola in *Shakespeare's Rome* (1983), studying the Roman works in their chronological order, not in the order of the historical events depicted in them, found that they were concerned with invasion and rebellion and with the Roman ideals of constancy, honour, and *pietas* but that Shakespeare's view of Rome underwent change, becoming increasingly critical.

Each of these scholars, I believe, has made a valuable contribution toward an understanding of Shakespeare's picture of Rome,[1] but each has only contributed a part of that picture. What I shall seek to do is to fit together the pieces of the picture, filing down those whose shape is not quite right and supplying whatever pieces are missing in the mosaic. Toward this end it will be useful first to present a quick sketch, necessarily simplified, of the material basis for the course of Roman history. This will help to explain the origin of the idea of Rome that Shakespeare derived from the Roman historians and their Christian successors.

The basis of Greco-Roman society was the slave, the 'speaking tool'. The development of slavery both rose from the low level of technique and set limits on the level of that technique. 'Productivity was fixed by the perennial routine of the *instrumentum vocalis*, which devalued all labour by precluding any sustained concern with devices to save it. The typical path of expansion in Antiquity, for any given state, was thus always a 'lateral' one – geographical conquest – not economic advance. Classical civilisation was in consequence inherently colonial in character: the cellular city-state invariably reproduced itself, in phases of ascent, by settlement and war. Plunder, tribute and slaves were the central objects of aggrandisement, both means and ends to colonial expansion.'[2]

Imperialist expansion enriched the members of the aristocratic Senate, the great landowners living in Rome, from whom the administrators of that empire were drawn, and of the equestrian order, who acted as money-lenders, traders, and contracted tax collectors. Great estates, the latifundia, were operated by inexpensive slave labour while the small farmers, who were conscripted into the army and whose land carried a heavy burden of debt, were ruined. Rome became swollen with hordes of dispossessed smallholders. Cliques of nobles vied for the spoils of empire while the disparity between the rich and the poor grew.

The chief factions in the competition for imperial riches were the 'optimates', the self-designated 'best people', and the 'populares'. The leaders of the 'populares' – the Gracchi, Marius, Cinna, Pompey for the greater part of his career before he allied himself with the noble clique dominant in the Senate, and Julius Caesar – appealed for support to the turbulent proletariat, which, unlike the modern industrial proletariat, was jobless as well as propertyless, and to the plebeian artisans and traders. These leaders were members of the nobility who were outside of the dominant group.[3]

'Liberation of the state from tyranny' was 'a popular theme in the speeches of both sides. In the emphasis on tyranny neither side went far wrong, for the question at stake was not senatorial versus popular government but the maintenance of the tyranny of an oligarchy versus the establishment of the tyranny of the individual.'[4] It is, however, the senatorial republican ideal of libertas that has come down to us as a still potent force.

Augustus effected what Julius Caesar sought to accomplish. 'He was able to rally a desperate urban plebs and weary peasant conscripts against a small and hated governing elite. . . and above all, he relied on the Italian provincial gentry. . . A stable, universal monarchy emerged from Actium, because it alone could transcend the narrow municipalism of the senatorial oligarchy in Rome.'[5] While Augustus made use of the lower classes to bring about a 'collapse of the hegemony' of the oligarchy, his state 'represented a compromise between the opposing forces',[6] the nobility being purged, tamed, and integrated into a broader ruling class. His autocracy claimed to be restoring the old republican traditions revered by the nobility, as he dispensed favours to members of the nobility, many of them sons of those killed by his proscriptions, who were willing to acquiesce to his rule.[7]

Under the principate, the early emperors who retained republican forms, the ruling class was further widened. More and more of the landed classes in the Western provinces outside of Italy were included in the circle of imperial power until even the emperors from Trajan to Marcus Aurelius were of Spanish or Southern Gallic background.[8] The empire was extended and consolidated. The public works and architectural accomplishments of Rome were reproduced in the cities of the various provinces. However, 'the tranquil magnificence of the urban civilisation of the Roman Empire concealed the underlying limits and strains of the productive basis on which it rested. . . With the final closure of the imperial frontiers after Trajan, the well of war captives inevitably dried up.' And, because of the limits of the slave mode of production, 'there was. . . no increase of production in either agriculture or industry within the imperial borders to offset the silent decline in its servile manpower, once external expansion had ceased.'[9]

The civil strife, the scramble for wealth, and the luxurious living of the upper classes in the imperial republic made writers look back nostalgically to an idealised earlier day. 'From the beginning of our era onwards the people of the Empire were obsessed with a vague feeling of deterioration. The elder Seneca (*c*55 BC–*c*AD 40), in a historical work now lost [but referred to by Lactantius], asserted that under the Emperors Rome had reached its old age and could look forward to nothing but death; and his pessimism merely echoed the repeated laments of late Republican poets and writers that Rome was no longer what she used to be.'[10]

Augustus, in claiming to be the restorer of the ancestral system, promoted the strange ambivalence toward Julius Caesar and his republican foes that Schanzer and Bullough noted without explaining. 'Cato, the symbol of the old republic, became a hero and received the homage of the nobles and the poets and historians of the new regime. And with this cult of Cato went almost a conspiracy of silence against the mighty Julius, the tyrant who had overthrown the republic. . . In general the poets, if they speak of Caesar, concern themselves with the impiety of his murder and the translation of his soul to heaven where the Julian star brings blessing to Rome and to Caesar's son and heir.'[11] Just as today Ronald Reagan looks back to the sturdy virtues of the American pioneering past, to the work ethic, the religious values, and the simple but bygone patriotism of the McGuffey readers while continuing to speak of the unique destiny of the United States,[12] just as he talks of returning to an era of smaller government while employing to the full the powers of what has been called 'the imperial presidency', so did the court poets and historians of Augustus look back to the stern grandeur of the early republic, its austerity, civic pride, and self-discipline, while proclaiming that Rome's destiny would be achieved under the new imperial regime.

While the Senate as an institution was only a hollow shell, the nobility maintained an 'oppositionism' that 'survived for centuries after the creation of the Empire', largely impotent though it was.[13] It looked back admiringly at the adherents of libertas but enjoyed the peace and security of the imperial rule. Since the nobility was the source of culture, later Roman historians, including those Hellenistic historians from the provincial aristocracy such as Plutarch and Appian, continued to have an ambivalent attitude toward Julius Caesar and his aristocratic assassins. In some instances this ambivalence came to extend to Augustus himself.

Thus Tacitus says in noncommittal fashion that opinion was divided about Augustus after his death. Some said that it was necessary for one man to have the rule for the sake of the commonwealth, but others said that Augustus's love for Julius Caesar and 'the corruption of the times' were only 'a cloak' for his 'ambition and desire of rule.'[14]

. Thus, too, Appian says: 'He [Augustus] showed himself to be another Caesar, yea, more mighty than Caesar was, as well touching the subjection of his own country as of all other nations. . .' But then, having said that Augustus subjected his own country in the same way that he subjected other countries, he reverses himself and states that, 'being settled in his state', Augustus became 'happy and beloved', as 'the commonwealth. . . came to unity and the rule of one.'[15]

St Augustine ministered further to the ambivalence with

which Western Christendom was to regard Rome. Christianity had started as a militant movement of the proletariat in the cities of the Empire. Its hatred of Rome was expressed in the Book of Revelation, a fiery prophecy of the downfall of Rome, in which it is presented as a harlot who has enriched traders from all over the world by buying luxurious goods from them and who has engaged in fornication with all of the kings of the earth. But in the course of time Christianity turned from militance to otherworldliness, promising the poor a kingdom not on earth but in heaven. It was then transformed into its opposite, a bulwark of the social order.[16] St Augustine quoted Cicero and Sallust on the degeneration of Rome long before the advent of Christianity as a defence of the church against the pagans who charged it with weakening the Empire. The moral deterioration that was eating away at the Empire, he said, came from paganism, not Christianity.

St Augustine, no doubt remembering the attack on Rome in the Bible, was, however, of two minds concerning the Empire. In book 3 of *The City of God*, in opposing pagan morality, he suggested that the glory of the Empire was not worth the price of enervating luxury and moral decline: 'But when in the last Punic War, Rome's rival in imperialism was destroyed . . ., Rome stands out as more hurt by Carthage in so speedy a fall, than in so long an opposition previously.'[17] He was even more explicit in condemnation of the glory gained in war in speaking of Rome's victory over Alba: 'Why are the words glory and victory used to veil the truth? The lust for mastery brings many veils upon the human race and grinds it down. Rome, conquered. . . by this lust, gave the name of glory to the memory of her crime. . .'[18] In book 5, however, when he came to discuss God's providence, he said that 'the one true and just God gave his aid to the Romans that they might win the glory of so great an empire, for they were good men by the particular standard of the earthly city.'[19]

In addition to his ambivalence of feeling about the glory of the Roman Empire, St Augustine repeated the Roman historians' ambivalent statement about republican liberty: 'Caesar Augustus. . . appears in every way to have wrested from the Romans that liberty which was no longer even in their own eyes glorious, but rather productive of discord and destruction, and now quite feeble and inert, and. . . introduced the totalitarian absolutism of kings, and, as it were, restored and renewed the republic when it was sunk in senile decay . . .'[20] Thus he sees Augustus as somehow having simultaneously wrested from the Romans their liberty, introducing totalitarian absolutism, and having restored the republic.

The Roman historians and St Augustine, then, established for later times a tradition of ambivalence not only toward the principals in Julius Caesar's assassination, as Schanzer and Bullough asserted, but toward Rome itself. But this ambivalence was particularly marked with regard to the assassination, the pivotal event in the transition from republic to empire.[21] On occasion, however, one side or other of the ambivalent view of the event might be emphasised to meet the political needs of the writer. So Dante, upholding the Holy Roman Empire in his time and finding its authority to be derived from the God-given supremacy of the classical Roman Empire, placed Brutus and Cassius in the lowest circle of hell together with Judas Iscariot, even though he was enthusiastic about Cato but not about Julius Caesar. The Renaissance humanists of the republic of Florence were hostile to Caesar, but the humanists attached to the courts of the Italian princes were admirers of his. Luther, in conflict with the German emperor, regarded Caesar as the tyrannical destroyer of the Roman commonwealth.

The work that Shakespeare used as the basis of his Roman plays, North's translation from Amyot of Plutarch's *Lives*, and the two works that it has been plausibly argued he also made use of, a translation of Appian's history and Elyot's *The Governor*,[22] maintained the tradition of ambivalence but set it in an Elizabethan frame of reference for monarchy. Although North's Plutarch states flatly at one point that Caesar's acquisition of the title 'perpetual dictator' was 'a plain tyranny',[23] he contradicts this at another point, declaring that Caesar had only seemed, before he gained power, as if he might prove to be a tyrant.[24] '. . . [I]t seemed he rather had the name and opinion only of a tyrant than otherwise that he was so indeed. For there never followed any tyrannical nor cruel act, but, contrarily, it seemed that he was a merciful physician whom God had ordained of special grace to be governor of the Empire of Rome and to set all things again at quiet stay, the which required the counsel and authority of an absolute prince.'[25] The words 'authority of an absolute prince' have greater resonance when we read in North's dedicatory epistle to Queen Elizabeth his statement of the effect of reading in Plutarch about the 'whole armies' who 'cast away their lives. . . for the pleasure of their princes': 'Then well may the readers think: if they have done this for heathen kings, what should we do for Christian princes?'[26]

The title page of the Elizabethan translation of Appian's history reads: 'An Ancient History and Exquisite Chronicle of the Romans' Wars, Both Civil and Foreign. . . in the which is declared their greedy desire to conquer others; their mortal malice to destroy themselves; . . . all the degrees of sedition and the effects of ambition; a firm determination of fate through all the changes of fortune; and, finally, an evident demonstration that people's rule must give place and prince's power prevail.' Here, in a nice balancing, is a condemnation of imperialist conquest coupled with an assertion that the rise of Rome was providentially designed and a censure of both sedition below and ambition above that culminates in the statement that Rome is an illustration of the transience of 'people's rule' and the inevitability of 'prince's power.'

So, too, Elyot, after declaring that Caesar 'subverted the best and most noble public weal of the world', states: 'Brutus and Cassius, two noble Romans and men of excellent virtues,. . . slew Julius Caesar. . . , supposing thereby to have brought the Senate and people to their pristinate liberty, but it did not so succeed to their purpose. But by the death of so noble a prince happened confusion and civil battles.'[27] Caesar, despite his subversion of the renowned Roman republic, turns out to be a prince whose assassination must bring disorder.

For the Elizabethans, then, Rome in both the moral grandeur of the early republic and the splendid glory of the empire was guided by providence, as was stated both by Virgil and Tacitus and by St Augustine. Philemon Holland in his translation of Plutarch's *Morals* states that Plutarch shows 'the great wonders of God's providence in sustaining the Roman Empire and the notable aid of an infinite number of instruments, which the said divine providence employed in planting, raising up, and pulling down so mighty and renowned a dominion.'[28] William Fulbecke in his epitome of the history of Rome until the accession of Augustus speaks of the early republic as a time when there flourished 'most admirable examples of abstinency, modesty, justice, fortitude', but concludes that with the accession to power of Augustus, 'civil enmities' were 'extinguished, foreign wars fully ended, justice recalled, destiny satisfied. . .' [29]

But the destiny of Rome did not end with Augustus. He and succeeding emperors only arrested the decline of Rome. The warnings of the Romans who saw Rome as sunk in senile decay and the prophecy of the Book of Revelation were realised.[30] This is most clearly brought out in Edmund Spenser's 'Ruins of Rome', which has been overlooked by students of Shakespeare's Roman plays.

Just because Spenser was not tied down to the recounting of historical events, he was able to give in his lament the best expression of the Elizabethan idea of Rome. The two words Spenser uses repeatedly for Rome, words also to be used by Shakespeare, are 'greatness' and 'pride'. The 'great spirit' (1. 66) that animated the 'renowned nurslings' of Rome in 'her youthly days' (1.131) caused them to continue their conquests until 'Rome was the whole world, and all the world was Rome' (1.359). The 'glory' of Rome, the greatest city in the history of the world, was 'fairest of all earthly thing' (1. 14). But, 'puffed up with pride', Rome 'seemed above heaven's power itself to advance' (11.143-44). In challenging heaven's power, Rome brought about its own ruination.

Cato the Censor, the great-grandfather of Cato of Utica, Julius Caesar's foe, to whom Spenser refers without naming, called for the destruction of Carthage lest its luxury corrupt Rome. 'He well foresaw how that the Roman courage, / Impatient of pleasure's faint desires, / Through idleness would turn to civil rage, / And be herself the matter of her fires. / For in a people given all to ease, / Ambition is engendered easily' (11.313-18). When Rome was 'swollen with plenty's pride' (1.321), the Roman spirit turned against Rome itself. Just as 'huge flames' to 'the heavens' do 'spire', so 'did this monarchy aspire /. . . Till it by fatal doom adown did fall' (11.219-24). The words 'doom', 'fates', and 'destiny' echo throughout the poem, as does the word 'fall', which in each of the three instances it appears comes at the end of the stanza, reverberating ominously.

Providence in Shakespeare's Roman plays

In 'the world of the [Shakespearean] classical history play,' says Hugh M Richmond, 'men's acts' do not 'seem to be related. . . to any providential order.'[31] The contrary is true. Although it is not heavily insisted upon, each of the Roman history plays suggests a providence at work behind human actions.

In the very first scene of *Coriolanus*, Menenius tells the plebeians,

You may as well
Strike at the heaven with your staves as lift them
Against the Roman state, whose course will on
The way it takes, cracking ten thousands curbs
of more strong link asunder than can ever
Appear in your impediment.
(1.1.68–73)

His words produce the impression of a mighty force proceeding along its predestined way, a historical force that cannot be stopped by any power. It is futile even to try to do so.

In the final act of the play, having seen Coriolanus seemingly implacably resolved to destroy Rome, Menenius tells the tribune Sicinius (5.4.1–6), 'See you yond coign o' th' Capitol, yond cornerstone?. . . If it be possible for you to displace it with your little finger, there is some hope the ladies of Rome, especially his mother, may prevail with him.' His prediction is dramatically ironic, since we have just seen Volumnia, unknown to Menenius, prevail over Coriolanus. But there is a further irony. The Capitol itself is to be the cornerstone of a great empire, and yet its apparent stability is illusory. Rome can – indeed, if it continues in its present factiousness, must – fall. 'This is the way to lay the city flat,' said Cominirus to the tribunes in response to their call for the banishment of Coriolanus (3.1.203-6); 'To bring the roof to the foundation, / And bury all which yet distinctly ranges, / In heaps and piles of ruin.'

The reflective members of the audience were reminded of the Rome of their own day, in which, in the words of Spenser, the 'old walls, old arches', and 'old palaces' were in their wreckage melancholy reminders of the 'mighty power' that had 'tamed all the world' (11.31-35). Rome was to come to this as a result of the spirit of factiousness that was present in it from the very beginning. The path of imperial glory from which Rome could not be deflected led but to the 'heaps and piles of ruin' in which, once more in the words of Spenser (1. 65), 'the corpse of Rome' was 'entombed.'

Julius Caesar has many omens, most of which are rejected by the characters and all of which prove true. Toward the end Cassius, who had told Brutus that their being underlings was not the fault of the stars but of themselves, now tells Messala that he no longer accepts Epicurus's scepticism that external supernatural forces affect the fortunes of human beings. He at least partly believes that the carrion birds flying thick above their heads before the battle of Philippi presage death and disaster. 'The gods today stand friendly,' he wishes, speaking to Brutus, and Brutus in turn speaks (5.1.93, 106–7) of 'the providence of some high powers / That govern us below.' But the gods are not to be friendly, and providence is not to order things so that they win.

Schanzer denies that 'Destiny or the hand of God. . . contributes to the defeat of the conspirators.'[32] But why, then, do Cassius and Brutus talk of providence just before their defeat if not to suggest that providence is against them? The dramatic context suggests the aptness of Plutarch's comment on Cassius's mistakenly believing that Brutus's wing of the army has been defeated: 'Howbeit the state of Rome in my opinion being now brought to that pass that it could no more abide to be governed by many lords but required one only absolute governor, God, to prevent Brutus that it should come to his government, kept this victory from his knowledge. . .'[33]

Schanzer himself points out some highly significant allusions without, it seems, understanding their significance. Caesar's words, 'Good friends, go in and taste some wine with me; / And we, like friends, will straightway go together,' he says, 'call up memories of the ceremonial sharing of wine before another betrayal, memories which are strengthened by the kiss which Brutus gives to Caesar in the Capitol ("kiss thy hand, but not in flattery, Caesar"), and later by Antony's reproach of Brutus at Philippi:

In your bad strokes, Brutus, you give good words;
Witness the hole you made in Caesar's heart,
Crying "Long live! Hail, Caesar!"
(5.1 30–32)

("And forthwith he came to Jesus, and said, Hail master; and kissed him." Matthew 26:49).'[34] What do these allusions suggest if not that the assassination of Caesar was a most heinous crime, comparable to the crucifixion, that must be punished by God, just as in Dante's hell Brutus and Cassius are chomped together with Judas in Satan's three sets of fangs?

To be sure, Shakespeare does not present Brutus and Cassius as villainously wicked. On the contrary, he presents them, especially Brutus, as noble and well intentioned. This is in keeping with the tradition of ambivalence, which made Appian speak of Brutus and Cassius as 'most noble and worthy Romans and, but for one fact, ever followed virtue.' But, having said this, Appian goes on to say that in killing Caesar they not only killed their friend and benefactor, who was 'the chief ruler, such an officer as never was the like, so profitable *126* to all men to. . . his country and empire', but 'an holy man, having on an holy vesture.' The religious awe evoked by the sudden downfall of so great a man as Caesar is compounded by the fact that as pontifex maximiis he was the head of the state religion. The crime is all the greater because of this, and for it, says Appian, 'God did punish. . . them and many times gave tokens of it.'[35] In Shakespeare the carrion birds and the irony of the swords that killed Caesar being turned against Brutus and Cassius themselves, as the poisoned foil was turned in *Hamlet* against Laertes and Claudius, are just such tokens.

One other omen in *Julius Caesar* warrants discussion. Calphurnia has dreamt that Caesar's statue gushed forth blood in which many Romans bathed and entreats him not to go to the Senate. One of the conspirators, Decius Brutus, tells him (2.3.87-89), however, that the dream signifies that from Caesar 'great Rome shall suck / Reviving blood, and that great men shall press / For tinctures, stains, relics, and cognizance.' Calphurnia's dream, of course, foretells the conspirators' bathing their hands in Caesar's blood. Ironically, however, Decius Brutus's interpretation of the dream, which is meant to entice Caesar to go to the Senate by flatteringly reassuring him, is also prophetic in a way in which he is not aware. Great men will indeed proclaim themselves the avenging followers of Caesar, wearing proudly the 'cognizance', the vassals' marks of identification that identify them as such, and Caesar's 'relics', the venerated belongings of a martyr, will be much sought after. So Antony tells the populace that when Caesar's will is known Romans will dip their handkerchiefs in his 'sacred blood' (3.2.134) and beg for a hair of him to leave in their wills as a precious thing. And, indeed, Caesar's body is burned 'in the holy place' (3.2.254), as befits the funeral rites of a martyr. The 'reviving blood' that 'great Rome' will suck would seem, then, to be also prophetic and to refer to Augustus, Caesar's grand nephew and adopted son.[36]

Antony and Cleopatra, too, contains intimations of a providence working through the actions of men. Schanzer asserts: 'Neither can I agree with Bradley that "[Octavius] Caesar is felt to be the Man of Destiny, the agent of forces against which the interventions of an individual would avail nothing." This is how he sees himself and how Plutarch presents him, but it is not, I think, how Shakespeare makes us view the matter.'[37] But it is not only Caesar who views himself as a man of destiny; both Antony and Cleopatra also view him as such. Antony accepts the word of the soothsayer that Caesar's fortunes will rise higher than his. He says (3.13.169) that he 'will oppose his [Caesar's] fate', that is, challenge his destiny. Cleopatra says (5.2.4) that Caesar is 'a minister of her [Fortune's] will', echoing Caesar's earlier statement (3.6.87-89) that 'the high gods. . . makes his ministers / of us.'[38] Moreover, Augustus's assertion of his destiny is corroborated by the dramatic circumstances. When he says (4.6.5), just before the battle of Actium, 'The time of universal peace is near', the fact that we know his words prove to be correct, that with his victory there did indeed come about a time celebrated for its peace and prosperity, gives credibility to his confidence in his destiny. This is a Caesar who was destined to be proclaimed Augustus, a title hitherto reserved for the gods.

In *Cymbeline*, which, like the other romances, concludes with peace, harmony, and reconciliation, it is seen that during the period of universal peace under Augustus Rome's imperial destiny is for the time being essential to Britain's destiny. Indeed, as St Augustine's friend and disciple Orosius had argued, the Roman Empire was God's means for saving the whole world. As Walbank says, paraphrasing him: 'Was it not under Augustus that Christ himself had become incarnate – "and a Roman citizen"? Accordingly it became clear that Christians must accept and support the Empire, for on it depended the fate of the universe.'[39]

The relationship of the British princess Imogene, as the page Fidele, to the Roman commander Lucius reflects the relationship of Britain to Rome. Lucius, accepting her into his service, promises (4.2.395) to 'rather father thee than master

thee.' His words, 'Be cheerful; wipe thine eyes. Some falls are means the happier to arise', prove prophetic for both her and Britain. At the conclusion, she says to him (5.5.403-4), 'My good master, I will yet do you service', the disclosure of her identity and that of her brothers having prompted Cymbeline, moved by the spirit of reconciliation, to indicate that he will be merciful to his Roman captives. Britain will continue to serve Rome, the time for her to be independent of Rome's beneficent rule not yet having come.

The vision of the soothsayer, made known immediately before Lucius found Fidele, is seen at the end not to have meant that the gods willed a Roman victory but that they willed peace through mutual agreement:

The Roman eagle,
From south to west on wing soaring aloft,
Lessen'd herself, and in the beam o' th' sun
So vanished; which foreshadowed our princely eagle,
Th' imperial Caesar, shall again unite
His favour with the radiant Cymbeline,
Which shines here in the west.
(5.5.470-76)

But in the fact that the Roman eagle disappears in the light of the sun, the radiance of Cymbeline, there is perhaps also a hint to the audience that the greatness of the Roman Empire will eventually be absorbed in the glory of Britain.[40]

The theme of ingratitude in the Roman plays

The existence of intimations of providential design in Shakespeare's Roman plays is denied by Schanzer because he believes that such intimations must negate the characters' responsibility for their actions. 'Error and human frailty,' he says, 'are shown to be the causes of Antony's defeat, not the workings of destiny.'[41]

But this is to ignore the Elizabethan belief, discussed above in relation to the English history plays, that providence, generally hidden from men except on extraordinary occasions, is ordinarily perceived as the natural consequence of the deeds of men. Spenser's 'Ruins of Rome' speaks of destiny as having operated through the great virtues and great vices possessed by Rome.

'Rome in the time of her great ancestors' (1. 259) had in potentiality, 'like a Pandora', 'all good and evil.' 'Destiny' released from the Pandora's box both the Romans' 'heavenly virtues' and 'their great sins.' It was their virtues that brought them their 'good hap' and their sins that were 'the causers of their pain.'

In Shakespeare's Rome the sin of ingratitude is throughout the cause of disaster, not only in *Coriolanus*, where it has been frequently pointed out, but in the other plays.[42] King Lear's exclamation (3.4.14-16); 'Filial ingratitude, / Is it not as this mouth should tear this hand / For lifting food to't?' is significant for an understanding of this recurrent theme. Rome is the fostering mother, the alma mater, of her citizens, and for any of her children to rise up against her is monstrous ingratitude.[43] Roman society is not only a family; it is, as Menenius tells the plebeians in the first scene of *Coriolanus*, a body whose members, which owe gratitude toward each other for their mutual helpfulness, cannot be at odds with each other if the body is to endure.[44] These ideas, explicitly expressed in *Coriolanus*, underlie the representations of ingratitude in the other plays.

Menenius, when the tribunes demand Coriolanus's death, exclaims:

Now the good gods forbid
That our renowned Rome, whose gratitude
Towards her deserved children is enrolled
In Jove's own book, like an unnatural dam
Should now eat up her own!
(3.1.289–93)

Ingratitude is accursed, just as gratitude is loved by the

gods, and for Rome to eat her own children, like a sow devouring her young, would be monstrously unnatural. But by the same token it is unnatural for the child to kill the mother. So the tribunes charge Coriolanus with unnatural filial behaviour in calling him (3.1.263–65) a 'viper / That would depopulate the city and / Be every man himself', that would wipe out Rome and replace it by himself. Vipers were thought to eat their way out of their mothers' wombs. The viper gnawing at its mother's insides is as hideously monstrous as the sow eating its own young.

The accusations both of Menenius and of the tribunes are seen to be justified. 'What is the city but the people?' says the tribune Sicinius (3.1.198). His concept of Rome does not extend beyond the common people. *Coriolanus*, on the other hand, using animal imagery indicative of his contempt, says (3.1.237-38) that the plebeians are 'barbarians', 'though in Rome littered.' Each fails to perceive Rome as an organic unity that needs each of its parts.

Body imagery is used later in the same scene. When Sicinius says that Coriolanus is 'a disease that must be cut away', Menenius replies (3.1.295-96), 'O, he's a limb that has but a disease; / Mortal, to cut it off; to cure it, easy.' Later he says (3.1.305-7), echoing the tribunes' sentiments with bitter irony: 'The service of the foot / Being once gangrened is not then respected / For what before it was.' Each part of the body politic deserved grateful respect for past services.

In the climactic scene in which Volumnia prevails against Coriolanus, she takes on the aspect of Rome itself. Earlier she had said in urging him to dissemble with the plebeians for the sake of the other patricians (3.2.64–65), 'I am in this / Your wife, your son, these senators, the nobles.' So now, too, she is standing in place of all the patricians, indeed of the entire society. She reminds him that she had fostered and shaped him, making him what he is (5.3.62–63): 'Thou art my warrior; / I holp to frame thee.' Her reference to Rome as 'our dear nurse' recalls that Rome also is a fostering mother. For him to 'triumphantly tread on thy country's ruin' will entail that he 'tread. . . on thy mother's womb / That brought thee to this world.'

There is perhaps also the suggestion in Volumnia's speech that Coriolanus's assault upon Rome, 'tearing / His country's bowels out', would be a kind of ravishment of the mother who gave birth to him. So 'Ruins of Rome' asserts (11.151-52) that the Gothic nation, which had been incorporated into the Roman Empire and had sworn allegiance to Rome, in assaulting it 'was beating down these walls with furious mood / Into her mother's bosom.' So, too, Plutarch has it that Caesar, before he crossed the Rubicon, the frontier of Italy, 'dreamed a damnable dream that he carnally knew his mother.'[45] The invasion of one's own country its like an incestuous rape.

In *Julius Caesar*, as in *Coriolanus*, ingratitude is present on all sides. The tribunes rebuke the plebeians for being disloyal to Pompey the Great, forgetting Pompey's services to Rome, in greeting Caesar after his victory over him and declare (1.1.55–56): 'Pray to the gods to intermit the plague / That needs must light on this ingratitude.' Antony tells the crowd (3.2.185-86) that when Caesar saw Brutus join in the attack upon him 'Ingratitude, more strong than traitors' arms, / Quite vanquished him.' Antony himself, however, suggests to Octavius that they use Lepidus, the third member of the triumvirate, to bear the burden of actions for which they would be blamed and then, having made use of him, drive him off as an ass who has performed his function. Gratitude is not a consideration when each person is concerned only with himself.

In *Antony and Cleopatra* the son of Pompey the Great takes it upon himself to 'scourge the ingratitude that despiteful Rome / Cast on my noble father' (2.5.22–23). His words on the ingratitude of Rome are shown to be justified by the fact that he himself now draws the allegiance of those who were formerly supporters of the triumvirate. 'The hated, grown to strength,' says Antony (1.3.48–49), 'Are newly grown to love.' The hated come to be loved as they grow in strength while those who were formerly loved for their ability to dispense favours are deserted as they lose power. Pompey himself, despite his talk of avenging his father, betrays his followers by making a soft peace with the triumvirate, giving up his power and paying tribute to them in return for the Sicily and Sardinia that are already his.

There is no gratitude anywhere. Both Antony and Octavius Caesar make the point that the masses' fickleness is exemplified by their having deserted Pompey the Great and by their flocking to his son in the name of his father, of whom he is unworthy. The aristocrats, however, with their shifting alliances are just as changeable and lacking in gratitude. Fulvia, Antony's wife, fights against his brother and then joins with him against Caesar. Antony repudiates the actions of his brother and his dead wife and makes a compact with Caesar, sealed by his marriage to Caesar's sister Octavia, but he and Caesar soon fall out. After the peace with Pompey, made when Pompey's strength was at its greatest, Caesar and Lepidus make war on him and despoil Sicily, one of Antony's grievances being that he has not received his share of the spoils. After Caesar had used Lepidus in the war against Pompey, he turns on him and imprisons him. Antony now regrets that his officer has killed Pompey,[46] for Pompey would have been useful in the coming war with Caesar. In this world it is every one for himself, with no gratitude for past benefits or sentiment for present relationships.[47] Nor is there any gratitude for Rome, the mother of them all.

In *Titus Andronicus*, when Titus rejects all claims to the empire and designates Saturninus as the emperor, Saturninus exclaims:

Thanks, noble Titus, father of my life! . . .
when I do forget
The least of these unspeakable deserts,
Romans, forget your fealty to me.
(1.1.253-57)

The lines are dramatically ironic. He is shortly to turn against his proclaimed father shamefully, forgetting all he owes him, and Romans will for their part turn against him.

His treacherous Gothic queen Tamora, however, persuades him (1.1.446-49) to dissemble for the time being 'lest then the people, and the patricians too, / Upon a just survey, take Titus' part, / And so supplant you for ingratitude, / Which Rome reputes to be a heinous sin.'

Lucius, the son of Titus, who has been banished by Saturninus, raises an army of Goths to revenge himself against Saturninus and 'his ungrateful country' (4.1.111). However, on finding how much Rome hates the tyrannical Saturninus and longs for him to be emperor, his purpose changes. He announces to the assembled Romans:

I am the turned-forth, be it known to you,
That have preserved her welfare in my blood,
And from her bosom took the enemy's point,
Sheathing the steel in my advent'rous body.
(5.3.109–12)

This seems to be a reminiscence of the story of Coriolanus, to whom Lucius is explicitly compared (4.4.68), for Coriolanus did suffer death at the hands of the Volscians, but we have not seen Lucius to have been in any way injured by the Goths for seeking to preserve Rome. The words 'her bosom' suggest once more the idea of Rome as the nurturing mother to whom filial gratitude and love are due.

The greatness and degeneration of Shakespeare's Rome

The idea of providence and the theme of ingratitude are constant throughout Shakespeare's Roman plays. They are the expression in Roman history of the ever-present tension between the order of things created and upheld by God and the disorder threatened by human beings' propensity to sin, the product of the fall of man. But with these constants in Roman history there is also portrayed an evolution of Rome, a portrayal that Shakespeare derived from the Roman historians and their successors.

Surprise has sometimes been expressed that Shakespeare chose a relatively obscure person in Roman history like

Coriolanus as the subject of one of his tragedies. But Appian points out in his preface that Coriolanus's march on Rome was the 'only feat of force'[48] in the political contentions of the republic prior to the Gracchi.

134 Just as British imperialism was able in the nineteenth century to buy off a 'labour aristocracy' from its superprofits abroad, so the Roman republic in its first two and a half centuries, says Walbank, 'solved' the conflict between patricians and plebeians 'in a typical compromise by which the richer plebeians were absorbed into the ruling group. . . while the economic demands of the poorer classes were either shelved or diverted towards the plunder of foreign wars.'[49] The Roman republic became celebrated in history as a 'mixed state', with a strong executive of elected consuls, sometimes compared to kings, an aristocratic senate, and a popular assembly, a state that combined features of monarchy, oligarchy, and democracy to achieve a remarkable stability,[50] so much so that even in the time of the American Revolution the founding fathers of the United States were influenced in their framing of a constitution by the description of the well-balanced Roman constitution by the late-republic historian Polybius. Shakespeare, aware of what Fulbecke called the 'good and temperate constitution' of the early republic and of the 'universal unity and agreement'[51] that flourished under it, chose the story of Coriolanus as a dramatic foreshadowing of the conflicts and discord of later history, which were embryonically present even then.

But, although *Coriolanus* foreshadows the discord of later Roman history, its world is far different from that of later Rome. It is a simple Rome, a self-contained city whose urban setting is conveyed through references to the lead roofs, cement buildings, water conduits, stone walls, and city gates. Provincial though this Rome is, it is, however, warlike, engaged in constant struggle with Antium, its rival city-state.

Coriolanus, its warrior-hero, possesses the virtues of early Rome. 'It is held,' says Cominius in his encomium of him (2.2.83-84), 'That valour is the chiefest virtue', and this indeed was the credo of Rome, as can be seen from the fact that the word *virtue* is derived from the Latin *virtus*, manly strength. Coriolanus's martial spirit rises to the needs of the occasion. Overcome by the fatigue of his heroic exertions, 'his doubled spirit / Requick'ned what in flesh was fatigate.' This is the 'great spirit' that Spenser says was possessed by the 'renowned nurslings' of Rome in 'her youthly days' and that enabled them to conquer the world.

Coriolanus has been trained by his mother to seek honour in battle and to be ready to die for Rome. It was these characteristics that St Augustine saw as the basis of the Roman Empire: 'God willed that an empire. . . should arise,. . . splendid for its extent and greatness. To overcome the grievous vices of many nations he granted supremacy to men who for the sake of honour, praise, and glory. . . did not hesitate to prefer her [Rome's] safety to their own.'[52] The spoils of war, wealth, and luxury mean nothing to Coriolanus. Martial combat is all he knows, and he is content with less than poverty has to offer. In the words of Cominius, 'He covets less / Than misery itself would give, rewards / His deeds with doing them.'

In *Julius Caesar*, however, set in the time of the late republic, corrupt greed or the scandal of it is widespread. Brutus publicly disgraces a friend of Cassius for having taken bribes, and Cassius is offended because Brutus paid no attention to his pleas on behalf of his friend, saying that in a time of emergency small misdeeds must be overlooked. Brutus retorts that Cassius himself has been accused of selling state offices for money. He reminds Cassius that Caesar was struck down for protecting dishonest officials and says that it is not meet that they now sell their honour for bribes.

Octavius, Antony, and Lepidus arbitrarily condemn to death some of the leading men of Rome, including Lepidus's brother and Antony's nephew, confiscating their property. Antony, who demagogically made use of Caesar's bequest to Rome of seventy five drachmas for each citizen and his arbours and orchards for public places of recreation to incite the crowd, tells Octavius and Lepidus (4.1.8-9) that they will examine Caesar's will to 'determine / How to cut off some charge in legacies', to see how they can reduce some of the amounts of the bequests. Thus all of the main characters except Brutus are touched by corruption and greed – and even Brutus, after saying that he cannot extort money from peasants, rebukes Cassius for not having sent him money that he requested, money that he has just implied Cassius acquired by selling offices.

The money Brutus needs is to pay his legions. The army of conscripted small-holders of Coriolanus's day had been transformed by Marius into a professional long-service army to maintain the empire. In the time of rival commanders in the imperial republic, these armies owed their primary loyalties to their commanders, as is illustrated by the behaviour of Antony's soldiers in *Antony and Cleopatra*, just as the English lords under 'bastard feudalism' had their private armies. Their commanders paid them in part from the spoils of conquest, which enriched themselves as well as the state.[53] This is how Shakespeare's Brutus and Cassius lose at Philippi: Brutus's wing of the army, having acquired an advantage over Octavius, 'his soldiers fell to spoil' (5.3.7), failing to pursue their advantage because they are occupied with looting, while Cassius's wing of the army is surrounded by Antony's troops. The corrupt system exacts its toll.

In *Antony and Cleopatra* the degeneration of Rome deepens. It is often said that Egypt represents pleasure-seeking, luxury, and self-indulgence and that Rome represents civic duty, responsibility, and self-discipline. This is true, but Egyptian values invade Rome. Livy, in a passage echoed by St Augustine,[54] had described how as early as 187 BC 'the beginnings of foreign luxury were introduced into the City by the army from Asia. . . [B]anquets. . . began to be planned with greater expense. . . Yet those things which were then looked upon as remarkable were hardly even the germs of the luxury to come.'[55] The Lucullan banquet, deriving its name from the general who came back from his conquests and administrative positions in the East with immense wealth, became a byword for lavish entertainment. So in *Antony and Cleopatra* even the soldier Enobarbus – who stands for the Roman devotion to duty although, untrue to his own nature, in the general falling away from Antony he deserts him – brings back to Rome the eating and drinking habits of the East. Pompey proposes that he, Antony, Lepidus, and Octavius Caesar compete in feasting each other but concedes in advance that Antony's 'fine Egyptian cookery' (2.6.63) will win the prize.

The carousal scene on Pompey's galley, an 'Alexandrian feast' (2.7.97), is worth examining in detail as a symbolic picture of the Roman world corrupted by Eastern luxury. While the generals at the outposts of the empire are, as the next scene shows, extending its boundaries, taking care, however, that their conquests be not too large lest their chiefs in this self-seeking society become jealous of them, the lords of the world are being overcome by the 'conquering wine.' The 'loud music' of the 'Egyptian Bacchanals' sounds as a 'battery' to their ears, and each man joins in the chorus 'as loud / As his strong sides can volley.' The military imagery and the refrain in honour of Bacchus, 'With thy grapes our hairs be crown'd', emphasise the contrast between these 'world-sharers' and the general Ventidius, who enters in the next scene 'as it were in triumph.' The constant expanding movement necessary to maintain the centre of empire while that centre is collapsing is graphically shown. 'Cup us, till the world go round', sing the revellers. The whole world is indeed set spinning precariously as a result of the unsteadiness at its central point.

The drunken behaviour of Lepidus reflects this unsteadiness. As the revellers quarrel in their cups, Lepidus, says one of the servants, maudlinly 'reconciles them to his entreaty, and himself to the drink', which drowns his understanding. This is an accurate picture of his role in the drama of empire. The politically blind Lepidus, concerned with keeping the peace between his two powerful partners, does not see that he keeps his own position only by their sufferance. They make him 'drink alms-drink', carry more than his share of the burden of drink in the drinking bout, just as they have used him to ease themselves of disagreeable tasks in carrying the burden of empire.

138 But, while he has served this purpose, his political position is as unsteady as his physical position. 'Some o'their plants are ill-rooted already,' says a servant. 'The least wind i' the world will blow them down.' 'The third part of the world' is indeed not very firmly planted on his feet; after receiving a few more 'healths' from his drinking companions he is ignobly borne away. So, too, does he leave the stage of history. Antony's words in his guying him about the wondrous quicksands of Egypt, the last spoken to him, are a kind of epitaph: 'These quicksands, Lepidus / Keep off them, for you sink.' Lepidus, a small man outside of his proper element, is indeed engulfed by the quicksands of politics.

While Antony is saying this to Lepidus, Menas is whispering to Pompey, 'Wilt thou be lord of all the world?' Antony's advice about keeping away from quicksands acts as a comment on the temptation contained in the question. Pompey rejects Menas's suggestion that he take advantage of the meeting of the triumvirate on his galley to have them murdered but not because of any firmly grounded moral principles. He would accept the world if it were given to him by Menas, no matter how criminally got, but he believes that it would sully his honour to reach out for it himself. This is what 'honour' comes to at this time of scrambling for position.

Pompey's moral obtuseness and half-heartedness in crime parallels his political obtuseness and half-heartedness in the struggle for empire. After having stated (2.1.10-11), 'My powers are crescent, and my auguring hope / Says it will come to the full', he had lowered his sails while the tide of his fortune was swelling, letting his chance slip away. Menas's comment is apt (2.6.110): 'Pompey doth this day laugh away his fortune.' So much does he give himself up to the spirit of mirth, calling three times for a cup of wine for Lepidus, that it is with the greatest difficulty that Menas is able to get him away to tell him that he can have the world if he wishes it. Oblivious to the effect on Menas of his waving the world aside, he returns to his fun of getting Lepidus dead drunk. In everything except in frivolous pleasure he cannot steer a straight course. His last words on leaving the galley – and the drama – sum him up: 'O Antony, / You have my father's house, – But what? we are friends.' Although he is uneasily aware that he has made a dishonourable peace, he permits himself to be robbed of his patrimony in drunken goodfellowship—only subsequently to have his boon companions renew their war against him and kill him.

The contrast between the behaviour of Caesar and of Antony in this scene is prophetic of the victory of Caesar, which will bring social peace and a temporary halt to Rome's decline.[56] 'Be a child o' the time', Antony urges Caesar. The words are not merely an urging that Caesar give himself up to the spirit of merrymaking. Antony is a child of his time, a time of imperial decadence. Caesar is superior to the distractions and the disorder of the time, as he urges Octavia to be superior to its heartaches when he informs her that Antony has left her. 'Be you not troubled with the time,' he tells her,

which drives
O'er your content these strong necessities;
But let determined things to destiny
Hold unbewail'd their way.
(3.6.82-85)

Always he is in full control of himself, strong in his knowledge of his destiny to restore order to the empire. He holds his own in the drinking bout, although the custom is repugnant to him, breaks off, saying, 'Our graver business / Frowns at this levity', and, after a warm farewell to Antony, ironic in view of the enmity between them that Antony's abandonment to the soft beds of the East[57] and Caesar's own drive for power are to breed, departs with dignity, the only sober man of the company.

Antony, however, leaves to renew the drinking bout with Pompey on shore. Enobarbus's warning to him, 'Take heed you fall not', as Pompey says 'Come, down into the boat' would seem to have a dramatically ironic meaning: Antony's lack of responsibility in permitting himself to be swayed by the intoxicating Cleopatra will cause him to take to the boats instead of fighting by land and will result in his fall. Admirable as he is in his generosity and capacity to love and elicit love, he illustrates Rome's decline from virtue.

In *Cymbeline* the traditional ambivalence about Rome is neatly resolved by Rome being split into two. In this romance set as much in a never-never land as in primitive Britain or ancient Rome, the villain Iachimo is not an ancient Roman but an accomplished courtier of Renaissance Italy who has the cynicism, cunning, deceitfulness, and slanderousness that Italianate Englishmen were alleged to have brought from abroad. He is never spoken of as a Roman but as an Italian. The words 'Italian' and 'Italy' have connotations throughout of decadence and vice: 'false Italian, As poisonous-tongued as handed' (3.2.4–5), 'drug-damned Italy' (3.4.15), 'slight thing of Italy' (5.4.48), 'Italian brain' (5.5.196; to suggest Machiavellian subtlety and underhandedness), 'Italian fiend' (5.5.210).

Lucius, on the other hand, is a commanding though colourless figure. His Roman legions are consistently differentiated from the 'gentlemen of Italy' (4.2.338), the gentry from the Italian border regions, who serve under the captainship of Iachimo. 'Rome' and 'Roman' throughout have connotations of grandeur. The only exceptions are the phrases 'Romish stew' (1.6.152) and 'Roman courtesan' (3.4.126), which possibly recall the Protestant identification of the Whore of Babylon in the Book of Revelation with the contemporary Roman Catholic Church.[58]

Titus Andronicus, written very early in Shakespeare's career and without a historical source, 'seems to be,' as T J B Spencer says, 'a quintessence of impressions derived from an eager reading of Roman history rather than a real effort at verisimilitude,' as contrasted with 'the care and authenticity' of the later Roman plays.[59] The political institutions in it are derived from many periods in Roman history. Marcus, Titus's brother, speaks as a tribune for 'the people of Rome' (1.1.20) and announces that they have elected Titus emperor at a time when the dignity and rights of tribunes had vanished, the 'tribunician authority' having been taken over by the emperors. When Titus declines and begs the people to choose Saturninus emperor instead, the 'patricians and plebeians' (1.1.231) do so by acclamation as if Rome were still a primitive community electing its king in the comitia curiata before the republic came into being. But, if the political institutions are confused, the picture of a decadent and disunited Rome whose civilisation is threatened from within rather than from without is entirely clear.

Titus, valorous, noble, loyal to the state, is representative of the ancient Roman virtues generally absent in his society. Surnamed the Pius and referred to as 'the good Andronicus' by the tribunes of the people and in public proclamation, he embodies the spirit of Aeneas, the ancestor of Rome. He comes back after ten years of war against the Goths to a country whose princes are competing for the throne and whose patricians are divided. Despite the people's choice of him as emperor, he properly supports the older prince as the legitimate heir of his dead father.

The new emperor, Saturninus, however, is degenerate. He falls in love with Tamora, 'the subtle Queen of Goths' (1.1.392), and she teaches him the Machiavellian art of dissembling his resentment at the slight to his honour by Titus's sons, who aided his brother, Bassianus, to run away with their sister, Lavinia, although she had been promised to Saturninus by Titus. Under Tamora's tutelage he plots revenge against Titus and his family.

Dedicated to 'villainy and vengeance' (2.1.121), Tamora brings destruction to Rome. In this she is served by the Moor Aaron, a devil whose soul is as black as his face, to whom she has given herself up. The atheism of the 'barbarous Moor' (2.3.78; 5.3.4) and his cunning Machiavellian 'policy and stratagem' (2.1.104) demonstrate the unity in diabolical evil between a decadent, overly sophisticated civilisation such as that of Renaissance Italy and barbarism. So does the marriage of Saturninus and Tamora.

These two, 'proud Saturnine and his empress', are the fit rulers of 'proud Rome' (3.2.298, 291). The tribunes before whom Titus pleads for his sons' lives are as unmindful of his services to the state and as inflexible as Saturninus himself. There is reason for Titus's inveighing against Rome as 'a wilderness of tigers' (3.1.54). Rome, proud of its might, has become ungrateful to its champions and pitiless to its enemies.

Titus himself, paragon of virtues though he was, had been unmoved by Tamora's entreaties, insisting that the ghosts of his sons demanded the sacrifice of her first-born son. 'Ambitious Rome', personified in Titus, acting, as Tamora says (1.1.132, 130), with 'cruel, irreligious piety', had been without mercy to the Goths, quite unlike the British Cymbeline's mercy toward his Roman captives. The words of Tamora, villainous though she is, implicitly set Roman pitilessness in its imperial conquests against Christian mercy. The imperial city will be punished by suffering at the hands of the now helpless Goths.

In having Tamora's son killed, Titus started the entire train of bloody events, as revenge was succeeded by counter – revenge. His horrible vengeance wipes the slate clean, as he goes down together with his victims in the grand debacle. The conclusion wipes the slate clean not only for himself but for Rome. Lucius, 'Rome's young captain' (5.3.94), comes with the promise that he will knit the commonwealth's 'broken limbs again into one body' (5.3.72). In the reign of Saturninus and Tomora, however, there is an indication of the eventual victory of the Goth over a slack and degenerate civilisation.

The 'Romanness' and non-'Romanness', of Shakespeare's characters

Shakespeare, says Alexander Pope, echoing Nahum Tate and John Dryden, was 'very knowing in the customs, rites, and manners of antiquity. In *Coriolanus* and *Julius*

Caesar not only the spirit but manners of the Romans are exactly drawn, and still a nicer distinction is shown between the manners of the Romans in the time of the former and of the latter.'[60] This is what Paul A Cantor in developing Pope's observation has called the 'Romanness' of Shakespeare's Romans.

Shakespeare indeed captured the spirit of Rome while differentiating (except in *Titus Andronicus*) between the manners of different times in the history of Rome. Parallels could be drawn, in the manner of Plutarch and in accordance with the Elizabethan idea of historical patterns that repeat themselves, between the characters of Shakespeare's Roman history plays and those of his English history plays: Coriolanus with Hotspur, Julius Caesar with Richard II (although here the similarities are solely in situation, not in personality), Octavius Caesar with Bolingbroke, Titus Andronicus with Sir John Talbot, but the Roman characters remain Roman. Thus Coriolanus is like Hotspur in that both lead armies against their countries, are great warriors but not military strategists, desire military glory more than anything else, have high regard for their honour, are indifferent to humanistic pursuits, and are contemptuous of social classes other than their own, and yet he is a Roman patrician and Hotspur is a feudal noble. As a feudal noble, Hotspur is ready to divide up England with his fellow nobles; he does not have the pride in his country and devotion to it in which Coriolanus was brought up and which only the shame of having been booted out of Rome by the despised plebeians causes him to relinquish, thereby leaving him with only his sense of personal honour as a guide. And who could imagine Coriolanus joking with his wife, as Hotspur does, about God helping him to find his way to another woman's bed? He has too much Roman gravitas and sense of the sacredness of the family.

But, as Cantor fails to see, Shakespeare does not always adhere to 'Romanness'. I refer here not merely to anachronisms noted by eighteenth century editors such as the clock striking in *Julius Caesar* or Cleopatra playing at billiards, details about which Shakespeare, a fast-writing playwright rather than a finicky pedant, was sometimes careless. I refer to something that goes to the heart of his technique, his treatment of the lower classes.

144 George Gordon, writing about the 'alternation between Nowhere and England' in the romantic comedies, gives the key to it: '[T]here was a tacit understanding at that time between audience and the stage that the entrance of the comic characters indicated a temporary suspension of the romantic or historical fiction on which the serious action was based; that the assumption of a strange country or a different period of history had been dropped. . . Such was the porter in *Macbeth*, with his jokes about Garnett the Jesuit and last year's harvest. No one supposed him to be a porter of ancient Scotland. Here was a primitive convention which Shakespeare maintained.'[61] This idea of a convention by which the comic members of the lower classes – the quick-witted servants, the professional fools, the good-natured logic-chopping artisans, the bumbling rustic clown – remain in England, not in the country and historical period being represented, is confirmed by what J Dover Wilson has to say, writing of the 1595 drawing of a production of *Titus Andronicus*: 'It may tell. . . something of the costumes adopted in the production of Roman plays; the lower classes being played apparently in "modern dress", whereas every effort was obviously made. . . to attain accuracy in the attire worn by the patricians.'[62]

At the time of *Coriolanus* the plebeians were predominantly small farmers who lived within the city walls but went out every day to cultivate their fields. At the time of *Julius Caesar* the city had grown enormously with the influx of dispossessed farmers and uprooted people from other portions of Italy who constituted a propertyless and jobless proletariat. Shakespeare could have learned about the class character of his 'Roman citizens' from Plutarch and Appian.[63] However, he was not concerned about a historical depiction of them; they were to be timeless London artisans. They are like Jack Cade's men, good-humoured and delighting in the bandying of witticisms but easily inflamed and manipulated.

In *Coriolanus* the emphasis Shakespeare gives to the plebeians' complaints about the grain shortage, which has no basis in Plutarch, probably is designed to remind his audience of the Midlands peasant uprising of 1607, which was supported by the populace of several towns.[64] On the other hand, Shakespeare refers only glancingly to the plebeians' complaints about usury, through which, Livy states, the Roman farmers were losing their farms, especially those serving in the army.[65] Usury was not an issue in the Midlands uprising.

In *Julius Caesar* the killing of Cinna the poet, like the hanging by Cade of the clerk of Chatham for knowing how to read and write, would have been regarded by Shakespeare's audience as an indication of what culture can expect at the hands of the mob, whether that mob be composed of Roman plebeians or radical Puritans, the precursors of the Civil War Levellers. For the members of this audience, as Brents Stirling says, were 'told in sermons' and 'heard it rhymed in season and out that Jack Cade, Jack Straw, the Roman mobs, and the Anabaptists' were 'all one and that together or individually they spell out the Puritan, "Presbyterial", or Brownist disciplines, all of which are to be lumped together.'[66]

Through the anachronistic depiction of his Roman mobs, Shakespeare made the events of the past have relevance to the Elizabethan present and made the events of the Elizabethan present have a universal significance. The 'simple countryman' (5.2.138) who brings Cleopatra the asps has another function. He represents that ordinary humanity which continues to do its work while the great ones of the earth struggle for power. Queens and emperors come onto the stage of history, command the spotlight while they put on their bravura performances, but then leave it forever. The clown always returns, his familiar appearance acting as a cheerful reassurance about the survival of humanity. In *Antony and Cleopatra*, unaware of his contribution to history in bringing the asps, he can in his amusing garrulousness scarcely be shooed off the stage by Cleopatra, eager to go through with her great moment. He is no Egyptian fellah but blood-brother to the Dogberry who, on providentially learning of Don John's plot, almost fails to communicate it to Don Pedro in his incessant palaver.

146

The fall of Shakespeare's heroes and the fall of Rome

The upper-class characters of Shakespeare's Roman plays are, then, truly Roman and the lower-class characters are English. But the heroes of these plays are not merely Romans; they are epitomes of Rome. More 'deeply flawed', as Willard Farnham phrased it,[67] than the heroes of almost all of Shakespeare's other tragedies, they possess both the great virtues and the great vices that Spenser and others found in Rome. In their falls, in which they are at their noblest and most Roman, they simultaneously contribute to the renewal of Rome and foreshadow Rome's own eventual fall.

Coriolanus, says Aufidius in his summing up of him just before Coriolanus's climactic meeting with Volumnia (4.7.35-57), 'could not carry his honours even', could not carry the weight of his honours without losing his balance. The 'pride' that 'ever taints/ The happy man', that always infects the one blessed by prosperity, together with his natural want of judgment and the temperament that did not allow him to behave differently in peace than in war, contributes to his fall from his high position in Rome. But 'he has a merit / To choke it in the utt'rance', a merit that chokes the recital of his faults even as they are being uttered. His merits are so intermixed with his faults and his faults with his merits that he is destroyed by the very qualities that brought him honour: 'strengths by strengths do fail.'

Pride, spirit, and sense of honour are carried by Coriolanus to an extreme that makes his virtues defects. His pride makes him superior to compromise with principle for the sake of expediency, but it deprives him of a feeling for humanity and makes him incapable of ruling. His spirit causes him to perform wonders on the battlefield, but it makes him subject to uncontrollable bursts of anger that are his undoing. His sense of honour prevents him from doing anything he thinks ignoble, but it causes him to seek revenge against the country that has humiliated him and to become a traitor.[68]

So, too, Rome was said to have been destroyed both by the defects of the virtues that enabled it to conquer the world and by the pride resulting from that conquest. Its strength was then turned against itself. The 'pride of Roman hardy head [hardihood],' said Spenser (11.433, 290), brought it about that Rome's 'power itself against itself did arm'. Just as Aufidius said that Coriolanus's pride in his prosperity caused his own strengths to destroy him, so Florus said in his *Roman Histories*, a work known to every Elizabethan schoolboy, 'too much rankness of prosperity' caused the Roman people 'to grow to such greatness as to become consumed with their proper strengths.'[69]

In acceding to his mother, Coriolanus is acting in accordance with the noblest Roman ideals of civic duty and the sacredness of the family. In doing so, he becomes a tragic scapegoat who consciously sacrifices himself to save Rome (5.3.187-89): 'But, for your son, believe it, O, believe it, / Most dangerously you have with him prevail'd, / If not most mortal to him. But let it come.' Instead of being eternally dishonoured as the destroyer of his country, he gains, as stated in the last words of the play 'a noble memory', the immortal fame and glory that mean so much to him. However, his imprecation on being banished (3.3.128-34) pronounces the ultimate doom of ungrateful Rome: 'Have the power still / To banish your defenders, till at length / Your ignorance. . . deliver you as most / Abated captives to some nation / That won you without blows!' His sacrifice saves Rome for the moment and enables it to achieve its glorious destiny, but finally it will fall, primarily through its own weaknesses and the loss of its early martial virtues embodied in such heroes as Coriolanus.

Julius Caesar typifies the greatness and the pride of Rome. 'We all stand up against the spirit of Caesar', says Brutus to the other conspirators (2.1.167). The spirit of Caesar of which he speaks is what Fulbecke calls the 'haughtiness of his thoughts', which were 'most like to Alexander the Great.'[70] So Plutarch has Caesar weeping after reading of Alexander the Great because Alexander at his age had already conquered so many countries. The same spirit caused him, says Elyot, to brook 'no superior' in Rome.[71] The 'spirit of Caesar' is for the republican Brutus the spirit of tyranny. But this spirit of Caesar is, after all, the spirit of Rome itself. As St Augustine said, 'that passion for rule which among the other vices of mankind was found more concentrated in the Roman people one and all. . .'[72]

Shakespeare presents Caesar at the end of his career, when he had risen to such a peak of success that, looking out upon his conquests, he had become intoxicated with his own glory. Elyot, using the same figure as Shakespeare's 'could not carry his honours even' for Coriolanus, wrote that Caesar's 'felicity' at this period made him unable 'to sustain the burden of fortune.' The consequence was that he 'abandoned his natural disposition and. . . sought new ways how to be advanced above the estate of mortal princes. Wherefore little and little he withdrew from men his accustomed gentleness, becoming more sturdy in language and strange in countenance than ever before had been his usage.'[73]

This is Shakespeare's Caesar, of whom Cassius complains (1.2.115-18) – and his words accurately describe Caesar's behaviour – 'This man / Is now become a god, and Cassius is / A wretched creature and must bend his body / If Caesar carelessly but nod on him.' He disregards omens and prophecies and stalks blindly to his doom. As Calphurnia says (2.2.49), his 'wisdom is consum'd in confidence.' His proud inflexibility, his vaunt that he is not like other men, who are 'flesh and blood' and subject to being moved by entreaties (3.1.66–70), are dramatically ironic, as the conspirators group themselves about him while he is declaiming, preparing to strike him down and to prove that he is but flesh and blood, after all.

So Rome proceeded along its course, heedless in its pride of the many prophecies of doom. As Fulbecke said, 'then proud ambition mounted her plume of disdain upon the top of the Capitol, then their excessive pride. . . for their victories. . . were as bellows to puff up their swelling humours.'[74] Just as the 'conquests, glories, triumphs, spoils' of Caesar, Antony found (3.1.149–50), were 'shrunk' to the 'little measure' of his dead body, so were the conquests and glories of Rome itself reduced to nothingness. 'The corpse of Rome', said Spenser (11.65, 208–10), was now 'entombed' in those wreckages over which he exclaimed 'behold the ruin'd pride / Of these old Roman works' that are now 'naught else but heaped sands.' So, too, the corpse of Caesar is saluted by Antony (3.2.254–57), in an implicit comparison to the remains of a decayed and fallen building, as 'thou bleeding piece of earth, /. . . the ruins of the noblest man / That ever lived in the tide of times.'

Caesar's fall at the hands of the conspirators was prefigured by his fall in the marketplace when, after having been offered the crown, his 'falling-sickness' (1.2.254) came upon him. The zoologist Aldrovandi, who was famous in Shakespeare's time, stated: 'This affliction [epilepsy, the "falling sickness"] must beyond doubt be likened to the disease of pride which in truth can be called a sacred disease, since it triumphs over saintly and perfect men. Likewise, epilepsy is called a damage. . . of the upper regions. . . since it has cast down the highest angels. For we read in Holy Script: The Lord has destroyed the seats of proud princes.'[75] Pride, whether of great men or great states, goes before a fall. Yet the awareness of preeminence or the desire to gain it triumphs over the noblest men, being, as Milton was to say, 'the last infirmity of noble mind.' So St Augustine declared that the love of praise, honour, and glory spurred the early Romans to gain an empire and 'overcame the love of money and many other vices', but 'even the love of praise is a vice.'[76]

What Caesar stands for is victorious despite his fall. 'Caesar's spirit, ranging for revenge', Antony predicts

(3.1.270–73), 'With Ate by his side come hot from hell, / Shall in these confines with a monarch's voice, / Cry "Havoc", and let slip the dogs of war.' Caesar's spirit speaks with a monarch's voice because hunting with hounds is the sport of
150 princes but also because that spirit represents the monarchic principle.[77] This principle, it is implied, will be realised through Augustus and will save Rome, but at the same time Caesar's fall is the fall of Rome itself and foreshadows the ultimate fall of the Roman Empire. 'O, what a fall was there, my countrymen!' exclaims Antony (3.2. 194–96). 'Then I, and you, and all of us fell down, / Whilst bloody treason flurish'd over us.'

Although the empire had to be, the passing of the republic, identified with the ancient Roman virtues despite its present corruption, is mourned elegiacially. 'The sun of Rome is set. Our day is gone. . . our deeds are done!' says Titinius over Cassius's dead body (5.3.63–64) before he kills himself. Brutus exclaims over Cassius (5.3.99): 'The last of all the Romans, fare thee well!' In Brutus's own suicide he gains victory in defeat, for he, who has been at war with himself throughout the play, becomes master over himself. 'Brutus only overcame himself', says Strato (5.5.56–57), 'And no man else hath honour by his death.'[78]

In committing suicide in accordance with the creed of Stoicism, Brutus, 'the noblest Roman of them all', as he is called by Antony (5.5.68), is being most nobly Roman. Stoicism was a philosophy that was in vogue among the nobility during this time and for some time thereafter and was associated with republicanism. 'The most eminent Stoics were usually found in the ranks of the opposition, carrying on against the Caesars the hopeless struggle to which as a party and a sect they had been committed by Cato of Utica', whose calm suicide gave impetus to the vogue.[79]

During this time of violent ups and downs of fortune, the Stoics declared that virtue, not the external things of the world such as wealth, which can be lost, or selfish pleasure, which is fleeting, was the highest good. The 'idea of nature' as 'a simple, universal Order,' says John Herman Randall Jr, 'meant that Providence intended Rome to rule the world: it was the idea of what Americans have called manifest destiny. It gave the Romans a comfortable feeling of high responsibility: it was the Romans' burden to act as agent for Nature and Providence.'[80]

The virtue of which the Stoics spoke was the ancient Roman virtue of the idealised republic brought up to date. In the Stoical philosophy suicide under certain circumstances was called for by honour and duty. 'When a life in accordance with nature is no longer possible,. . . when we can only live by a loss of personal honour or through dereliction of duty, then we must obey the call and go. Under such circumstances to remain in life is an act of cowardice as heinous as if we shrink from death for country or friend . . .'[81]

Brutus in his public spiritedness, his aristocratic contempt for money, his noble superiority over the vicissitudes of life, and his rational and resolute acceptance of the inevitable that enables him to die honourably rather than to live shamefully embodies the spirit of republican Stoicism. In a number of ways Stoicism is an aristocratic version of some aspects of Christianity – its rejection of the vanities of this world, its belief in the rule of divine providence, and its resigned acceptance of the will of God – both doctrines having risen in the same climate of opinion and having subsequently interacted upon each other. When Brutus speaks (5.1.105-7), therefore, of 'arming myself with patience / To stay the providence of some high powers / That govern us below', his words refer to an impersonal providence and Stoic endurance, but for a Christian audience they could also be suggestive of a divine providence and Christian resignation. This helped to dispose the Elizabethan audience, although the taking of one's life was contrary to its religious beliefs, to regard his suicide sympathetically as an act of courage in accordance with the highest creed available to his time.

'I shall have glory by this losing day', says Brutus (5.5.36–38), 'More than Octavius and Mark Antony / By this vile conquest shall attain.' Indeed, although he loses the world by his defeat, he gains immortal fame, the drama itself being a testimony that the pre-eminence of his nobility has endured through history. At the same time his defeat enables Rome, which needs the monarchic rule of Augustus, to be renewed.

Antony in *Antony and Cleopatra* epitomises the magnificence and the decadence of Rome. His fall is at once 'a spacious mirror' in which Octavius Caesar can 'see himself' (5.1.34–35), can see the fall of empire in the fall of this extraordinary man, and a lamentable necessity for the regeneration of Rome. 'O Antony!' exclaims Caesar with regret, stirred in his princely magnanimity, 'I have follow'd thee to this; but we do lance / Diseases in our bodies.'

Despite his faults Antony has much of the ancient Roman in him. He had in the past, Caesar recalls early in the play, led an army in famine, drinking with Stoic endurance horse urine to keep alive and bearing it like a soldier. Although he is now given over to revelry, he is still a valiant warrior much loved by his men. Egypt and Rome vie with each other within him. His 'taints and honours' (5.1.30–31), his shameful defects and his praiseworthy virtues, are equally matched in him.

Barroll notes that 'Antony and Cleopatra were universally condemned in various compendia of exempla, in Roman history, in mediaeval history, in Renaissance versions of ancient history, and in the popular dictionaries. . . [I]t is difficult to believe that even Shakespeare would have glorified Antony and Cleopatra at the expense of Augustus.'[82] But Barroll fails to see that Antony, while pointed to as an outstanding example of the prince who brings his own ruin through self-indulgence, was also regarded as a glorified figure in one of the famous tragedies of romantic love. Chaucer had told his story in *The Legend of Good Women*, where Cleopatra was one of Cupid's saints and he, a true knight and model chivalric lover, 'for the love of Cleopatras' 'al the world. . . sette at no value' (11. 601-2). So, too, both the Countess of Pembroke's translation of Garnier's *Antonius* and Samuel Daniel's *Cleopatra* treated the lovers sympathetically, although in the Countess of Pembroke's Garnier Cleopatra dies primarily for love and in Daniel Cleopatra, who has learned to love Antony truly only after his death, dies primarily for honour. Shakespeare succeeds in amalgamating the idea of the infatuated Antony ruined by the seductive Cleopatra with the idea of the two as lovers whose glorious death lives in history.[83]

The death of each not only is in keeping with the demands of romantic love; it meets the standard of Roman virtue, to which their love had previously been opposed. Love and honour are at the end reconciled, and through reconciliation their love is transmuted. Antony, in killing himself, is finally being true to his love by following Cleopatra to the very end and also being true to his honour by being the only one to conquer himself, 'a Roman by a Roman / Valiantly vanquished' (4.15.57-58).

He had vowed to break off from 'this enchanting queen' (1.2.132), had married Octavia, pledged himself to be her faithful husband, shunted Cleopatra from him after she had cost him the battle at Actium, raged against her when he found her dealing with Caesar behind his back and allowing her hand to be kissed by Caesar's messenger, thought to kill her when he believed she had betrayed him. Now, in conquering himself he accepts her completely, not questioning her about whether or not she had betrayed him, not reproaching her for having sent false news of her death, trustfully advising her to seek from Caesar life with honour. Captive reason no longer tries to tear away from enchaining passion but is united to it in sovereignty. Antony follows Cleopatra in her supposed death not madly, frantically, as he did when she left the naval battle, but with Stoical self-mastery in the rational conviction that he is doing what is right, and he expires in that spirit.

If Antony had sought to free himself of Cleopatra and had been suspicious of her, she had doubted his love, seeking to stimulate it by keeping him constantly uncertain, and had shown her own lack of steadfastness in her flight and in her reception of Caesar's messenger. In killing herself Cleopatra too is being faithful to her love although, to be sure, what gives her the strength to be faithful is the realisation that, aside from suicide, her only future is to be exhibited as a spectacle to the Roman populace. Although her method of suicide

is in keeping with her character (she had investigated painless ways of dying, as she had experimented in pleasurable ways of living), by her death 'after the high Roman fashion' (4.15.87) she and her love are transfigured. She, who had been presented as the essence of femininity in the changeableness of her mood, says as she is waiting for the clown to bring the asps (5.2.238–40): 'My resolution's placed, and I have nothing / Of woman in me: now from head to foot / I am marble-constant.' She is 'marble-constant' like the statue of a Roman hero. Ceasing to be a woman in one sense, she gains true womanhood in another. The dazzling Egyptian courtesan-queen who had scornfully said of Antony's Roman wife (1.3.20), 'What says the married woman?' is able to call (5.2.290) 'Husband, I come' before she dies with the asp at her breast in the posture of a nursing mother.

She commits suicide in the eager expectation of meeting her loved one after death, fancying she sees him 'rouse himself' and call her. It is the same vision of an after-life as the one Antony sees, as he prepares to die:

I come, my queen: – Eros! – Stay for me:
Where souls do couch on flowers, we'll hand in hand,
And with our sprightly port make the ghosts gaze:
Dido and her Aeneas shall want troops,
And all the haunt be ours.
(4.14.50-54)

The reference to ghosts and to Dido and Aeneas gives a classical underworld colouration to this vision, but it also resembles the heaven of true lovers described by the mediaeval theorists of chivalric love in making their religion of love parallel to Christianity: 'The meadows were very beautiful and more finely laid out than mortal had ever seen. . . On a throne made of gold and every sort of precious stones sat the Queen of Love, wearing a gorgeous crown on her head, dressed in very costly robes, and holding a golden sceptre in her hand. . . The Queen of Love received him [the King of Love] with an embrace. . . For each of the women there was prepared a most beautiful couch on which to sit, and the knights chose for themselves the seats they preferred.'[84] The meadows, the crown, the splendid robes and sumptuous regalia, the embrace between the royal pair, the couches for their attendants in this description are in accord with Antony and Cleopatra's final speeches and Cleopatra's costuming herself for meeting Antony after her death. Antony and Cleopatra are imagined as displacing Aeneas and Dido and becoming the new king and queen of love. But Aeneas and Dido were not only the classical exemplars of romantic love; Aeneas was the ancestor of Rome, and Antony in following Aeneas is being true to his Roman heritage as well as to his love.

Antony and Cleopatra, then, are represented as having lost a mortal empire and having gained an immortal one. The Elizabethan audience could accept this imaginative concept more readily because it is mingled with the Stoic concept of rising above the evils of this world, expressed in familiar Christian de contemptu mundi terms. Among the greatest of the earth's kings and queens, solely concerned with this world and given over to the life of the senses, Antony and Cleopatra are reduced from their positions of might and stripped of everything. Adversity teaches them, however, to despise mundane things and to escape from the world's giddy whirl. 'My desolation', says Cleopatra,

does begin to make
A better life, 'Tis paltry to be Caesar;
Not being Fortune, he's but Fortune's knave,
A minister of her will.
(5.2.1-4)

'The world' she now regards as 'vile' and 'not worth leave-taking' (5.2.300-301, 317).

Antony had expressed in the first scene contempt for the kingdoms of this earth as dross, but his dismissal of imperial power had been a rejection of all order. 'Let Rome in Tiber melt', he had exclaimed, as he embraced Cleopatra,

and the wide arch
Of the ranged empire fall! Here is my space.
Kingdoms are clay: our dungy earth alike

Feeds beast as man: the nobleness of life
Is to do thus.
(1.2.34-37)

The 'space', the empire, he embraces is the slender waist of Cleopatra – but her body, 'this mortal house', as she calls it in the last scene (5.2.51), using the same figure as did Antony in speaking of Julius Caesar's corpse as 'ruins' and a 'piece of earth', too is a thing of clay. Antony cannot really reject the world until his love has been transmuted.

The world is well lost for Antony and Cleopatra not when they throw off the cares of government to drown themselves in pleasure; it is well lost when they renounce its pomps and pleasures for the spiritual values they attain in death. In giving up the world, they are paradoxically immortalised in its history, for they have given it an example of the self-sacrifice and regeneration in which lies its hope. Antony in being most true to Roman values in his death transcends these values.

Conclusion: Shakespeare's Roman plays and the modem world

Understanding the idea of Rome that Shakespeare inherited helps us to understand his Roman plays. But his plays in their turn help us to understand Roman history. Using the information he obtained from his sources, Shakespeare was able to project himself into the world of ancient Rome and make it come alive. By doing so, he makes it take on meaning for our own world.

In *Coriolanus* Shakespeare shows the class struggle that was present in the early Roman republic. He also shows that the 'mixed' government of this republic was in essence the rule of an oligarchy despite the democratic forms. The three men standing for consul compete to get the vote of the plebeians, but they are all patricians nominated by the Senate,

and the choice of the plebeians is merely a choice between those approved by the nobility. It is a 'custom', a 'ceremony' (2.2.136, 141), for the nominees of the Senate to stand in the marketplace, dressed in 'the gown of humility' (2.2.42), soliciting the votes of the people. The trouble in Coriolanus's case
is that he is incapable of going through with this empty ritual.

The two tribunes of the people are well integrated into the system. They are hostile to Coriolanus because they realise that he is an 'innovator, / A foe to th' public weal' (3.1.174-75), one who would upset the status quo to return to the days before there were tribunes and popular ratification of consul nominees, who is what today would be called a member of the 'radical right.' 'Our office,' says Brutus (2.1.225-26), 'may, / During his power, go sleep.' Moreover, the distribution of free grain that the patricians gave as a sop to the restless plebeians during hard times Coriolanus would not permit as a matter of principle. A revocation of this concession would stir up the plebeians, disturbing the tribunes' working relationship with such liberal patricians as Menenius. It might even cause the plebeians to take matters into their own hands, disregarding the tribunes, who, significantly, are not present in the first scene, in which rebellious plebeians appear armed with staves, clubs, and other weapons.

Having incited the plebeians against Coriolanus, the tribunes, once he is exiled, make haste to disperse them, only too eager to return to their cosy relationship with the patricians. 'Bid them all home,' says Sicinius (3.2.1-3), 'he's gone, and we'll no further. The nobility are vexed, whom we see have sided / In his behalf.' Brutus replies: 'Now we have shown our power, / Let us seem humbler after it is done / Than when it was a-doing.'

Looking upon Shakespeare's picture of the Roman republic and then trying to look with some historical distance upon our own republic will uncover some resemblances. What is in essence a plutocracy although democratic in form nominates professional politicians, lawyers, and businessmen through parties dominated by that plutocracy, which also dominates the opinion-moulding mass media. It would be as unthinkable for these parties to nominate an auto worker or a steel worker as it would have been for the Roman Senate to nominate a plebeian. The nominees wear 'the gown of humility' during their campaigning, coming on as 'just folks' and genial 'nice guys', seeking to ingratiate themselves with the electorate, and vowing to prove themselves worthy of the great American people, just as the candidates for the consulship were 'supple and courteous to the people', seeking to win their way into their esteem 'without any further deed' than to have 'bonneted' to them (2.1.26-28).

The Roman tribunes of the people may be compared to the bureaucratic chieftains of the trade unions who are more at home hobnobbing with the representatives of big business than with their membership. They seek as best they can while maintaining their relationships with the political parties to save the welfare measures that come under attack from the 'radical right'. But, once having mounted a demonstration such as the 1981 Washington 'Solidarity Day' demonstration against the cuts in social benefits, they 'seem humbler after it is done / Than when it was a-doing.'

If Shakespeare's depiction of the Roman republic in *Coriolanus* suggests comparison with bourgeois democracy, his depiction of Julius Caesar suggests comparison with modern dictators. The intoxication with his own power that made Caesar blind to his doom caused Hitler to make such an extraordinary error as to strike at the Soviet Union while engaged in the West and caused Stalin to make such an extraordinary error as to trust Hitler although he trusted no one else. If Shakespeare indeed, as has been conjectured, in response to Ben Jonson eliminated the line 'Caesar did never wrong but with just cause', which Jonson found ridiculous, then it was unfortunate, for it is just such an absurdity as a power-intoxicated dictator might have uttered. Deification works havoc on men's judgments, making them lose touch with reality.

Finally, and above all, Shakespeare's depiction of the

decline of Rome underscores the fact that, despite Augustus's proclamation that Eternal Rome 'was destined to prove the final form of organised society'[86] and Reagan's similar belief in what he euphemistically calls 'the American free enterprise system', social systems are only stages in the development of human society. The power and might of the rulers of a great nation who dominate the world, extracting profits from the impoverished countries under their economic overlordship, are hollow if they themselves are faced with mounting internal social contradictions to which they wilfully blind themselves. The arrogance of power creates its own nemesis.

Summary and conclusion

The idea of cosmic order, which lies behind both the English history plays and the Roman history plays, was a rationalisation of the social position of the new aristocracy, the ruling class under Tudor absolutism. Although Shakespeare's history plays as well as his other plays were shaped by the Christian humanist ideology of the new Tudor aristocracy, they were not simple preachings of Tudor orthodoxy but complex works of art. The deposition of Richard II and the assassination of Julius Caesar are presented as violations of the cosmic order, but neither Richard nor Caesar engages the audience's unambivalent sympathy

Both English and Roman history are shown as guided by providence, spoken of in Christian terms by the characters of the English history plays but not by the pagan characters of the Roman history plays. Providence is the working out of the established order of things, of which the social order is a part. It works not through miracles but through a natural law in accordance with which each of the actions of the actors on the stage of history has its necessary effects. The perception of cause and effect often conveys a sense of historical inevitability, and yet the actors in the drama of history are not reduced to puppets.

What human beings can do is limited by all that has gone before, by the past that determines current circumstances. Because choices are limited, necessity may force even Christian kings to take harsh measures to defend the social order, whose maintenance is of paramount importance.

Society is constantly threatened by the evil passions of

men, the consequence of the fall of Adam and Eve. In the Roman plays the threat to the social order is expressed through the theme of ingratitude toward other members of the social organism and, above all, toward Rome, the nurturing mother of all Romans.

The idea underlying the English history plays is that the suffering which England undergoes in the feudal strife of the Wars of the Roses will only cease with the coming into being of a new kind of monarchy under Richmond, the founder of the Tudor line, a monarchy adumbrated although not enduringly realised by the Lancastrian kings, Henry IV and Henry V. The idea underlying the Roman history plays is that of the greatness of Rome and of its subsequent degeneration, a degeneration that caused its fall. This fall was only temporarily staved off by the accession of Augustus, who brought unity, internal peace, and prosperity to Rome. The story of Rome, unlike the story of England, which ended happily, was a tragedy, and the heroes of the Roman plays partake of the tragic grandeur of Rome. They are deeply flawed though noble, for they epitomise Rome itself, which Shakespeare in accordance with inherited tradition regarded ambivalently.

Parallels can be drawn between Shakespeare's English historical characters and his Roman historical characters, but his upper-class Romans are distinctively Roman. His lower-class comic Roman characters, however, are London artisans or English peasants. Like the comic lower-class characters of the English history plays, they make the historical past relevant to the Elizabethans and universalise the contemporary.

Although Shakespeare does not show the collapse of serfdom, the ultimate although not the only cause of the baronial wars and of the decline of feudalism, or the exhaustion of the possibilities of the slave mode of production, the ultimate although not the only cause of the fall of Roman civilisation, he is very much aware of the changes taking place in the two societies. Monarchy, aristocracy, and bourgeoisie undergo a process of evolution in the English history plays that affects their relationship to each other. The Roman nobility, which has evolved from the patrician oligarchy of the old Roman republic, is locked in a fierce inner struggle that recalls that of the feudal nobility of the English history plays. The corrupted Roman republic needs an emperor, as feudal England needs a strong king.

Although Shakespeare portrays the struggle of classes in both feudal England and ancient Rome, his characters are complex creations, not merely spokesmen for social classes. Falstaff is a degenerate member of the feudalistic aristocracy, but his resilience makes him become representative of the irrepressible spirit of ordinary humanity coping with the blows of life. Richard III is of the feudal house of York, but his use of commercial images and financial terminology and his business language and attitudes identifies him with the most aggressive section of the bourgeoisie.

Understanding the concepts that govern Shakespeare's view of history helps us to understand his history plays, but the plays themselves, on the other hand, help us to understand English and Roman history. Shakespeare makes the worlds of feudal England and ancient Rome come alive, and thereby causes them to take on contemporary meaning. His history plays provide a heightened appreciation of the drama of history, of the crucial role of individuals, and of the constraints imposed by the historical past. The English history plays suggest the harshness of history's choices and the immense difficulties entailed in the attempt to suppress the evils inherited from previous societies. The Roman history plays suggest that economic and political systems, whose rulers in their blindness regard them as everlasting, are only stages in the development of society. The question posed by Shakespeare's depiction of the decline of feudalism and of the fall of Roman civilisation is: will late capitalism be succeeded, in Engels' words, by 'socialism or barbarism', by a new Renaissance or by a new Dark Ages?

Notes

Preface

1. See below p 16.

Chapter 1. Marxism and Shakespearean criticism

1. Terry Eagleton, *Marxism and Literary Criticism* (Berkeley: University of California Press, 1976); Raymond Williams, *Marxism and Literature* (New York: Oxford University Press, 1977).
2. In Karl Marx, *Selected Works* (New York: International Publishers, n.d.) 1:392.
3. René Wellek, 'The Aims, Methods and Materials of Research in the Modern Languages and Literature', *PMLA* 67 (1952): 23. This misstatement is all the more extraordinary in that it was not only written by an eminent historian of literary criticism but was part of a collective effort by distinguished scholars under the auspices of the Modern Language Association to state the principles concerning the study of literature. For a fuller discussion of Wellek's comments on Marxist literary criticism, see my introduction to *Leon Trotsky on Literature and Art* (New York: Pathfinder Press, 1970) pp 8-15.
4. *Leon Trotsky on Literature and Art*, ed. Paul N Siegel (New York: Pathfinder Press) p 68.
5. Ibid., p 37.
6. Frederic Jameson, introduction to Henri Arvon, *Marxist Aesthetics* (Ithaca: Cornell University Press, 1973) p xiii.
7. Robert Weimann, 'Past Significance and Present Meaning in Literary History', *Preserve and Create: Essays in Marxist Literary Criticism*, ed. Gaylord C LeRoy and Ursula Beitz (N Y: Humanities Press, 1973) p 41.
8. Jameson, *Marxist Aesthetics*, p xiv.

Chapter 2. Marx, Engels, and the historical criticism of Shakespeare

1. Christopher Hill, 'Historians on the Rise of British Capitalism', *Science and Society* 14 (1950): 318n.
2. Karl Marx, 'Moralising Criticism and Critical Morality: A Polemic Against Karl Henzen', *Selected Essays*, tr. H J Stenning (London: Leonard Parsons, 1926) pp 148ff.
3. Marx, 'The English Revolution', *Selected Essays*, pp 204-5. 'It placed at the disposal of the middle class the necessary population' refers to the expropriation of the peasants from the soil. Cf Capital (Chicago: Kerr, 1909) 1:315.
4. Marx, *Gesamtausgabe*, Abt. 1, Bd. VII, S. 493. Quoted by Christopher Hill, 'The English Civil War Interpreted by Marx and Engels', *Science and Society* 12 (1948): 136.
5. R H Tawney, 'The Rise of the Gentry', *Economic History Review* 11 (1941): 9.
6. Ibid., p 10.
7. Lawrence Stone, 'The Anatomy of the Elizabethan Aristocracy.' *Economic History Review* 18 (1948): 39.
8. Stone. 'The Elizabethan Aristocracy – A Restatement', *Economic History Review* 22 (1952): 320.
9. H R Trevor-Roper, 'The Gentry. 1540 – 1640', *Supplement to the Economic History Review* April 1953, p 51ff.
10. Cf Christopher Hill, *Puritanism and Revolution* (London: Secker & Warburg, 1958) p 8. See also my analysis of the controversy, *Shakespearean Tragedy and the Elizabethan Compromise* (New York: New York University Press, 1957; Washington, D C: University Press of America, 1983) pp 191-93.
11. Karl Marx and Friedrich Engels, 'The Communist Manifesto'. *Basic Writings on Politics and Philosophy* ed. Lewis S Feuer (Garden City. N Y: Doubleday, 1959) p 9.
12. Marx, 'Moralising Criticism'. p 152.
13. Siegel, *Shakespearean Tragedy*, pp 26-29.
14. A F Pollard, *The History of England* (154 –1603) (New York, 1910) p 458.
15. Patrick Cruttwell, *The Shakespearean Moment* (London: Chatto and Windus, 1954) p 1.
16. G B Harrison, 'The National Background', *A Companion to Shakespeare Studies*. ed. H Granville-Barker and G B Harrison (Garden City, N Y: Doubleday. 1960) p 180.
17. Cf Siegel, *Shakespearean Tragedy*, pp 25-40, 55-70.
18. 'The Communist Manifesto', p 26.
19. Marx and Engels, *The German Ideology*, ed. Roy Pascal (New York:

International Publishers 1939) p 39.

20. Cf Alfred Harbage, *Shakespeare's Audience* (New York: Columbia University Press, 1941) p 90.

21. Alfred Harbage, *Shakespeare and the Rival Traditions* (New York: Macmillan. 1952) p141.

22. Cf E K Chambers, 'Sir Thomas Wyatt', *Sir Thomas Wyatt and Some Collected Studies* (New York: Russell & Russell, 1965) p 100; Paul N Siegel 'English Humanism and the New Tudor Aristocracy', *Journal of the History of Ideas* 13 (1952): 454-56 (later incorporated into *Shakespearean Tragedy*, pp 41-13): Fritz Caspari, *Humanism and the Social Order in Tudor England* (Chicago: University of Chicago Press, 1954) pp 8-10.

23. Cf Siegel, *Shakespearean Tragedy* , pp 48-54.

24. 'The Communist Manifesto', pp 9-10.

25. Engels, 'On Historical Materialism', *Basic Writings*, pp 54,55.

26. Hill, 'The English Civil War', p 154.

27. *Capital* 1:315.

28. *The Works of Heinrich Heine*, tr. Charles Godfrey Leland (New York: Dutton, 1906) 2:277.

29. Cf *Capital* 3:388.

30. Marx, 'On the Jewish Question', *Selected Essays*, p 95.

31. Cf Tawney's editorial introduction, Thomas Wilson, *A Discourse Upon Usury* (New York: G Bell, 1925) pp 1-172.

32. Ibid., p 177. I have modernised Elizabethan spelling and punctuation throughout for the convenience of my readers, who I hope will not be confined to Elizabethan specialists.

33. Ibid., p 178.

34. John Russell Brown, in *The Merchant of Venice* (New York: Random House, 1964) p xliii. See also John W Draper, 'Usury in The Merchant of Venice', *Modern Philology* 33 (1935): 37-47, and E C Pettet, 'The Merchant of Venice and the Problem of Usury', *Essays and Studies* 31 (1946): 19-33.

35. E E Stoll, *From Shakespeare to Joyce* (Garden City, N Y: Doubleday, Doran, 1944) p 134. Cf Hermann Sinsheimer, *Shylock: The History of a Character* (New York, 1947) p 86; Siegel, *Shakespeare in His Time and Ours* (Notre Dame, Ind: University of Notre Dame Press, 1968) pp 237-54; Peter Milward, *Shakespeare's Religious Background* (Bloomington: Indiana University Press, 1973) pp 158-61.

36. Cf Brown's citations, p liii.

37. C L Barber, *Shakespeare's Festive Comedy* (Cleveland: World Publishing Co, 1966) p 167.

38. Max Plowman, 'Money and The Merchant', *The Adelphi* 2 (September 1931): 510.

39. Barbara K Lewalski, 'Biblical Allusion and Imagery in The Merchant

of Venice', *Shakespeare Quarterly* 13 (1962): 339-40. For other discussions of the traditional Christian aspects of the play, see John D Rea, 'Shylock and the Processus Belial', *Philological Quarterly* 8 (1929): 311-13; Israel Gollancz, *Allegory and Mysticism in Shakespeare*, ed. A W Pollard (London: G W Jones, 1931) pp 13-68; Nevill Coghill, 'The Basis of Shakespearean Comedy', *Essays and Studies* 3 (London, 1950) pp 18-23.

40. All Shakespeare quotations and line references are from *The Complete Signet Classic Shakespeare*, ed. Sylvan Barnet (New York: Harcourt Brace Jovanovich, 1972).

41. For a discussion of the world of the romantic comedies as derived from the dream of the ideal court of the Renaissance courtesy books, see Siegel, *Shakespeare in His Time and Ours*, pp 175-80.

42. *Marx, Early Texts*, ed. David McLellan (New York: Barnes and Noble, 1971) pp 180-81.

43. Kenneth Muir, 'Timon of Athens and the Cash-Nexus', *The Singularity of Shakespeare and Other Essays* (Liverpool: Liverpool University Press, 1977) p 75.

44. Cf Francelia Butler, *The Strange Critical Fortunes of Shakespeare's Timon of Athens* (Ames: Iowa State University Press, 1966) pp 75-93.

45. Cf, however, Siegel, *Shakespeare in His Time and Ours*, p 156, who sees Timon as 'an idealisation of the new Tudor aristocracy, which practised old-time hospitality as one of the feudal traditions it assimilated.'

46. E C Pettet, 'Timon of Athens: The Disruption of Feudal Morality', *Review of English Studies* 23 – (1947): 32~30. Cf John W Draper, 'The Theme of Timon of Athens', *Modern Language Review* 29 (1934): 20-31. For Marx's comments on *Timon of Athens* in Capital, as well as other Shakespearean references in that work (none with the pregnant implications of the one on *The Merchant of Venice*) see M Nechkina, 'Shakespeare in Karl Marx's *Capital*', *International Literature* no. 3 (1935) pp 75-81. For other Shakespearean references in Marx, see S S Prawer, *Karl Marx and World Literature* (London: Oxford University Press) passim.

47. For other comments on the Christian implications of *Timon of Athens*, see G Wilson Knight, *The Wheel of Fire* (New York: Oxford University Press, 1949) p 235, and Siegel, *Shakespeare in His Time and Ours*, pp 51-54.

48. *Marx & Engels on Literature & Art*, ed. Lee Baxandall and Stefan Morawski (St Louis: Telos Press, 1973) p 109.

49. T A Jackson, 'Marx and Shakespeare', *International Literature*, no. 4 (1936) p 87. Jackson seems unaware of Engels's reference to Falstaff.

50. Cf Siegel, *Shakespearean Tragedy*, pp 86-87, and Georg Lukacs, *The Historical Novel* (Boston: Beacon Press, 1963) p 153.

51. Since Edwin Muir presented *King Lear* as mirroring the conflict between 'the mediaeval world with its communal tradition' and 'the

modern individualist world' (*The Politics of King Lear* [Glasgow: Jackson, 1947], p 7) this view has been developed by other critics. See C H Hobday, 'The Social Background of King Lear,' *Modern Quarterly Miscellany*, no. 1 (1947) pp 37-56; John F Danby, *Shakespeare's Doctrine of Nature* (London: Faber and Faber, 1961); Siegel, *Shakespearean Tragedy*, pp 166-68; Rosalie L Colie, 'Reason and Need: King Lear and the "Crisis" of the Aristocracy', *Some Facets of King Lear*, ed. Rosalie L Colie and F T Flahiff (Toronto: University of Toronto Press, 1974) pp 185-219; Paul Delany, 'King Lear and the Decline of Feudalism', *PMLA* 92 (1977): 429-40.

52. E M W Tillyard, *Shakespeare's History Plays* (London: Chatto & Windus, 1961) and Lily B Campbell, *Shakespeare's 'Histories'* (San Marino, Calif : Huntington Library, 1947) have shown the great contemporary significance of Shakespeare's dramas of English history for his audience, which feared new civil wars.
53. For a discussion of *All's Well That Ends Well* in relation to the neochivalric cult of honour of the old aristocracy and of other Shakespearean plays in relation to this cult, see Siegel, *Shakespeare in His Time and Ours*, pp 122-62.
54. A Smirnov, 'Shakespeare, the Renaissance and the Age of Barroco', *Shakespeare in the Soviet Union*, ed. Roman Samarin and Alexander Nikolyukin (Moscow: Progress Publishers, 1966) pp 58-59.
55. *Marx & Engels on Literature & Art*, p 107. Cf Engels' letter to Lassalle, p 109.
56. Ibid., pp 115-16.

Chapter 3. The Marxist approach and Shakespearean studies today

1. Richard Levin, *New Readings vs. Old Plays: Recent Trends in the Reinterpretation of English Renaissance Drama* (Chicago: University of Chicago Press, 1979) pp 196, 199-200.
2. 'Introduction', *His Infinite Variety: Major Shakespearean Criticism since Johnson*, ed. Paul N Siegel (Philadelphia: Lippincott, 1964) pp 2-3.
3. Levin, *New Readings*, p x.
4. Ibid., p 200.
5. *Understanding Fiction*, ed. Cleanth Brooks, Jr, and Robert Penn Warren (New York: Appleton-Century-Crofts, 1943) pp 286-87. Cleanth Brooks and Robert B Heilman say much the same thing in *Understanding Drama* (New York: Henry Holt, 1948) p 102, but less fully.
6. Brooks and Heilman, *Understanding Drama*, p 658.

7. Levin, *New Readings*, p 234.
8. Marvin Rosenberg, *The Marks of King Lear* (Berkeley: University of California Press, 1972) pp 5, 328.
9. Cf Cleanth Brooks, *The Well Wrought Urn* (New York: Reynal & Hitchcock, 1947) pp 93-94.
10. Levin, *New Readings*, p 80.
11. Brooks and Heilman, *Understanding Drama*, pp 378-79.
12. Cf below, pp 86-92 and 76-77.
13. Leon Trotsky, *Literature and Revolution* (New York: International Publishers, 1925) p 164.
14. Robert B Heilman, *This Great Stage: Image and Structure in King Lear* (Baton Rouge: Louisiana State University Press, 1948) pp 332, 279-81.
15. *Leon Trotsky on Literature and Art*, p 38.
16. Northrop Frye, *A Natural Perspective: The Development of Shakespearean Comedy and Romance* (New York: Columbia University Press, 1965) pp 40, 41.
17. Ibid., p 40.
18. Cf Siegel, *Shakespeare in His Time and Ours*, pp 163-211.
19. Levin, *New Readings*, pp 211, 223.
20. Siegel, *Shakespearean Tragedy*, pp 215-16.
21. Levin, *New Readings*, p 244, n 9.
22. Ibid., p 226.
23. Siegel, *Shakespeare in His Time and Ours*, pp 50-51.
24. Cf below, p96.
25. *King Richard II*, ed. Peter Ure (Cambridge, Mass: Harvard University Press, 1956) p xlviii.
26. *King Richard II*, ed. J Dover Wilson (Cambridge: Cambridge University Press, 1957) p xviii.
27. Extracts from Holinshed, Appendix 1, *King Richard II*, Arden ed, pp 193, 189.
28. It might be noted that, just as the modern study of Shakespeare's imagery can be traced back to William Whiter, so anticipations of the modern understanding of Shakespeare's use of biblical allusions to suggest comparisons between some of his characters and Christ can be found in the eighteenth century. Stevens remarked, without discussing its significance, that the First Stranger's comment on the ingratitude of Timon's friends echoes Christ's foretelling of his betrayal by Judas, anticipating G Wilson Knight's perception that the premisanthropic Timon is a Christ figure, one piece of evidence being this biblical allusion. *Timon of Athens*, ed. H J Oliver (Cambridge: Harvard University Press, 1965) p 60n; Knight, *The Wheel of Fire*, p 235 and n. Theobald said that Othello's statement over the dead Desdemona that there should be eclipses and earthquakes referred to the eclipses and earthquakes at the

time of the crucifixion, adding, 'Let the Poet account for the profhenation, if he has committed any', not realising that Elizabethans were accustomed to such biblical analogies. *The Works of Shakespeare*, ed. Lewis Theobald (London, 1773) 8:361n.

29. Levin, *New Readings*, pp 224-25. Levin here ignores such explicit comparisons as that between Macbeth and Lucifer made by Malcolm (4.3.22-24) and that between Claudius and Cain made by Claudius himself (3.3.37-38) in circumstances that clearly indicate to the audience that we are to accept them. Instead of regarding the dramatic experience itself, he demands external evidence from nonexistent Elizabethan dramatic criticism of the plays.

30. Quoted by Elbert N S Thompson, *The Controversy between the Puritans and the Stage* (New York: Russell & Russell, 1966) p 82. See also pp 69, 106, 140, 144.

31. For a reevaluation of the English Renaissance that finds as many mediaeval as modem strands in its complex of ideas, see Douglas Bush, *The Renaissance and English Humanism* (Toronto: University of Toronto Press, 1956). For the influence of the morality play tradition, see Willard Farnham, *The Mediaeval Heritage of Elizabethan Tragedy* (Oxford: B. Blackwell, 1970) and Bernard Spivack, *Shakespeare and the Allegory of Evil* (New York: Columbia University Press, 1958). For the lesser influence of the miracle play tradition, see Robert Grams Hunter, *Shakespeare and the Comedy of Forgiveness* (New York: Columbia University Press, 1965). Cf also S L Bethell, *Shakespeare and the Popular Dramatic Tradition* (Durham, N C: Duke University Press, 1944).

32. There are many anticipations of the 'Christian' interpretation of Shakespeare in earlier criticism. Coleridge and De Quincey, who, like Lamb, scorned the view that Shakespeare was 'true to nature' in the sense of ordinary everyday life portrayed by a Lillo, regarded his chief characters as titanic figures and, in so doing, made them more than human beings, suggestive of the Christian supernatural. Cf S T Coleridge, 'Lectures', *Shakespeare Criticism 1623 – 1840*, ed. D Nichol Smith (London: Oxford University Press, 1961) pp 268-69, and Thomas De Quincey, 'On the Knocking at the Gate in Macbeth', *Shakespeare Criticism 1623 – 1840*, pp 334-36. Cf also A C Bradley's discussion of Providence in *Hamlet* and of the 'intimation' in the tragedies of a 'vaster life' than 'the limited world of ordinary experience.' See *Shakespearean Tragedy* (New York: Fawcett, 1966) pp 145-47, 269-73.

33. Levin, *New Readings*, pp 164, 194-95.

34. Jonathan Dollimore's *Radical Tragedy: Religion, Ideology and Power in the Drama of Shakespeare and His Contemporaries* (Chicago: University of Chicago Press, 1984) a highly ambitious and sophisticated attempt to apply Marx, Foucault, and Derrida to the study of Elizabethan drama, would seem, at least superficially considered, to contradict my thesis. It

finds (pp 3-4) that 'a significant sequence of Jacobean tragedies, including the majority of Shakespeare's. . . subjected' the 'established institutions of State and Church' to 'sceptical, interrogative and subversive representations.' But, although we disagree on much, I believe a reconciliation to be possible. Dollimore concedes (p 83) that 'providentialism' was the 'dominant discourse' of the time while I have stated (*Shakespearean Tragedy*, p 78) that 'the conflict between the Christian humanist values and the outlook on life represented by Marston and Donne . . . furnished the emotional material for later Elizabethan and Jacobean tragedy.' Nevertheless, while I regard Dollimore's book with respect, I believe it to be out of focus. John F Danby's Marxist influenced *Shakespeare's Doctrine of Nature and Poets on Fortune's Hill*, which comes much closer to my position, is, I believe, better balanced.

35. E M W Tillyard, *The Elizabethan World Picture* (London: Chatto & Windus, 1943) p1.

36. G Wilson Knight, *The Shakespearian Tempest* (London: Oxford University Press, 1932) passim.

37. G Wilson Knight, *Shakespearian Production with Special Reference to the Tragedies* (Evanston: Northwestern University Press, 1964) p 157.

38. *The Ancient Bounds* (London, 1645) reprinted in A S P Woodhouse, Puritanism and Liberty (London: J M Dent, 1957) p 248.

39. Cf *Certain Sermons or Homilies Appointed to be Read in Churches in the Time of Queen Elizabeth of Famous Memory* (London, 1864) pp 63, 66, 148, 442.

40. Cf the quotations from Frank Kermode, Alvin Kernan, Kenneth Muir and J Dover Wilson in 'Introduction to the 1983 Edition', *Shakespearean Tragedy and the Elizabethan Compromise* (Washington DC: University Press of America, 1983) pp xiv-xv.

41. The controversy has been much less intense in the discussion of the comedies. Key statements of the 'Christian' view are Nevill Coghill, 'The Basis of Shakespearian Comedy', *Shakespeare Criticism 1935 – 1960*, ed. Anne Ridler (London: Oxford University Press, 1963); G Wilson Knight, *The Crown of Life: Essays in Interpretation of Shakespeare's Final Plays* (London: Methuen, 1918); Lewalski, 'Biblical Allusion and Allegory in The Merchant of Venice.' All of these are listed as suppliers for Levin's anonymous quotations.

42. *Shakespeare Studies* VIII, ed. J Leeds Barroll III (New York: Burt Franklin, 1975) pp 426, 432-33, 438.

Chapter 4. Shakespeare's view of English history

1. E M W Tillyard. *Shakespeare's History Plays* (1944); Lily B Campbell, *Shakespeare's Histories: Mirrors of Elizabethan Policy* (1947); Derek Traversi, *Shakespeare from Richard II to Henry V* (1957); G Wilson Knight, *The Sovereign Flower* (1958); M M Reese, *The Cease of Majesty: A Study of Shakespeare's History Plays* (1961); S C Sen Gupta, *Shakespeare's Historical Plays* (1964); H M Richmond, *Shakespeare's Political Plays* (1967); James Winny, *The Player King: A Theme of Shakespeare's Histories* (1968); Henry A Kelly, *Divine Providence in the England of Shakespeare's Histories* (1970); David Riggs, *Shakespeare's Heroical Histories: 'Henry VI' and Its Literary Tradition* (1971); Robert Pierce, *Shakespeare's History Plays: The Family and the State* (1971); John Bromley, *The Shakespearean Kings* (1971); Robert Ornstein, *A Kingdom for a Stage* (1972); Moody E Prior, *The Drama of Power: Studies in Shakespeare's History Plays* (1973); Michael Manheim, *The Weak King Dilemma in the Shakespearean History Play* (1973); Edward I Berry, *Patterns of Decay: Shakespeare's Early Histories* (1975): Larry S Champion, *Perspective in Shakespeare's English Histories* (1976); David L Frey, *The First Tetralogy: Shakespeare's Scrutiny of the Tudor Myth* (1976); George Joseph Becker, *Shakespeare's Histories* (1977); James L Henke, *The Ego-King: An Archetype Approach to Elizabethan Political Thought and Shakespeare's Henry VI Plays* (1977); Peter Sacchio, *Shakespeare's English Kings* (1977); Edna Zwick Boris, *Shakespeare's English Kings, the People, and the Law* (1978); John Wilders, *The Lost Garden: A View of Shakespeare's English and Roman History Plays* (1978); James L Calderwood, *Metadrama in Shakespeare's Henriad* (1979); Larry S Champion, *Perspective in Shakespeare's English Histories* (1980); H R Coursen, *The Leasing Out of England: Shakespeare's Second Henriad* (1982); C G Thayer, *Shakespearean Politics: Government and Misgovernment in the Great Histories* (1983).
2. Tillyard, *The Elizabethan World Picture*, p 1.
3. Siegel, *Shakespearean Tragedy*, pp 41-54.
4 James Chace, 'How "Moral" Can We Get?' *New York Times Magazine*, May 22, 1977, p 42.
5. Tillyard, *Shakespeare's History Plays*, pp 61-64, and M M Reese, *The Cease of Majesty* (London: Edward Arnold, 1961) pp 60-62. All future Tillyard references are to *Shakespeare's History Plays* unless otherwise noted.
6. Tillyard, p 10.
7. Ibid., pp 9, 10.
8. 'Bastard feudalism' Elton defines (*England under the Tudors*, [London: Methuen, 1974], p 3) as 'the patronage system' in which, although 'superficially the relationship continued to be feudal, relying on

personal loyalties', in actuality it 'was based on payment, though the unstable tendencies in it were balanced by the persistence of personal and family ties.' 'Bastard feudalism' resulted in 'the creation of private magnate armies' that threatened the stability of the kingdom.

9. Ibid., pp 7-8.

10. Charles Barber, 'Prince Hal, Henry V, and the Tudor Monarchy', *The Morality of Art: Essays Presented to G Wilson Knight*, ed. D W Jefferson (London: Routledge & Kegan Paul, 1969) p 67.

11. Cf Tillyard, p 91.

12. Henry Ansgar Kelly, *Divine Providence in the England of Shakespeare's Histories* (Cambridge: Harvard University Press, 1970) passim.

13. Cf Ibid., pp 136-37.

14. Geoffrey Bullough, *Narrative and Dramatic Sources of Shakespeare* (New York: Columbia University Press, 1960) 3: 409.

15. Leonard F Dean, 'Tudor Theories of History Writing', *Univ. of Michigan Contributions in Modern Philology* no. 1 (1941) pp 12-13.

16. Sir Walter Raleigh, *The History of the World*, ed. C A Patrides (Philadelphia: Temple University Press, 1971) p 76.

17. Ibid., p 201.

18. Edmund Bolton, 'Hypercritica, or a Rule of Judgment for Writing or Reading our Histories' (1618?) in *Critical Essays of the Seventeenth Century*, ed. J E Spingarn (Bloomington: Indiana University Press, 1968) 1:84.

19. Quoted by Dean, pp 19-20.

20. Samuel Daniel, *The Civil Wars*, ed. Laurence Michel (New Haven: Yale University Press, 1958) bk 1, st 3.

21. Francis Bacon, *The Advancement of Learning*, Second Book, 3:3.

22. Moody E Prior, *The Drama of Power* (Evanston: Northwestern University Press, 1973) pp 44-53.

23. Cf Eleanor Prosser, *Hamlet and Revenge* (Stanford: Stanford University Press, 1967) p 200.

24. Prior, *The Drama of Power*, p 53.

25. John Davies of Hereford, 'Microcosmos', *Complete Works*, ed. Alexander B Grosart (Edinburgh: Edinburgh University Press, 1878) 1: 57b.

26. Tillyard, p 208.

27. Historically, however, the killing of children did not end, for Clarence's son, the young Earl of Warwick, was killed by Henry VII.

28. Cf *3 Henry VI*, 2.5, in which a son laments a father whom he has unwittingly killed and a father laments a son he has unwittingly killed.

29. Kelly, *Divine Providence*, p 210.

30. Ibid., p 300. Cf Robert Ornstein, *A Kingdom for a Stage* (Cambridge: Harvard University Press, 1972) p 18.

31. Kelly, *Divine Providence*, pp 1-2.

32. Ibid., p 299.

33. Bullough, *Narrative. . . Shakespeare*, 4:279.

34. Daniel, *The Civil Wars*, bk 2, st 103.

35. Ibid., bk 3, st 24. He is even more explicit in the second and third editions: 'Leave with your mischief done and do not link / Sin unto sin, for heaven and earth will dash / This ill-accomplished work ere it be long.'

36. See, for example, *Richard II*, 5.5. 47-48, and *Henry V*, 1.2.180-83.

37. See, for example, *1 Henry IV*, 111-4, and *2 Henry IV*, 3.1.31, 38-41.

38. See, for example, *3 Henry VI*, 2.5.8-13; *Richard II*, 3.2.36-53, 3.3.62-67; *1 Henry IV*, 1.2.217-23.

39. Tillyard, pp 88-89.

40. Quoted by Irving Ribner, *The English History Play in the Age of Shakespeare* (Princeton: Princeton University Press, 1957) p 313.

41. Davies of Hereford, *Complete Works*, 1:60a, n 5.

42. Kenneth H Vickers, *England in the Later Middle Ages* (New York: Barnes & Noble, 1961) p 493. Shakespeare is true enough to history to have Richard refer to Richmond's men as 'these overweening rags of France, / These famished beggars' (5.3.328-29). However, these are presented as the scornful words of 'God's enemy' (253). Richmond's Bretons are regarded quite differently than the Frenchmen who Pandulph says will act as the nucleus for a revolt against John (3.3.173-75): 'If but a dozen French / Were there in arms, they would be as a call / To train ten thousand English to their side.' The editor of the New Arden edition perceptively comments on these lines (*King John*, ed. E A J Honigmann [Cambridge: Harvard University Press, 1962], p 87n): 'The verb [*"train"*] was influenced by the substantive train treachery, guile, deceit. After *call* ["decoy"] this suggests "a decoy to trap 10,000 English in treachery": Shakespeare's comment is there behind Pandulph's words. "Circumstances do indeed alter cases!"'

43. Elton, *England under the Tudors*, p 19.

44. Bullough, *Narrative. . . Shakespeare*, 3:15.

45. Ibid., 4: vii.

46. Cf Ribner, *The English History Play*, p 311.

47. Cf Ibid., pp 314-18.

48. S C Sen Gupta, *Shakespeare's Historical Plays* (New York: Oxford University Press, 1964) p 7. Sen Gupta says of York in *Richard II* (p 117) 'Since Shakespeare makes such a spineless, vacillating old man an exponent of the philosophy of order, his own attitude to that philosophy cannot be without an element of irony.' If York, however, is ineffectual in his old age against overwhelming opposing force and indeed against the dictates of history itself, he is clearly to command our full sympathy. Before he appears on the scene, he is referred to by Gaunt as 'good old

York' (1.2.67); Northumberland also calls him 'good old York' (2.3.52); the gardener vouches for the authenticity of the news of Richard's coming deposition by saying it comes from 'a dear friend of the good Duke of York's' (3.4.70). Richard, who speaks contemptuously of the 'outward pity' (4.1.240) other nobles show him, says to York (3.3.202-3): 'Uncle, give my your hands. Nay, dry your eyes. / Tears show their love, but want their remedies.'

49. Ornstein, *A Kingdom for a Stage*, p 25.

50. Ibid., p 13.

51. See G B Harrison, 'A Last Elizabethan Journal 1599 – 1603', *The Elizabethan Journals* (London: George Routledge, 1938) pp 144-50, 155-66.

52. John Harvard, *The Life and Reign of King Henry IV* (London, 1599) pp 287-88. Quoted by Tillyard, pp 243-44.

53. *A Mirror for Magistrates*, ed. Lily B Campbell (Cambridge: Cambridge Univ. Press, 1938) p 178.

54. Davies of Hereford, *Complete Works*, 1 : 53b.

55. Raleigh, quoted by Dean, 'Tudor Theories', p 20.

56. Davies of Hereford, *Complete Works*, 1: 55b.

57. John C Bromley, *The Shakespearean Kings* (Boulder: Colorado Associated University Press, 1971) p 43n.

58. Quoted above, p 51.

59. Quoted above, p 60.

60. Cf Macbeth's statement (1.7.8-10) that in murdering Duncan to gain the throne 'we but teach / Bloody instructions, which being taught return / To plague the inventor.'

61. The term comes from Jan Kott, *Shakespeare Our Contemporary* (Garden City, NY: Doubleday, 1966) chapter 1, passim. He does not, however, see that it is the disturbance of the natural order that sets the 'grand mechanism' going.

62. Quoted by Ribner, *The English History Play*, p 161.

63. Davies of Hereford, *Complete Works*, 1: 60b.

64. Ibid., p 53b.

65. Ibid., p 56a.

66. Davies, like Shakespeare, regarded Henry VI (p 56a) as a passive weakling 'o'erul'd' first by 'his uncles (more like fathers)' and then by his wife, 'a woman most improvident', until 'hate and factions o'ergrew government.'

67. Ibid., p 61a.

68. Ibid.

69. Ibid., p 57a.

70. Felix Raab, *The English Face of Machiavelli* (Toronto: University of Toronto Press, 1964) p 67.

71. Michael Manheim, *The Weak King Dilemma in the Shakespearean*

History Play (Syracuse: Syracuse University Press, 1973) pp 11-12.
72. Prior, *The Drama of Power*, p 223, quoting the damning document from Antonia Fraser, *Mary Queen of Scots*.
73. Cf Tillyard, p 23.
74, Ibid., p 186.

75. Herbert Howarth, *The Tiger's Heart* (New York: Oxford University Press, l970) pp 177, 266.
76. Tillyard, p 22, believes that Spenser used Machiavelli as a guide in writing this work.
77. Paul Jorgensen, 'The "Dastardly Treachery" of Prince John of Lancaster', *PMLA* 76 (1961): 490-91. Prince John said of the rebels' capture as a result of his ruse (*2 Henry IV*, 4.2.121) 'God, and not we, hath safely fought today.'
78. Elton, *England under the Tudors*, p 147. Like the Northern Rebellion in Elizabeth's reign and like the rebellion in *2 Henry IV* the Pilgrimage of Grace was an uprising in the semifeudal North Parts of England.
79. Jorgensen, 'The "Dastardly Treachery", ' p 492.
80. Of recent critics who have voiced these views, see Sen Gupta, *Shakespeare's Historical Plays*, p 148; Herbert Howarth, *The Tiger's Heart*, pp 35-37; Bromley, *The Shakespearean Kings*, pp 85-92; Ornstein, *A Kingdom for a Stage*, pp 182, 185, 189-91.
81. Prior, *The Drama of Power*, p 244.
82. Davies of Hereford, *Complete Works*, 1: 56b, n 1
83. It has been alleged by those who believe Shakespeare is critical of Henry that Henry evades the issue of the justice of the war raised by the soldier Williams to whom he speaks disguised before Agincourt. But the point that Henry is making is that the justice of the war is irrelevant to the salvation or damnation of the individual soldier, who is responsible for his own soul and owes obedience to the king regardless of the rights or wrongs of the war, into which it would be presumptuous for him to inquire. Almost three hundred years later Tennyson was still able to express much the same sentiment: 'Theirs not to reason why, / Theirs but to do and die.' If the individual soldier goes into battle religiously prepared to die, he will be saved if he does die or be an example of proper behaviour to other men if he survives. Henry's argumentation convinces Williams and Bates and inspires them to the heroism of Agincourt ('I do not desire he [the king] should answer for me,' concludes Bates [4.1.200-201], 'and yet I do determine to fight lustily for him') just as two scenes later, when he contradicts Westmoreland's wish that they had 10,000 more men by saying he would not have one more, he inspires his officers.
84. Vickers, *England. . . Middle Ages*, p 350.
85. *Bromley, The Shakespearean Kings*, p 131.
86. Kelly, *Divine Providence*, p 31. It should be added that in the

passage cited (Deut, 20: 10-14) the Israelites were also enjoined by God to take all women and children as the spoils of war. The horrors threatened by Henry have biblical warrant. Those who believe that Henry's threats are too terrible to be Christian might furthermore consider whether there was a storm of protests in American pulpits the Sunday after an atomic bomb was dropped on Hiroshima – without the warning Henry gave Harfleur – creating horrors on a scale far greater than even Shakespeare was capable of imagining.

87. For statements that the English were the chosen people of God, see Tillyard, pp 142-3. Elizabethans accepted the idea of the collective guilt of a people. For the frequent predictions that the people of London, old and young, would be destroyed by God, as were the people of Sodom, Gomorrah, and Jerusalem, if London did not repent of its sins, see Siegel, *Shakespeare in His Time and Ours*, pp 191-92.

88. Campbell, *Shakespeare's Histories*, p 280.

89. Cf the Chorus's description of Henry (Act l, Prologue, 11. 6-8) at whose heels; 'Leashed in like hounds, should famine, sword, and fire / Crouch for employment.'

90. 'Introduction', *King Henry V*, ed. J H Walter (Cambridge: Harvard University Press, 1961) p xxvii.

91. Quoted above. Cf Cranmer's prediction about the royal infant Elizabeth (*Henry VIII*, 5.5.3l): 'She shall be loved and feared.' To be sure, the next lines make clear that she will be loved by her countrymen and feared by her foreign enemies. The king, like God, bears different aspects on different occasions.

92. Siegel, *Shakespearean Tragedy*, p 50.

93. Zdenek Stribrny, 'The Idea and Image of Time in Shakespeare's Early Histories', *Shakespeare Jahrbuch* (Weimar) 110 (1974): pp 129-30. See also his follow-up article, 'The Idea and Image of Time in Shakespeare's Second Historical Tetralogy', *Shakespeare Jahrbuch* (Weimar) 111 (1975): pp 51-66.

94. Quoted by Tillyard, p 19.

95. Caroline Spurgeon, *Shakespeare's Imagery and What It Tells Us* (Cambridge: Cambridge University Press, 1958) pp 216-44.

96. Tillyard, *The Elizabethan World Picture*, p18.

97. Stribrny, *The Idea and Image of Time in Shakespeare's Early Histories*, p131.

98. Tillyard pointed out (p 43) the dramatic quality of Hall's chapter titles, which sum up the reigns of each of his kings: 'The Unquiet Time of King Henry the Fourth', 'The Victorious Acts of King Henry the Fifth', 'The Troublous Season of King Henry the Sixth', and so forth. The titles are an expression of 'the Renaissance discovery of time', to use the title of Ricardo Quinones's book, a sense of the drama of changing times unknown to the mediaeval analysts. Cf the opening

words of *1 Henry VI*, 'Hung be the heavens with black', referring to the black curtains used on the stage when a tragedy was being shown, and *2 Henry IV*, 4.5.198-99, 'For all my reign hath been but as a scene / Acting that argument', a dumb show acting out the central theme of his drama, the theme of his reign being its unquietness.

99. Cf the Bastard in *King John* (1.1.207-8): 'For he is but a bastard to the time / That doth not smack of observation', he is not a true child of the time who does not keep his eye on the main chance, who is not a time-server.

100. Cf Siegel, *Shakespearean Tragedy*, pp 55-60.

101. Campbell, *Shakespeare's Histories*, pp 231-37, and Siegel, *Shakespeare in His Time and Ours*, pp 135-36.

102. Siegel, *Shakespeare in His Time and Ours*, pp 134-38.

103. William Hazlitt, *The Characters of Shakespeare's Plays* (New York: Wiley and Putnam, 1845) pp 133-44.

104. Marx, 'The Eighteenth Brumaire of Louis Bonaparte', *Basic Writings on Politics & Philosophy*, p 320.

Chapter 5. Richard III and the spirit of capitalism

1. W H Clemen, *The Development of Shakespeare's Imagery* (Cambridge: Harvard University Press, 1951) p 135n.

2. 'Cooke's Richard the Third', repr. in *Richard III*, ed. Mark Eccles (New York: New American Library, 1964) p 213.

3. *The Complete Works of Shakespeare*, ed. Irving Ribner and George Lyman Kittredge (Waltham, Mass.: Ginn, 1971) p 639.

4. 1.2.249, 255, 259, 262; 3.7.157; 4.2.34; 4.3.34; 5.3.11.

5. Cf G Wilson Knight, *The Shakespearian Tempest* (London: Oxford University Press, 1932) pp 72ff.

6. Foreign trade was permitted as an occupation for gentlemen, for whom it was regarded as improper to stand behind the counter of a shop Cf Ruth Kelso, 'The Doctrine of the English Gentleman in the Sixteenth Century', *University of Illinois Studies in Language and Literature* 14 (1929): p 68ff.

7. Shakespeare in his early sonnets plays with the idea of physical beauty as a treasure freely loaned by nature that must be freely spent. The youth is a 'beauteous niggard' and a 'profitless usurer' (Sonnet 4) because he hoards his beauty instead of marrying and begetting sons like himself. The 'use' of his 'beauty's treasure' in marriage would not be 'forbidden usury' (Sonnet 6) for the loan of his body would make his wife happy, unlike the loans made to the victims of genuine usurers.

8. Compare the attitude toward the military profession of the

mercenary soldier Iago with that of the romantic warrior Othello, who speaks of the 'pride, pomp and circumstance of glorious war' (3.3.351). Iago, using mercantile language and imagery, speaks of the 'trade of war' (1.2.1) and advises Roderigo to use money as a weapon in besieging Desdemona: 'Put money in thy purse. Follow thou the wars' (1.3.334-35). Earlier he had used such terms as 'lined their coats [with money], 'cashiered', and 'I know my price.' (1.1.50, 45, 10).

9. Marx and Engels, *Basic Writings*, p 9.
10. Ibid., p 10.
11. Ibid., p 10.
12. Ibid., p 9.
13. Siegel, *Shakespearean Tragedy*, pp 55-62.
14. Robert Greene, *The Life and Complete Works*, ed. Alexander B. Grosart (London: Huth Library, 1881-83) 12:104.

Chapter 6. Falstaff and his social milieu

1. *King Henry IV Part I*, ed. A R Humphreys, New Arden ed. (New York: Random House, 1967) pp xli-xliii.
2. John W Draper, 'Sir John Falstaff', *Review of English Studies* 7(1932): 414-24; Lily B Campbell, *Shakespeare's 'Histories'*, pp 245-54; Paul Jorgensen, *Shakespeare's Military World* (Berkeley: University of California Press, 1956) pp 64-71, 130-43.
3. T A Jackson, 'Marx and Shakespeare', *International Literature*, no. 2 (1936): 86.
4. Ibid., p 96.
5. Samuel Rowlands, 'The Melancholy Knight', in *Complete Works* (Glasgow: Hunterian Club, 1880) 2:18.
6. Ibid., p 22.
7. Karl Kautsky, *Thomas More and His Utopia* (New York: Russell & Russell, 1959) p 33.
8. William Green, *Shakespeare's Merry Wives of Windsor* (Princeton: Princeton University Press, 1962) pp 7-20.
9. Geoffrey Chaucer, *The Canterbury Tales*, General Prologue, 11. pp 331-60.
10. Susanne K Langer, *Feeling and Form* (New York: Charles Scribner's Sons, 1953) p342.

Chapter 7. American revolutionists and the political ideology of Shakespeare's English and Roman history plays

1. The Tudor political theorists, while raising the king from a mere feudal overlord to God's vicegerent, thereby strengthening his authority against the old aristocracy and the Catholic Church, did not grant him the unlimited absolutism assigned him by the Stuart theorists of the divine right of kings. Cf Franklin Le Van Baumer, *The Early Tudor Theory of Kingship* (New Haven: Yale University Press, 1940) p 92. Fulke Greville, looking back during the reign of James I to the golden age of Elizabeth, contrasted the 'moderate form of monarchy' of her England with the 'precipitate absoluteness' of France. Sir Fulke Greville, *Life of Sir Philip Sidney* (London: Oxford University Press, 1907) pp 52-54.
2. Bernard Bailyn, *The Ideological Origins of the American Revolution* (Cambridge: Harvard University Press, 1967) pp 22-54.
3. Ibid., p311.
4. Ibid., pp 314-18.
5. Ibid., p317.
6. Ibid., p 311.
7. *King Richard II*, ed. J Dover Wilson (Cambridge: Cambridge University Press, 1966) p lix.
8. Bailyn, *Ideological Origins*, p 125.
9. Ibid.
10. *The Works of John Milton* (New York: Columbia University Press, 1933) 8:7, 47.
11. Bailyn, *Ideological Origins*, p 26.
12. Ibid.
13. For a more detailed discussion of the ambivalent Elizabethan view of Rome, see pp 115-121
14. Bailyn, *Ideological Origins*, p 287.
15. *Shakespeare's Appian*, ed. Ernest Schanzer (Liverpool: Liverpool University Press, 1956) Henry Bynnerman's title page.
16. Bullough, *Narrative. . . Shakespeare* 5:22,24.
17. Brents Stirling, *Unity in Shakespearean Tragedy* (New York: Columbia University Press, 1956) p 50. For a discussion of the suggestions that Caesar's assassination, like Richard's deposition, is reminiscent of Christ's crucifixion, see below, p 109.
18. Cf below, pp 125, 127-28, 132-39, 149-51.
19. Bailyn, *Ideological Origins*, p 78.
20. The Catholic feudal lords who led the Northern Rebellion protested that 'new-set-up nobles', newly made peers, had 'put down the ancient nobility of this realm' and turned the queen away from 'God's word.' Quoted by Campbell, *Shakespeare's Histories*, pp 234-35.

21. Cf John Locke, *The Second Treatise of Government* (Oxford: Basil Blackwell, 1956) p 110: 'The reason why men enter into society is the preservation of their property. Whensoever, therefore, the legislative shall . . . endeavour to grasp themselves or put into the hands of any other an absolute power over the lives, liberties, and estates of the people, by this breach of trust they forfeit the power the people had put into their hands . . . What I have said here concerning the legislative. . . , holds true also concerning the supreme executor.' Note that Locke's 'lives, liberties, and estates' is echoed by the Declaration of Independence's 'life, liberty and the pursuit of happiness.'
22. Marx, *Capital*, 1: 195.
23. Cf Sacvan Bercovitch, *The Puritan Origins of the American Self* (New Haven: Yale University Press, 1975) pp 146-48.

Chapter 8. Shakespeare's view of Roman History

1. G Wilson Knight's *The Imperial Theme* (1931) Maurice Charney's *Shakespeare's Roman Plays* (1961) and Derek Traversi's *Shakespeare: The Roman Plays* (1963) are concerned with a close examination of language and imagery in the individual plays rather than with Shakespeare's view of Roman history, but such insights as Knight's observations on the urban imagery in *Coriolanus*, Charney's observations on the suicides as a manifestation of the Roman spirit, and Traversi's observations on the treachery and corruption of Roman society in *Antony and Cleopatra* are useful for defining that view.
2. Perry Anderson, *Passages from Antiquity to Feudalism* (London: Verso Editions, 1981) p 28. Keith Thomas's encomium of Anderson's Marxist historical analysis in the New York Review of Books – 'the breath-taking range of conception and architectural skill with which it has been executed makes this work a formidable intellectual experience' – is entirely justified.
3. Lily Ross Taylor, *Party Politics in the Age of Caesar* (Berkeley and Los Angeles: University of California Press, 1949) p 21.
4. Ibid., p 23. Cf *Sallust History*, 1.12, quoted by St Augustine, *The City of God against the Pagans*, 3:17 (Loeb ed., 1:337): 'a few powerful men,. . . masquerading as supporters of Senate or people, pursued the goal of tyranny.'
5. Anderson, *Passages*, p 70.
6. M Rostovtzeff, *The Social and Economic History of the Roman Empire* (London: Oxford University Press, 1963) 1:xi-xii. Rostovtzeff saw the 'opposing forces' as the 'Italian bourgeoisie and the Italian proletariat' on the one side and the 'large half-feudal landowners and

business men who owed their material prosperity to the exploitation of the resources of the state' on the other side. Anderson deplores (p 83rf) 'the insistent anachronism' of Rostovtzeff's 'analytic concepts, which incongruously turn municipal landowners into a "bourgeoisie" and imperial legions into "peasant armies" arrayed against it . . .' Cf Meyer Reinhold, 'Historian of the Ancient World: A Critique of Rostovtzeff', *Science and Society* 10 (1946): 361-91, a Marxist critique of Rostovtzeff's work as well as a tribute to it.

7. Taylor, *Party Politics*, p 178. Cf *Tacitus Annals*, bk 1 (Bullough, *Narrative and Shakespeare*, 5: 145).
8. Anderson, *Passages*, p 75.
9. Ibid., pp 76, 82. Cf F W Walbank, *The Awful Revolution: The Decline of the Roman Empire in the West* (Toronto: University of Toronto Press, 1969) p 57, on the limitations of the slave mode of production as the ultimate cause of that 'awful revolution', the decline and fall of the Roman Empire, which Gibbon found so impressive.
10. Walbank, *The Awful Revolution*, p 11.
11. Taylor, *Party Politics*, p 178.
12. 'I have always believed that this land was placed here between the two great oceans by some divine plan. It was placed here to be found by a special kind of people' (*New York Times*, Sept. 22, 1980).
13. Anderson, *Passages*, p 73.
14. Bullough, *Narrative. . . Shakespeare*, 5:146.
15. *Shakespeare's Appian*, ed. Ernest Schanzer (Liverpool: Liverpool University Press, 1956) p 9.
16. Cf Karl Kautsky, *The Foundation of Christianity* (New York: S A Russell, 1953) pp 350-96.
17. *The City of God*, 3.21 (Loeb ed.,1:367).
18. Ibid., 3.14 (1:315-17).
19. Ibid., 5.19 (2:243).
20. Ibid., 3.30 (1:393).
21. T J B. Spencer misses the point when he says ('Shakespeare and the Elizabethan Romans', *Shakespeare Studies* 10 [1957, 1:33]) 'It seems hardly legitimate to talk about "tradition", to refer to "traditional" opinions about Caesar and Brutus, when in fact the characters of each of them had been the subject of constant discussion.' What Schanzer and Bullough have shown is that most writers, beginning with the Roman historians, regarded Caesar and Brutus ambivalently. MacCallum and Phillips plucked pro-Caesar sentiments and J Dover Wilson anti-Caesar sentiments from contexts whose ambivalence they minimised.
22. Cf *Shakespeare's Appian*, pp xix-xxviii, and Kenneth Muir, *Shakespeare's Sources* (London: Methuen, 1957) p 195n.
23. Bullough, *Narrative. . . Shakespeare*, 5:78.
24. Historically, Caesar, like Augustus, sought to consolidate his power

by conciliating his former enemies such as Brutus and Cassius, who had been adherents of Pompey.

25. Bullough, *Narrative. . . Shakespeare*, 5: 133.
26. *The Lives of the Noble Grecians and Romans*, tr. Thomas North (London, 1595) pp ii-iii.
27. Bullough, *Narrative. . . Shakespeare*, 5: 166.
28. Quoted by J Leeds Barroll, 'Shakespeare and Roman History', *Modern Language Review* 53 (1958): 339.
29. William Fulbecke, *An Historical Collection of the Continual Factions, Tumults, and Massacres of the Romans and Italians during the Space of One Hundred and Twenty Years before the Peaceable Empire of Augustus Caesar* (London, 1601) pp 5, 209.
30. These warnings were repeated during the very time when Rome was succumbing to the barbarian onslaught. Cf Walbank, *The Awful Revolution*, p 13: 'Salvian (c. AD 400 – after AD 470), presbyter at Marseilles, writing when wide tracts of the Western Empire were already in the hands of the barbarians, chastises the Romans as being more to blame than their foes precisely because they are Christians and should know better. The barbarians are chaste, while cities of Rome are sinks of iniquity. In short, what are the barbarian invasions but God's judgment upon an Empire "already dead or certainly breathing its last"?'
31. H M Richmond, *Shakespeare's Political Plays* (New York: Random House, 1967) p 204.
32. Ernest Schanzer, *The Problem Plays of Shakespeare* (New York: Schocken Books, 1963) pp 35-36.
33. Bullough, *Narrative. . . Shakespeare*, 5:127.
34. Schanzer, *The Problem Plays*, p 30.
35. *Shakespeare's Appian*, p 66.
36. Cf John Anson, 'Julius Caesar: The Politics of the Hardened Heart', *Shakespeare Studies* 2 (1966):22.
37. Schanzer, *The Problem Plays*, p 172.
38. 'Makes', as the New Arden edition note points out, is an old plural, 'and its identity with the singular form may be responsible for his of the folios.'
39. Walbank, *The Awful Revolution*, p 12. Cf Robin Moffet, 'Cymbeline and the Nativity', *Shakespeare Quarterly* 13(1962): 207-18.
40. Cf Knight, *The Crown of Life*, p 166.
41. Schanzer, *The Problem Plays*, p 172.
42. St Augustine recalled (*The City of God*, 3.21 [Loeb ed., pp 366-651] how Scipio Africanus's 'thankless fatherland' exiled him despite his having vanquished Hannibal, and Thomas Heywood in *An Apology for Actors* (quoted by Clifford Chalmers Huffman, *Coriolanus in Context* [Lewisburg: Bucknell University Press, 1971] p 44n) cited Scipio Africanus as the prime example of one who deserved well of his country

but was 'evil requited.'

43. Cf Edmund Spenser, 'Ruins of Rome', 11. 299-300: 'Her [Rome's] nurslings did with mutinous uproar / Hearten against herself.'

44. Cf Ibid., 11. 429-31: 'Thou only cause [of Rome's fall], O civil fury, art Which. . . Didst arm thy hand against thy proper heart.'

45. Bullough, *Narrative. . . Shakespeare*, 5:69.

46. 3.4.19-20. In Plutarch, it is clear that the murder was at Antony's command; in Shakespeare, it is ambiguous, perhaps because Shakespeare did not want to alienate sympathy for Antony too completely.

47. In the Roman history plays, as in the English history plays, Shakespeare looks upon realpolitik unblinkingly. However, in the Roman plays there is a higher degree of detachment. There are no idealised heroes like Henry V and Richmond, and there are no utterly diabolic villains like Richard III.

48. *Shakespeare's Appian*, p 5.

49. Walbank, *The Awful Revolution*, p 2.

50. Cf Huffman, *Coriolanus in Context*, passim.

51. Fulbecke, *An Historical. . . Caesar*, pp 4, 5.

52. *The City of God*, 5.13 (Loeb ed., 2:207).

53. Rostovtzeff, *Social and Economic History*, 1:25.

54. *The City of God*, 3.21 (Loeb ed.,1:365).

55. *The Founding of the City*, 39.6 (Loeb ed., 11:235-37).

56. Shakespeare's depiction of Octavius Caesar is in accordance with the ambivalent way in which the Elizabethans regarded him. Cf Robert P Kalmey, 'Shakespeare's Octavius and Elizabethan Roman History', *Studies in English Literature 1500 – 1900*, 18 (1978): 287: 'Most of the historians damn Octavius' neglect of the commonweal while he strove to attain absolute power; most praise him for his care after he had obtained it. . . Mexia [Pedro Mexia, *The History of All the Roman Emperors* tr. W T [London, 1604] comprehends the complexity of Octavius: "he happened wisely and uprightly to govern that which by force and cunning he had gotten".'

57. 2.6.50: 'The beds i' th' East are soft.' Cf Fulbecke, *An Historical. . . Caesar* pp 5-19. 'Then the Asiatical triumphs did incorporate into the city a womanish wantonness. . . [The watchings of the camp were ended upon beds of down. . .]'

58. Cf Knight, *The Crown of Life*, pp 150-51.

59. Spencer, *Shakespeare and the Elizabethan Romans*, p 32.

60. Quoted by ibid., p 27.

61. George Cordon, *Shakespearean Comedy* (London: Oxford University Press, 1944) p51.

62. J Dover Wilson, 'Titus Andronicus on the Stage in 1595', *Shakespeare Survey* 1(1948): 21.

63. Cf Plutarch's statement about the 'confused and disorderly

multitude' in Rome, 'the flowing repair of all the people their neighbours thereabouts' (*Shakespeare's Plutarch*, ed. C F Tucker Brooke [New York: Duffield, 1909], 1:52) and Appian's statement (*Shakespeare's Appian*, p 24) about Rome being full of 'idle and needy vagabonds' and 'old worn soldiers out of wages.'

64. Cf E C Pettet, 'Coriolanus and the Midlands Insurrection of 1607', *Shakespeare Survey* 3 (1950): 34-42.

65. *The Founding of the City*, 2.23 (Loeb ed., 1:289-93).

66. Brents Stirling, *The Populace in Shakespeare* (New York: Columbia University Press, 1949) p 149.

67. Willard Farnham, *Shakespeare's Tragic Frontier: The World of His Final Tragedies* (Berkeley and Los Angeles: University of California Press, 1963) p 7.

68. He follows in this the dictates of the neochivalric cult of honour that guided Hotspur. Cf my *Shakespeare in His Time and Ours*, pp 149-55.

69. Bullough, *Narrative. . . Shakespeare,* 5:160.

70. Fulbecke, *An Historical. . . Caesar,* p 108.

71. Bullough, *Narrative. . . Shakespeare,* 5:167.

72. *The City of God*, 1.30 (Loeb ed., 1:127).

73. Bullough, *Narrative. . . Shakespeare*, 5:66. This is also the Caesar of Renaissance neo-Senecan drama.

74. Fulbecke, *An Historical. . . Caesar*, p 5.

75. Quoted by John Anson, 'Julius Caesar: The Politics of the Hardened Heart,' p 22.

76. *The City of God*, 5.13 (Loeb. ed. 2:207).

77. In keeping with the traditional ambivalence, Shakespeare shows Caesar as one who, as manifested by his self-intoxication, might well have become a tyrant but who was not one at the time of his assassination. Brutus himself admits the sovereignty of Caesar's reason over his passions, the prime attribute of the good ruler (2.1.20-21): 'I have not known when his affections sway'd / More than his reason.'

78. Cf 'Ruins of Rome', 1. 38: 'And only Rome of Rome hath victory.'

79. R D Hicks, *Stoic and Epicurean* (New York: Russell & Russell, 1962) p 369.

80. John Herman Randall Jr, *Hellenistic Ways of Deliverance and the Making of the Christian Synthesis* (New York: Columbia University Press, 1970) p 86.

81. Hicks, *Stoic and Epicurean*, p 100.

82. J Leeds Barroll, 'Shakespeare and Roman History', pp 341-43.

83. *Antony and Cleopatra*, like *Romeo and Juliet* and other Elizabethan tragedies of love, was influenced by contemporary adaptations of Italian novelle, which mixed a moralistic condemnation of passionate love with a glorification of it in accordance with the doctrine of the religion of love. Cf my *Shakespeare in His Time and Ours*, pp 65-85.

84. Andreas Capellanus, *The Art of Courtly Love*, ed. John Jay Parry (New York: Columbia University Press, 1941) pp 78-80.
85. Plutarch stated of Antony (Bullough, *Narrative. . . Shakespeare*, 5:255): 'He used a manner of phrase in his speech called Asiatic, which carried the best grace and estimation at that time and was much like to his manners and life, for it was full of ostentation, foolish bravery, and vain ambition.' In this and other speeches of love Antony displays the hyperbole that Plutarch deplores; however, it not only confirms the Roman censures of Antony's infatuation but in its poetic exaltation prepares for the transcendent love of the conclusion.
86. Charles Norris Cochrane, *Christianity and Classical Culture* (New York: Oxford University Press, 1957) p 74.

Works cited

Anderson, Perry. *Passages from Antiquity to Feadalism.* London: Verso Editions, 1981.

Anson, John. 'Julius Caesar: The Politics of the Hardened Heart.' *Shakespeare Studes* 2 (1966): pp 11-33.

Augustine, Bishop of Hippo. *The City of God Against the Pagans.* 7 vols. Cambridge: Harvard University Press (Loeb Library), 1957-72.

Bacon, Francis. *The Advancement of Learning*, edited by G W Kitchin. New York: Dutton, 1950.

Bailyn, Bernard. *The Ideological Origins of the American Revolution.* Cambridge: Harvard University Press, 1967.

Barber, C L. *Shakespeare's Festive Comedy.* Cleveland: World Publishing Co., 1966.

Barber, Charles. 'Prince Hal, Henry V, and the Tudor Monarchy. In The Morality of Art.' *Essays Presented to G Wilson Knight*, edited by D W Jefferson, pp 67-75. London: Routledge & Kegan Paul, 1969.

Barroll, J Leeds. 'Shakespeare and Roman History'. *Modern Language Review*, 53 (1958): pp 327–43.

Baumer, Franklin Le Van. *The Early Tudor Theory of Kingship.* New Haven: Yale University Press, 1940.

Becker, George Joseph. *Shakespeare's Histories.* New York: Ungar, 1977.

Bercovitch, Sacvan. *The Puritan Origins of the American Self* New Haven: Yale University Press, 1975.

Berry, Edward. *Patterns of Decay: Shakespeare's Early Histories.* Charlottesville:University Press of Virginia, 1975.

Bethel, S L, *Shakespeare and the Popular Dramatic Tradition*, Durham: Duke University Press, 1944.

Blanpied, John W. *Time and the Artist in Shakespeare's English Histories.* Newark: University of Delaware Press, 1984.

Bolton, Edmund. 'Hypercritica, or a Rule of Judgment for Writing or Reading Our Histories.' In *Critical Essays of the Seventeenth Century*, edited by J E Spingarn, 1:82-115. Bloomington: Indiana University Press, 1968.

Boris, Edna Zwick. *Shakespeare's English Kings, the People, and the Law.* Rutherford: Fairleigh Dickinson University Press, 1978.

Bradley, A C. *Shakespearean Tragedy.* New York: Fawcett, 1966.

Bromley, John C. *The Shakespearean Kings.* Boulder: Colorado Associated University Press, 1971.

Brooke, C F, Tucker, ed. *Shakespeare's Plutarch.* New York: Duffield, 1909.

Brooks, Cleanth. *The Well Wrought Urn.* New York: Reynal & Hitchcock, 1947.

— and Robert B. Heilman, eds. *Understanding Drama.* New York: Henry Holt, 1948.

— and Robert Penn Warren, eds. *Understanding Fiction.* New York: Appleton Century Crofts, 1943.

Bullough, Geoffrey, ed. *Narrative and Dramatic Sources of Shakespeare.* Vols 3 and 5. New York: Columbia University Press, 1960,1964.

Bush, Douglas. *The Renaissance and English Humanism.* Toronto: University of Toronto Press, 1956.

Butler, Francelia. *The Strange Critical Fortunes of Shakespeare's Timon of Athens.* Ames: Iowa State University Press, 1966.

Calderwood, James L. *Metadrama in Shakespeare's Henriad.* Berkeley: University of California Press, 1979.

Campbell, Lily B, ed. *The Mirror for Magistrates.* Cambridge: Cambridge University Press, 1938.

— *Shakespeare's Histories.* London: Chatto & Windus, 1961.

Capellanus, Andreas. *The Art of Courtly Love,* edited by John Jay Parry. New York: Columbia University Press, 1941.

Caspari, Fritz. *Humanism and the Social Order in Tudor England.* Chicago: University of Chicago Press, 1954.

Certain Sermons or Homilies Appointed to be Read in Churches in the Time of Queen Elizabeth of Famous Memory, London, 1864.

Chace, James. 'How "Moral" Can We Get?' *New York Times Magazine,* May 22, 1977.

Chambers, E K. 'Sir Thomas Wyatt' in *Sir Thomas Wyatt and Some Collected Studies.* New York: Russell & Russell, 1965.

Champion, Larry S. *Perspective in Shakespeare's English Histories,* Athens: University of Georgia Press, 1980.

Charney, Maurice. *Shakespeare's Roman Plays,* Cambridge: Harvard University Press, 1961.

Chaucer, Geoffrey, *The Works,* edited by F N Robinson. Boston: Houghton-Mifflin, 1961.

Clemen, W H. *The Development of Shakespeare's Imagery.* Cambridge: Harvard University Press, 1951.

Cochrane, Charles Norris. *Christianity and Classical Culture.* New York: Oxford University Press, 1957.
Coghill, Nevill. 'The Basis of Shakespearean Comedy.' *Essays and Studies,* n s 3 (1950): 18–23.
Coleridge, S T. 'Lectures.' *In Shakespeare Criticism 1623-1840*, edited by D Nichol Smith, pp 249–96. London: Oxford University Press, 1961.
Colie, Rosalie L. 'Reason and Need: King Lear and the Crisis of the Aristocracy.' In *Some Facets of King Lear* , edited by Rosalie L Colie and F T Flahiff, pp. l85-219. Toronto: University of Toronto, 1974.
Coursen, H R.. *The Leasing Out of England: Shakespeare's Second Henriad.* Washington, DC: University Press of America, 1982.
Cruttwell, Patrick. *The Shakespearean Moment.* London: Chatto & Windus, 1954.
Danby, John F. *Shakespeare's Doctrine of Nature.* London: Faber & Faber, 1961.
Daniel, Samuel. *The Civil Wars*, edited by Laurence Michel. New Haven: Yale University Press, 1958.
Davies, John of Hereford. 'Microcosmus', in *Complete Works*, edited by Alexander B Grosart, 1:1-88. Edinburgh: Edinburgh University Press, 1878.
Dean, Leonard F. *Tudor Theories of History Writing.* Ann Arbor: University of Michigan Press, 1947.
Delany, Paul. 'King Lear and the Decline of Feudalism.' *PMLA* 92 (1977): 42-40.
De Quincey, Thomas. 'On the Knocking at the Gate in Macbeth', in *Shakespeare Criticism 1623-1840*, edited by D Nichol Smith, pp 372-78. London: Oxford University Press, 1961.
Draper, John W. 'Sir John Falstaff'. *Review of English Studies* 7(1932): 414-24.
— 'The Theme of Timon of Athens'. *Modern Language Review* 29(1934): 20-31.
— 'Usury in The Merchant of Venice.' *Modern Philology* 33 (1935): 37-47.
Dollimore, Jonathan. *Radical Tragedy: Religion, Ideology and Power in the Drama of Shakespeare and His Contemporaries.* Chicago: University of Chicago Press, 1984.
Eagleton, Terry. *Marxism and Literary Criticism.* Berkeley: University of California Press, 1976.
Elton, G R. *England under the Tudors.* London: Methuen, 1974.
Farnham, Willard. *The Medieval Heritage of Elizabethan Tragedy.* Oxford: B Blackwell, 1970.

— *Shakespeare's Tragic Frontier: The World of His Final Tragedies.* Berkeley: University of California Press, 1963.

Frey, David L. *The First Tetralogy: Shakespeare's Scrutiny of the Tudor Myth.* The Hague: Mouton, 1976.

Frye, Northrop. *A Natural Perspective: The Development of Shakespearean Comedy and Romance.* New York: Columbia University Press, 1965.

Fulbecke, William. *An Historical Collection of the Continual Factions, Tumults, and Massacres of the Romans and Italians during the Space of One Hundred and Twenty Years before the Peaceable Empire of Augustus Caesar.* London, 1601.

Gianakaris, C G, Michael Manheim, and Robert P. Merrix. 'Reviews'. *Shakespeare Studies* 8 (1975): 42(i-36, 438-4.

Gollancz, Israel. *Allegory and Mysticism in Shakespeare,* edited by A. W. Pollard. London: C W Jones, 1931.

Gordon, George. *Shakespearean Comedy.* London: Oxford University Press, 1944.

Green, William. *Shakespeare's 'Merry Wives of Windsor'.* Princeton: Princeton University Press, 1962.

Greene, Robert. 'Greene's Groatsworth of Wit', in *The Life and Complete Works,* edited by Alexander B Gosart, 12:101-50. London: Huth Library, 1883.

Greville, Sir Fulke. *Life of Sir Philip Sidney.* Oxford: Clarendon Press, 1907.

Harbage, Alfred. *Shakespeare and the Rival Traditions.* New York: Macmillan, 1952.

— *Shakespeare's Audience.* New York: Columbia University Press, 1941.

Harrison, G B. *The Elizabethan Journals.* London: George Routledge, 1938.

— 'The National Background'. In *A Companion to Shakespeare Studies,* edited by H Granville-Barker and C B Harrison. Garden City, NY: Doubleday, 1960.

Hazlitt, William. *The Characters of Shakespeare's Plays.* New York: Wiley and Putnam, 1845.

Heilman, Robert B. *This Great Stage: Image and Structure in King Lear.* Baton Rouge: Louisiana State University Press, 1948.

Heine, Heinrich. 'Jessica in Shakespeare's Maidens and Women', in *The Prose and Poetical Works,* translated by Charles Godfrey Leland, 2:377-94. New York: Dutton, 1906.

Henke, James T. *The Ego-King: An Archetype Approach to Elizabethan Political Thought and Shakespeare's Henry VI Plays.* Salzburg: University of Salzburg, 1977.

Hicks, R D. *Stoic and Epicurean.* New York: Russell & Russell, 1962.

Hill, Christopher. 'The English Civil War Interpreted by Marx and Engels.' *Science and Society* 12 (1948): 130-56.
— 'Historians on the Rise of British Capitalism'. *Science and Society* 14 (1950): 307-21.
— *Puritanism and Revolution*. London: Secker & Warburg, 1958.
Hobday, C H. 'The Social Background of "King Lear". ' *Modern Quarterly Miscellany*, I (1974): 37-56.
Howarth, Herbert. *The Tiger's Heart*. New York: Oxford University Press, 1970.
Huffman, Clifford Chalmers. *Coriolanus in Context*. Lewisburg: Bucknell University Press, 1971.
Hunter, Robert Grams. *Shakespeare and the Comedy of Forgiveness*. New York: Columbia University Press, 1965.
Jackson, T A. 'Marx and Shakespeare'. *International Literature* 2 (1936): 75-97.
Jameson, Frederic. 'Introduction' to Henri Arvon, *Marxist Aesthestics*. Ithaca: Cornell University Press, 1973.
Jorgensen, Paul. 'The "Dastardly Treachery" of Prince John of Lancaster.' *PMLA* 76 (1961): 488-92.
— *Shakespeare's Military World*. Berkeley: University of California Press, 1956.
Kalmey, Robert P. 'Shakespeare's Octavius and Elizabethan Roman History.' *Studies in English Literature 1500-1900* 18 (1978): 275-87.
Kautsky Karl. *The Foundations of Christianity*. New York: Russell & Russell, 1953.
— *Thomas More and His Utopia*. New York: Russell & Russell, 1959.
Kelso, Ruth. *The Doctrine of the English Gentleman in the Sixteenth Century*. Urbana: University of Illinois Press, 1929.
Kelly, Henry Ansgar. *Divine Providence in the England of Shakespeare's Histories*. Cambridge: Harvard University Press, 1970.
Knight, G Wilson. *The Crown of Life: Essays in Interpretation of Shakespeare's Final Plays*. London: Methuen, 1948.
— *The Imperial Theme*. London: Methuen, 1963.
— *Shakespearian Production with Special Reference to the Tragedies*. Evanston: Northwestern University Press, 1964.
— *The Shakespearian Tempest*. London: Oxford University Press, 1932.
— *The Sovereign Flower*. London: Methuen, 1958.
— *The Wheel of Fire*. New York: Oxford University Press, 1949.
Kott, Jan. *Shakespeare Our Contemporary*. Garden City, NY: Doubleday, 1966.
Langer, Susanne K. *Feeling and Form*. New York: Charles Scribner's

Sons, 1953.

Lewalski, Barbara K. 'Biblical Allusion and Imagery in The Merchant of Venice.' *Shakespeare Quarterly* 13 (1962): 327-43.

Levin, Richard. *New Readings vs. Old Plays: Recent Trends in the Reinterpretation of English Renaissance Drama*. Chicago: University of Chicago Press, 1979.

Livy. *The Founding of the City*. 14 volumes. Cambridge: Harvard University Press (Loeb Library), 1919-59.

Locke, John. *The Second Treatise of Government*. Oxford: Basil Blackwell, 1956.

Lukacs, George. *The Historical Novel*. Boston: Beacon Press, 1963.

Manheim, Michael. *The Weak King Dilemma in the Shakespearean History Play*. Syracuse: Syracuse University Press, 1973.

Marx, Karl, and Friedrich Engels. *Basic Writings on Politics and Philosophy*, edited by Lewis S Feuer. Garden City, NY: Doubleday, 1959.

— *The German Ideology*, edited by Roy Pascal. New York: International Publishers, 1939.

— *On Literature & Art*. Edited by Lee Baxandall and Stefan Morawski. St Louis: Telos Press, 1973.

— Marx, Karl. *Capital*. 3 vols. Chicago: Kerr, 1909.

— *Early Texts*. Edited by David McLellan. New York: Barnes and Noble, 1971.

— *Selected Essays*. Translated by H. J. Stenning. London: Leonard Parsons, 1926.

— *Selected Works*. Vol. 1. New York: International Publishers, n.d.

Milton, John. 'Second Defense of the People of England', in *The Works*. Vol 8. New York: Columbia University Press, 1933.

Milward, Peter. *Shakespeare's Religious Background*. Bloomington: Indiana University Press, 1973.

Moffet, Robin. 'Cymbeline and the Nativity.' *Shakespeare Quarterly* 13 (1962): 207-18.

Muir, Edwin. *The Politics of King Lear*. Glasgow: Jackson, 1947.

Muir, Kenneth. *Shakespeare's Sources*. London: Methuen, 1957.

— *The Singularity of Shakespeare and Other Essays*. Liverpool: Liverpool University Press, 1977.

Nechkina, M. 'Shakespeare in Karl Marx's Capital.' *International Literature* 3 (1935): 711-81.

Ornstein, Robert. *A Kingdom for a Stage*. Cambridge: Harvard University Press, 1972.

Pettet, E C. 'Coriolanus and the Midlands Insurrection of 1607.' *Shakespeare Survey* 3 (1950): 34-42.

— 'The Merchant of Venice and the Problem of Usury.' *Essays and Studies* 31 (1945): 19-33.

— 'Timon of Athens: The Disruption of Feudal Morality.' *Review of English Studies* 23 (1947): 321-36.

Pierce, Robert. *Shakespeare's History Plays: The Family and the State.* Columbus: Ohio State University Press, 1971.

Plowman, Max. 'Money and TheMerchant.' *The Adelphi,* no. 2 (September 1931): 508-13.

Plutarch. *The Lives of the Noble Grecians and Romans.* Translated by Thomas North. London, 1595.

Pollard, A F. *The History of England (1547-1603).* New York: Longmans, Green, 1910.

Prawer, S S. *Karl Marx and World Literature.* Oxford: Clarendon Press, 1976.

Prior, Moody E. *The Drama of Power.* Evanston: Northwestern University Press, 1973.

Prosser, Eleanor. *Hamlet and Revenge.* Stanford: Stanford University Press, 1967.

Raab, Felix. *The English Face of Machiavelli.* Toronto: University of Toronto Press, 1964.

Raleigh, Sir Walter. *The History of the World*, edited by C A Patrides. Philadelphia: Temple University Press, 1971.

Randall, John Herman. *Hellenistic Ways of Deliverance and the Making of the Christian Synthesis.* New York: Columbia University Press, 1970.

Rea, John D. 'Shylock and the Processus Belial.' *Philological Quarterly* 8 (1929): 311-13.

Reese, M M. *The Cease of Majesty.* London: Edward Arnold, 1961.

Reinhold, Meyer. 'Historian of the Ancient World: A Critique of Rostovtseff.' *Science and Society* 10 (1946): 361-91.

Ribner, Irving. *The English History Play in the Age of Shakespeare.* Princeton: Princeton University Press, 1957.

Richmond, H M. *Shakespeare's Political Plays.* New York: Random House, 1967.

Riggs, David. *Shakespeare's Heroical Histories: Henry VI and Its Literary Tradition.* Cambridge: Harvard University Press, 1971.

Rosenberg, Marvin. *The Masks of King Lear.* Berkeley: University of California Press, 1972.

Rostovtzeff, M. *The Social and Economic History of the Roman Empire.* Oxford: Clarendon Press, 1963.

Rowlands, Samuel. 'The Melancholy Knight', in *Complete Works,* 2: 1-44. Glasgow: Hunterian Club, 1880.

Sacchio, Peter. *Shakespeare's English Kings.* New York: Oxford University

Press, 1977.

Schanzer, Ernest. *The Problem Plays of Shakespeare.* New York: Schocken Books, 1963.

— ed. *Shakespeare's Appian.* Liverpool: Liverpool University Press, 1956.

Sen Gupta, S C. *Shakespeare's Historical Plays.* New York: Oxford University Press, 1964.

Shakespeare, William. *The Complete Signet Classic Shakespeare,* edited by Sylvan Barnet. New York: Harcourt Brace Jovanovich, 1972.

— *The Complete Works of Shakespeare,* edited by Irving Ribner and George Lyman Kittredge. Waltham, Mass.: Ginn, 1971.

— *Henry IV Part 1.* New Arden ed. Edited by A R Humphreys. New York: Random House 1967.

— *Henry V.* New Arden ed. Edited by J H Walter. Cambridge: Harvard University Press 1961.

— *King John.* New Arden ed. Edited by E A J Honigman. Cambridge: Harvard University Press 1962.

— *The Merchant of Venice.* New Arden ed. Edited by John Russell Brown. New York: Random House 1964.

— *Richard II.* New Arden ed. Edited by Peter Ure. Cambridge: Harvard University Press 1956.

— *Richard II.* New Cambridge ed. Edited by J Dover Wilson. Cambridge: Cambridge University Press 1957.

— *Richard III.* Signet ed. Edited by Mark Eccles. New York: New American Library 1964.

— *Timon of Athens.* New Arden ed. Edited by H J Oliver. Cambridge: Harvard University Press 1965.

Siegel, Paul N. 'English Humanism and the New Tudor Aristocracy.' *Journal of the History of Ideas* 13 (1952): 450-68.

— *Shakespeare in His Time and Ours.* Notre Dame: University of Notre Dame Press, 1968.

— *Shakespearean Tragedy and the Elizabethan Compromise.* Washington, DC: University Press of America, 1983.

— ed. *His Infinite Variety: Major Shakespearean Criticism since Johnson.* Philadelphia: Lippincott, 1964.

Sinsheimer, Hermann. *Shylock: The History of a Character.* New York: B. Blom, 1963.

Smirnov, A. 'Shakespeare, the Renaissance and the Age of Barroco', in *Shakespeare in the Soviet Union,* edited by Roman Samarin and Alexander Nikolyukin, pp. 58-83. Moscow: Progress Publishers, 1966.

Spencer, T J B. 'Shakespeare and the Elizabethan Romans.' *Shakespeare*

Survey 10 (1957): 27-38.

Spenser, Edmund. *Poetical Works*, edited by J C Smith and E De Selincourt. London: Oxford University Press, 1958.

Spivack, Bernard. *Shakespeare and the Allegory of Evil.* New York: Columbia University Press, 1958.

Spurgeon, Caroline. *Shakespeare's Imagery And What It Tells Us.* Cambridge: Cambridge University Press, 1958.

Stirling, Brents. *The Populace in Shakespeare.* New York: Columbia University Press, 1949.

— *Unity in Shakespearean Tragedy.* New York: Columbia University Press, 1956.

Stone, Lawrence. 'The Anatomy of the Elizabethan Aristocracy.' *Economic History Review* 18 (1948): 1-53.

— 'The Elizabethan Aristocracy – A Restatement.' *Economic History Review* 22 (1952): 302-21.

Stoll, E E. *From Shakespeare to Joyce.* Garden City, NY: Doubleday, Doran, 1944.

Stribrny, Zdenek. 'The Idea and Image of Time in Shakespeare's Early Histories', *Shakespeare Jahrbuch* (Weimar) 110 (1974): 129-38.

— 'The Idea and Image of Time in Shakespeare's Second Historical Tetralogy.' *Shakespeare Jahrbuch* (Weimar) 111 (1975): 51-66.

Taylor, Lily Ross. *Party Politics in the Age of Caesar.* Berkeley: University of California Press, 1949.

Tawney, R H. 'The Rise of the Gentry.' *Economic History Review* 11 (1941): 1-38.

— 'Introduction' to Thomas Wilson, *A Discourse Upon Usury.* New York: G Bell, 1925.

Thompson, Elbert N S. *The Controversy between the Puritans and the Stage.* New York: Russell & Russell, 1966.

Thayer, C G *Shakespearean Politics: Government and Misgovernment in the Great Histories.* Athens: Ohio University Press, 1983.

Tillyard, E M W. *The Elizabethan World Picture.* London: Chatto & Windus, 1943.

— *Shakespeare's History Plays.* London: Chatto & Windus, 1961.

Traversi, Derek. *Shakespeare from Richard II to Henry V* . Stanford: Stanford University Press, 1957.

— *Shakespeare: The Roman Plays.* Stanford: Stanford University Press, 1963.

Trevor-Roper, H R. 'The Gentry, 1540-1640.' *Supplement to the Economic History Review*, April 1953.

Trotsky, Leon. *Leon Trotsky on Literature and Art*, edited by Paul N. Siegel. New York: Pathfinder Press, 1970.

— *Literature and Revolution*. New York: International Publishers, 1925.

Tucker Brooke, C F, ed. *Shakespeare's Plutarch*. New York: Duffield, 1909.

Vickers, Kenneth H. *England in the Later Middle Ages*. New York: Barnes & Noble, 1961.

Walbank, F W. *The Awful Revolution: The Decline of the Roman Empire in the West*. Toronto: University of Toronto Press, 1969.

Weimann, Robert. 'Past Significance and Present Meaning in Literary History', in *Preserve and Create: Essays in Marxist Literary Criticism*, edited by Gaylord C LeRoy and Ursula Beitz, pp 30-53. New York: Humanities Press, 1973.

Wellek, René. 'The Aims, Methods and Materials of Research in the Modern Languages and Literature.' *PMLA* 67 (Oct 1952): 19-29.

Wilders, John. *The Lost Garden: A View of Shakespeare's English and Roman History Plays*. London: Macmillan, 1978.

Williams, Raymond. *Marxism and Literature*. New York: Oxford University Press, 1977.

Wilson, J Dover. 'Titus Andronicus on the Stage in 1595.' *Shakespeare Survey* 1 (1948): 17-42.

Winny, James. *The Player King: A Theme of Shakespeare's Histories*. London: Chatto & Windus, 1968.

Woodhouse, A S P. *Puritanism and Liberty*. London: J M Dent, 1951.

Index

Historical characters in Shakespeare's plays are indexed under the plays in which they appear, which are listed alphabetically. Their originals in history are indexed alphabetically.

REDWORDS